Loving Andrew: A Fifty-Two-Year Story of Down Syndrome

ISBN-10: 1478298340
ISBN-13: 978-1478298342

Library of Congress Control
Number: 2012919427

CreateSpace Independent
Publishing Platform,
North Charleston, SC

Book Design by James
Alexander of Jade Design
(www.jadedesign.co.uk)

**A Fifty-Two-Year
Story of Down
Syndrome**

Loving
Andrew

Romy Wyllie

Foreword by Brian Chicoine, MD

*For Margaret Class
With best wishes & appreciation,*

Romy Wyllie

To Andrew

"To know Andrew was to love him."
—Rev. Patricia Snickenberger

Contents

Illustrations

Foreword

Romy Wyllie's *Loving Andrew: A Fifty-Two-Year Story of Down Syndrome* is about her son Andrew, who was born with Down syndrome in 1959. The reader is given an in-depth look into Andrew's life. We not only get to know Andrew the person, but we also get to know Andrew as part of a family and part of the developing Down syndrome community.

As the medical director of the Adult Down Syndrome Center (of Advocate Lutheran General Hospital and Advocate Medical Group), a facility that has served the medical and psychosocial needs of over five thousand adolescents and adults with Down syndrome, I have had the opportunity to get to know many people with Down syndrome and their families. However, I always appreciate any occasion to get a more in-depth look into the lives of those individuals and their families. This book is one such opportunity.

Romy Wyllie has shared Andrew's journey with us but also her journey and that of her family. I was blessed to know Andrew, to be part of his life, and to experience joy and discomfort with him. Even knowing all that, I learned from reading this book. I have a better understanding of Andrew, and with that I can bring this enriching experience to the next person with Down syndrome I serve.

Andrew was born just a few months after Dr. Jérôme Lejeune published his finding that Down syndrome is caused by an extra twenty-first chromosome. Since then there has been much discussion of the implication of having an extra chromosome. What does it mean? What are the genetic ramifications, the individual and family opportunities and challenges, and the societal issues? How is Down syndrome defined? How can we loosen the bonds of that definition?

Families of a younger person with Down syndrome have often commented that their experience is very different from that of a family with an older adult with Down syndrome. While the genetics has not changed, the lives of people with Down syndrome have changed tremendously. I described that difference by the phrase "two syndromes." When my great-uncle Leo was born in 1907, he was called a "mongoloid," the term of the time. He had Down syndrome. My great-great-grandmother was told that Leo would probably not live past ten years of age, would never walk, would never talk, would have no school opportunities, and would certainly not live beyond his parents, so there was no need to plan for the future. Hopefully this is not what parents are being told today, and certainly it is not the experience of this generation of children with Down syndrome. The genetics is the same; the experience different. Why the change? Mrs. Wyllie gives us much insight into those questions through her description of Andrew and his opportunities, his achievements, and the challenges he faced.

To understand who we are, it is helpful to know where we have been. The language in the sections of the book describing Andrew's youth, now considered outdated, helps one understand the times. Will future generations look at us now and also be puzzled? Previous generations were no more completely wrong than we are completely right today. Instead of following medical advice and placing their offspring in an institution, the Wyllies and other families raised and loved their special children, and in doing so made a generous gift that propelled forward the societal view of and approach to people with Down syndrome. It is a process, an evolution. Mrs. Wyllie writes, "Once again our preconceived notions about the limitations of Down syndrome were being cast aside." How often can we continue to say that today?

In chapter 21, Mrs. Wyllie describes the requests, in 1982 and again in 1995, of her family and other parents for married housing at Lambs Farm where Andrew lived. These are still issues we are grappling with today without resolution at most supported residences. We are on a journey.

This book is about the hope of that journey, and it is told through the life of an amazing, delightful, loving, fun, and caring man. Each person has a story. Andrew certainly had his. In this book, you will get to know Andrew, learn his story, appreciate him, and love him. Perhaps you, too, will experience the journey, the hope, and the casting aside of preconceived notions.

Brian Chicoine, MD
Medical Director
Adult Down Syndrome Center
Advocate Lutheran General Hospital
Advocate Medical Group
Park Ridge, Illinois

Preface

"When I left the airport, they went in the other plane with my air ticket. Both of them follow me to California. They are here and trying to take me back to Chicago, but my parents won't let them." Andrew, our son with Down syndrome, was writing a postcard to his girlfriend in Chicago, where they both lived at the Lambs Farm in Libertyville. This was in the summer of 2000. Andrew had turned forty-one in April and since his thirty-ninth year had been suffering a mental illness characterized by delusions and auditory hallucinations. The postcard talked about two of "them" following him just when he had expected to leave "them" behind in Chicago and be able to enjoy his vacation in California free of his demons.

Between high school graduation and his thirty-eighth birthday, Andrew had been a highly successful man with Down syndrome, working full time in a regular job and leading an enjoyable and rewarding life under the umbrella of an adult residential organization for the developmentally disabled. With the onset of later years (he turned fifty in 2009), he faced the additional challenges of paranoid schizophrenia and Alzheimer's disease. Despite these setbacks, he was still happy and full of love.

The purpose of this book is to give a full account of the challenges and rewards of bringing up a child with a disability. In 1959, at a time when parents were urged to institutionalize their "mongoloid" babies because the prognosis for their development was so grim, we chose to bring up our son as an integral part of our family. Although friends had urged us to write our story ever since Andrew was small and it became clear that we were going to help him make the best of his handicap, I had hesitated to tackle the project. Then in October 1993, a devastating wildfire swept through our neighborhood, destroying six of the eight houses immediately around us. Our house remained intact in the center of a ring of fire. While our neighbors sifted through their ruins for a treasured ring or shred of a family photograph, we thanked God and a guardian angel for our good fortune. I thought of all the letters, photographs, notebooks, and articles I had been saving over the years with the intention of someday using them as source material. Realizing that I still had my collection, I heard a voice saying, *Your house was saved for a reason; it's time to stop procrastinating and get on with that book.* The book was completed in 1995 but for various reasons was shelved until new challenges in our son's life inspired me to add to his story.

As molecular biologists make continuing advances in gene identification and medical technology improves the procedures for prenatal testing, many of today's families are faced with heartbreaking choices. It appears that a couple's freedom to become loving parents may be replaced by a bureaucratic requirement that a fetus meet or exceed some standard of minimum quality. I hope our story will provide encouragement to families who decide to keep their less-than-perfect baby and will inspire them to cope with the challenges ahead. These include the many hurdles that all parents face as well as those extra challenges associated with a child who has a handicap.

The narrative is made more relevant for young parents by comparing our experiences fifty-two years ago with those of two families who have children born in 1980 and 1994. Today, couples have the advantage of information emanating from the ongoing medical research into causes and treatments of the various forms of developmental disabilities, greater public awareness and acceptance of the handicapped, and support services unheard of in the 1960s. But this does not make them any less vulnerable to the onerous responsibility of caring for a handicapped child or relieve them of the burden of guilt. For us, the most important lessons were learning to accept our child for what he was and exerting patience and perseverance to encourage Andrew to climb up the staircase of life and become a contributing member of society.

We should remember that someone with Down syndrome is first and foremost a person—a human being with a life to live and a role to play. I have written this book for parents, grandparents, siblings, friends, teachers, social workers, caretakers, medical practitioners, employers, and above all for those delightful men, women, and children who have Down syndrome or another type of disability.

Author's Note

The terminology throughout the book is intended to be appropriate for the period in which it is used. Although "mongol" and "mongoloid" may shock today's readers, these names were common usage when our son was born in 1959. With greater acceptance of the mentally handicapped following the legislation from the early 1970s to the present time, the names "Down's syndrome" and "Down syndrome" have superseded the earlier terminology. Now the medical profession has deleted the possessive s from all syndromes named after their discoverers unless that person had the syndrome or suffered from the disease (as in Lou Gehrig's disease). Accordingly, in 1984, the National Down Syndrome Congress voted to drop the apostrophe s. A mentally handicapped individual who used to be classified as mongoloid is now referred to as a person with Down syndrome. I have also felt free to use the shortened Down's because Andrew said, "I am Down's."

Acknowledgments

Throughout the emotional journey of writing this book, I have encountered dozens of people who have contributed in a thousand ways to Andrew's story. It is impossible to name everyone, but if you read this book and recognize an event in which you played a part, please know that I am forever grateful. Except where it seemed important to respect a person's privacy, real names have been used. Andrew's family is especially appreciative of the roles played by his teachers; counselors; employers; doctors and nurses; Lambs Farm CEO Dianne Yaconetti, house manager Mike Impastato and other staff, members of House One, and all of Andrew's friends at Lambs; Rev. Patricia Snickenberger, Deacon MJ Lewis-Kirk, Helen Lloyd, and members of St. Lawrence Episcopal Church; and many family friends, especially Donald and Nancy Los, Lynn and Eva Maddox, Amir Nour, and Ann Morrison—all of whom were important influences in Andrew's life growing up in Chicago.

The following people read the manuscript and offered helpful comments: Lisa Behm, Michael Bérubé, Lolla Chimitris, Denise Clemen, Missy Jennings, Jenijoy LaBelle, Jenny Lawrence, Lynn Rodriguez, Elaine Wyllie, Dianne Yaconetti, Fran Yariv, and Carol Yeager. I thank the Rodriguez and Yeager families for allowing me to include incidents from the lives of their daughters with Down syndrome.

Brian Chicoine, MD, was good enough to take time out of his busy medical practice to read my book and write the foreword.

Nicholas Goodhue contributed his expertise as a copyeditor and made me feel a great deal more confident in the accuracy of the final version.

As readers will realize, Andrew's family was an integral part of his life.

I thank with sincerity and admiration the contributions of siblings Lisa and John and their families, cousins Aileen and Lolla, and most of all my patient and understanding husband, Peter.

Part I: Primary
Ages Zero to Six

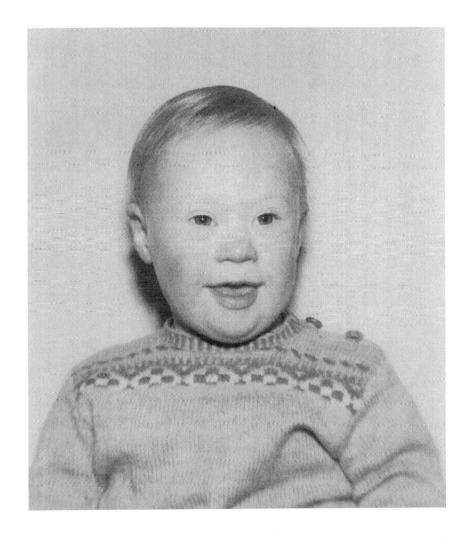

Chapter 1:
Our First Child

Lights twinkled in the great golden arches of Chicago's Auditorium Theater where Rudolf Nureyev had danced, Van Cliburn had played Tchaikovsky's first piano concerto, Count Basie had jumped around the clock, and punk groups had reduced the grandeur of the hall to a wild, echoing stadium. Tonight the faculty of Kenwood High School occupied the stage, and the auditorium seats were filled to overflowing by parents and families.

The line of students approached the platform, "Division 250, Special Education, Andrew Wyllie, Dean's Honor List." Attired in a pale blue cap and gown, his face beaming with pride, Andrew marched flat-footedly across the stage. He embraced and kissed his teacher, shook hands with the principal, and received a diploma that was proof of his graduation after four years in Kenwood High School.

As I stood to applaud, I felt immeasurably proud and wished I could encapsulate this special moment. Then tears clouded my vision as I remembered the occasion nineteen years earlier when we had waited all night in County Hospital, Bellefonte, Pennsylvania, for the birth of our first child. The date was April 21, 1959. At last the pregnancy was nearly over. I had looked forward to our baby's arrival with excitement and nervousness. As with most first babies, the labor was long and arduous, extending into the early morning hours. At 6:00 a.m., the doctor had just left to get some coffee when I felt a great urge to push. Hastily, I was wheeled into the delivery room and given some anesthetic.

Before I knew any more, I heard a voice saying, "Mrs. Wyllie, you have a baby boy."

"Can I see my baby?" I replied groggily.

"Oh, he's being cleaned up just now. You can see him in a little while," a nurse mumbled.

I vaguely recalled pictures of mothers holding their infants even before the umbilical cord was cut and wondered why I couldn't see my baby.

Drifting in and out of consciousness, I saw the bright lights in the hospital theater and was aware of a general mood of bustle and efficiency. Soon I was being taken out to the recovery room. As I lay on the hard, uncomfortable hospital cart, I became more fully conscious, and a feeling of euphoria came over me. I experienced an overwhelming sense of joy that our baby, the son I had hoped for, had been born.

At that moment the doctor and my husband, Pete, came and stood on either side of the gurney. As Pete took my hand, I smiled and started to say, "Isn't it wonderful? It's a boy." Pete's eyes looked strange, and his voice seemed to quaver as he spoke, "Yes, but we have some bad news."

I thought, *Oh my God, what's happened? Was something wrong with our baby?* In the distance I heard Pete saying, "Our baby isn't quite right; he's mongoloid. He is going to be physically and mentally handicapped."

"Mongoloid, handicapped! Why? What happened? What does it mean?"

I don't remember any more words, explanations, or expressions of sorrow. I just remember the awful feeling, a kind of sickness, the blankness and darkness of a candle flickering and sputtering and finally going out for lack of oxygen.

Several months later, Pete told me how the doctor had broken the news and put the burden on him as to how and what to tell me. Pete said, "I was waiting anxiously in the lounge, when Dr. Collins walked in and said, 'Congratulations, it's a boy.' I felt a glow of warmth and a distinct feeling of triumph for a new child before I heard the doctor saying, 'but come outside for a minute; I have something to tell you.'"

Pete remembered feeling worried. He told me, "Flashes of memories about the things that can go awry in Nature's great procreation experiments darted through my head." His first concern had been for me: "Is Romy all right?"

Dr. Collins had said reassuringly, "Oh yes, she's in good shape, but I'm afraid the boy is not quite right."

Pete recalled, "I felt sure our baby must be right. He had been born, and we were now parents. I felt bewildered as the doctor tried to explain, 'Your child is mongoloid. There are signs—the fingers, feet, eyes, shape of head.'"

Pete had asked the doctor what he meant by "mongoloid" and if there was anything that could be done. He told me, "I had faint memories of the term Mongolian monster being used to describe deformed kids and village idiots."

The doctor had painted a grim picture. "The child is mentally retarded. He will never grow up to be a normal adult. Sometimes the best policy is to inform the mother, before she even sees her baby, that the child has died and then place him immediately in an institution."

Pete told me, "I was confused. I thought about how we had made this baby together and you had grown him."

The doctor's suggestion to put him away forever was so shocking. How could we discard him? Who would want that? I imagined a tabloid report: *The doctor and the father conspire to destroy the evidence of the mother's labor. Nine months of production wasted. Mother told, "We are sorry, but your child was not perfect. We sent him away so that you can try again, unbothered by the knowledge and sight of your first, unfortunate error."*

Pete continued, "I felt my mind going numb. I used to wonder about the meaning of that phrase. How can the mind go numb? Now I know. It's like a creeping paralysis, questions half formed and never spoken. The electric impulses within the brain and from brain to tongue are derailed or shunted into cul-de-sacs. I heard the doctor's statements but didn't comprehend them."

Pete explained how the numbness slowly dissipated. "One thing became clear: I couldn't make this decision alone. I felt strongly that this baby was our joint responsibility. I decided you should be told right away because I knew you'd want to be involved."

We could only afford a semi-private room, but in the circumstances the hospital decided not to give me a roommate. As the nurses were helping me into bed, the doctor joined us and tried to explain. He knew little enough about "mongolism," now termed Down syndrome. Indeed, at that time there was little to know. He had witnessed only one other Down syndrome birth, and in that case the baby was taken away and the mother never saw her child. In spite of his limited experience, Dr. Collins was sure of his diagnosis because there were certain characteristics that distinguished a Down syndrome child from a normal child. He told us what he knew: the child's fingers were short and stubby, the toes unusual, the feet squat, abdominal muscles had an indication of an incipient congenital hernia, the head was small, the forehead narrow and flat, the nose almost nonexistent above a slack jaw, and the mouth was occupied by a tongue that was too large for it, with a "fissured," cracked surface. The facial features, up-slanting eyes, and a fold of skin at the inside corners were the obvious oriental touches that inspired the horrible phrase *Mongolian Monster* or *Mongolian Idiot*—one title fearsome, the other pathetic.

The doctor explained that in addition to being mentally handicapped, the boy would also suffer physical handicaps. He would have poor muscle tone, and all his joints would be slack or double-jointed. He told us Down syndrome children were usually susceptible to respiratory ailments and often died young from complications. (Was he trying to give us hope that our son might be overtaken by pneumonia at a young age?) He went on to recount some brighter aspects. The children were happy, cheerful, and easy to handle. They were children who never grew up, like Peter Pan and his friends in Never Never Land.

Dr. Collins suggested we get a second opinion, just to be certain. The local pediatrician eventually examined our baby on his rounds, confirmed the obvious, told us nothing directly, and later sent us a bill for $25 (a lot of money for a student in 1959).

I found it hard to concentrate on the doctor's explanation. My head felt heavy, my eyes stung, and my thoughts were fuzzy. I tried to rest but was too upset to be able to relax. When Pete returned in the evening, we tried to discuss our options sensibly, but we felt overloaded by emotion and confused by the lack of information. Following our natural nurturing instincts, we agreed unequivocally that we couldn't "put our child away" as the doctor suggested. We decided to keep him, at least for a few months, so we could give him a good start on life. We would make a final decision later when we were better informed and had a chance to see for ourselves how he might develop.

After Pete left and the nurse had turned out my light, I finally let go and cried myself to sleep, thinking that I would wake up to find the bad news was a horrible mistake, a nightmare that was not real. But as the morning light turned the window blinds into luminescent panels, the wailing of hungry newborns, like bleating lambs, reminded me all too clearly that my baby was different.

I waited anxiously for the nurse to bring him from the nursery. I had seen him only briefly, and then he was bundled up in blankets. Now with my dreams of a beautiful and perfect child cruelly shattered, I had mixed emotions when I looked at the tiny object in its hospital bassinet. It was ugly. In addition to the features that the doctor had described, the cheeks were plump with funny, full jowls covered in a kind of furry fuzz. But this strange thing was a baby—our baby. He breathed and squirmed. He made little gurgling noises and opened his mouth, searching for food. He was soft and warm to touch, and when I held him, carefully supporting his wobbly head, my nostrils were filled with the sweet perfume of baby lotion and talcum powder. How could we discard such a little creature? He was a human being. As a mother I felt an inescapable urge to protect and comfort him.

The next few days in the hospital were full of sadness and anxiety. After discarding our carefully selected list, we struggled to choose a name. We had planned to call our first son after my father, who had died suddenly on the eve of this fateful year. I had last seen him in Scotland three years earlier, just before we left on our sea voyage to America. As I hugged him and said good-bye, I had a disturbing premonition that I would never see him again. Now it did not seem right to perpetuate his name in our less-than-perfect son. In telepathic fashion, recalling the university where we met and the patron saint of our Scottish forebears, we chose the name Andrew.

— ★ —

Both Pete's grandfather and my father were Scottish. After serving in the medical corps in World War I (1914–18), my father had set up his practice as a general surgeon in Hull, England. He was highly regarded in the community and was known for pioneering orthopedic work with crippled children. He believed that children could be fitted with prostheses at a young age and taught to use them. The prostheses would be adjusted and enlarged as they grew. Sometimes he took me with him on his visits to the Hospital for Crippled Children.

Like most children, I reacted with curiosity and scorn when I saw odd looking people. I probably stared or snickered and then quickly looked away. No doubt my father felt that exposure to children who were physically deformed would teach me something about the reality of life outside the sheltered environment of my home. I remember that the children were always excited to see Doctor Blair. Invariably they were cheerful and eager to show off their activities using their new arms and legs. However, these children were not only crippled; they were poor. They came from the slums, the other side of the tracks. They were different, and their disabilities were something that would never touch me.

I admired my father's work, but I was never interested in pursuing any of the professions related to medicine. After spending eleven years at English boarding schools, I studied English and history at the University of St. Andrews in Scotland. I met Pete during my last year. We were married in 1956 on a cool gray June day in a small village church in Yorkshire, England. It was a formal affair, with the men attired in black tailcoats and gray top hats and the women showing off their milliners' best creations. I wore a long-sleeved cream brocade dress with beaded collar and cuffs. Two college friends were my bridesmaids, and a young cousin in kilt and sporran was my page. The reception for 150 guests was held in a marquee in the garden of my parents' home. The climax of the day came as we cut the wedding cake with my father's World War I ceremonial sword.

Before our wedding, my mother was a little shocked to learn that as members of the modern generation, we were going to plan our family. However, as Robert Burns wrote:

the best laid schemes o' mice an' men

Gang aft a-gley (Go oft astray)

An lea'e us nought but grief an' pain,

For promised joy.

Although Pete was still enrolled for his doctorate at the University of St. Andrews, Scotland, he had taken a full-time position as a research assistant in geology at the Pennsylvania State University in America. A Fulbright travel grant allowed us to stay in the United States for three years but stipulated that we must then return to England. We planned to wait two years to start our family so Pete could finish his PhD thesis and start his professional career. We decided that our first baby should be born a few months before the summer of 1959, our final year. In July and August of the previous year, we went on a six-week camping trip to explore the western states. It was an exciting journey for a young English couple, driving across the vast plains and endless prairie lands of the North American continent, and seeing the dramatic scenery of the Rockies and the spectacular beauty of the national parks. By the end of our trip, I knew I was pregnant. We decided that conception must have occurred one night in the Badlands of North Dakota, a location that seemed especially prophetic as we looked back.

Except for morning nausea and feelings of tiredness in the first trimester, my pregnancy was easy. We were both young and healthy and had no reason to anticipate any problems. In the 1950s, there was no way to determine the health of an unborn child because procedures for prenatal testing of an embryo had not yet been developed. The most our doctor recommended was a regular checkup and a sensible diet.

When I was eight months pregnant, we saw a film about a family with a handicapped son who was cared for by a black nanny. That night I dreamed we would have a developmentally disabled child, and somehow the presentiment never quite left me. But it was still far removed from reality; it was just a dream. One day I read a pamphlet about birth defects, but again I thought, *Oh, it won't happen to us.*

Now, to my horror, it had touched us. I had given birth to a mentally disabled child. I had failed in my role as a mother and bearer of this infant. I felt responsible for this tragedy and was wracked with shame and guilt. What had I done wrong? I had given up cigarettes and coffee. I had drunk milk every day and eaten detestable liver every week. Why had God punished us?

Pete was wonderfully supportive. Andy was his baby too, and we shared our emotions and talked about our feelings. Although we mourned for the perfect baby we had expected, Pete encouraged me not to think of this as God's punishment but as his gift. We had been chosen to bear this special child and give him the best life possible. Later we came to realize that, through our child, we could help other people. However, it was too early to look into the future. First we had to learn to accept our baby and make the best of him.

After six days in the hospital, we dressed Andy in his new garments, wrapped him in a beautiful shawl crocheted by a friend of my mother, and took him home to our small apartment in State College, Pennsylvania.

Chapter 2:
Parenting Challenges

Although we didn't have a choice regarding our less-than-perfect child before birth, we did have a choice after birth. In deciding to reject the doctor's recommendation of institutionalization and to care for our child ourselves, we had chosen to open one of the tightly closed doors in the long corridor of life. We could have walked through a door that was partly open and followed the example set by most parents, who sent their imperfect products to state-run homes. Only our imaginations told us what lay beyond that door: a dark, depressing, high-walled building where babies were kept in tightly barred cribs, their plaintive cries ignored, their soiled diapers unchanged, and their need for human contact cast aside. As evidenced by our doctor's statements, the society of the 1950s regarded the retarded as a subspecies, a group to be placed at the lower end of the spectrum of human beings.

Now, in this new millennium, are we about to discount all our efforts to assimilate the developmentally disabled into everyday life by discouraging plans to bring them into the world in the first place? It seems that in our anxiety to achieve human perfection, the cruel practice of institutionalization could be replaced by abortion as women of all ages are pressured to have prenatal tests to check for abnormalities. These tests are being constantly updated as research uncovers new and more accurate ways of identifying abnormalities. During my pregnancy, no such testing options existed. Even if they had existed, it is unlikely that my doctor would have suggested them because I was at the lowest end of the age statistics. I was only twenty-six when Andy was born.

Our only choice, a state-run organization or home care, had to be made in a haze of ignorance. After the initial shock of the doctor's words in the hospital, Pete had gone at once to the library in pursuit of more information, but only a few publications on the subject existed. He learned that "mongolism" was also referred to as Down syndrome and was a form of mental retardation distinguishable from other types by the physical characteristics, which the doctor had described. He read that in institutional living, "mongoloids" were forcibly sterilized to prevent their procreation.

In earlier historical times, survival of the fittest took precedence over sentiment. Tribal people practiced infanticide or allowed malformed children to die. In spite of history's perception that the Greeks were civilized, they slaughtered the aged, infirm, and handicapped in order to unburden themselves of added responsibilities. In a similar fashion, the Romans dropped mentally handicapped children into the River Tiber.

From ancient Egyptian times until the mid-eighteenth century, professional fools and jesters were often people who were deformed, mentally handicapped, or mad. Royal courts, private households, taverns, and brothels used them as a source of entertainment. A nobleman sometimes kept a disabled person in his home as a pet or for luck because his deformity could divert the evil eye. As well as being the butt of jokes, village idiots could be blamed for evil happenings or misfortune. Occasionally they were identified as witches or warlocks and were burned at the stake.

Until the Industrial Revolution changed society from an agrarian culture to a city-centered population in the later part of the eighteenth century, the handicapped often worked on farms and were cared for by family members. But as people thronged to the cities to find factory work, their disabled relatives became a burden and were placed in institutions, often with the mentally ill.

In 1883, Sir Francis Galton, a half-cousin of Charles Darwin, invented the term eugenics, a doctrine aimed at improving the human race through selective breeding. According to Adrian Woodridge, the author of the 2006 publication *Measuring the Mind: Education and Psychology in England 1860–1990*, the practice of eugenics through forced sterilization of unsuitable parents to forestall the "degeneration" of a particular race and "to spare the state the heavy cost of providing welfare for the backward and frail" was still on the statute books of several European countries until the mid-1970s. In Sweden, a country known for its high living standards, sixty thousand citizens were sterilized between 1935 and 1976. One canton in Switzerland had a law allowing compulsory sterilization of the mentally handicapped until the 1970s. After the US Supreme Court, in 1927, upheld a statute instituting compulsory sterilization of the unfit, including the mentally disabled, "for the protection and health of the state," more than thirty states in America legalized sterilization of the feeble-minded and the insane. In California such a law was on the books from 1909 until 1979. Ezra S. Gosney, a Pasadena financier, founded the Human Betterment Foundation in 1929. After Gosney's death in 1942, the foundation was liquidated, with its remaining funds establishing the Gosney Research Fund to support post-doctoral research in biology at the California Institute of Technology. The work of the Pasadena-based foundation inspired the leaders of the Nazi sterilization movement, who went far beyond the destruction of the malformed and mentally handicapped in their efforts to create a master race.

Hiding our disappointment as best as we could, we sent cables to our families about our newborn son and wrote to my brother, George, who was a doctor doing medical research in London. We asked him to help Mother understand the situation and to let us know of any new developments in the field of developmental disabilities. His reply of April 27, 1959, expressed deep sympathy, but his message was also full of encouragement and hope:

I'm so glad to hear Romy is well. How terribly sad for you that the babe is mongol. I can feel your disappointment very acutely. I immediately got in touch with my friend Cyril Williams, who works at the Fountain Hospital, the leading English institution that deals with mentally defective children.

Mongolism, as you have probably already discovered, is associated with a chromosome abnormality recently discovered by British and French workers. It is quite unrelated to mental disease and has no inherited basis. It represents some type—perhaps biochemical—of generalized retardation so that mongol children are delayed in development and never reach mental and physical maturity. Invariably they seem to be happy, affectionate, and responsive and give much reward for the care that is so often shown them. Perhaps some humans are a bit like rabbits and don't produce a perfect result the first "litter"; they need a sort of trial run. The defect is probably present at the time of conception.

The problem of mongolism as far as the parents are concerned is simply that they never grow up beyond a stage and so need prolonged care and attention. In large or very poor families institutionalization therefore becomes essential. The rich can obviously put the child out of sight if social or personal pressures are stronger than their feeling for what is so often a very gentle, handicapped, and dependent human being. Temporary residence in institutions to allow parents to holiday is quite commonly arranged. The Association for Mentally Handicapped Children offers many services for education. It has been shown, I believe, that mongols can have an economic value to society in protected employment in many cases. Although the condition is untreatable medically, it seems that the mongol is being accepted as a member of society and that he has quite a lot to offer in return for a more open-minded attitude to him.

This baby of yours is a challenge to us, Pete, because he, by being handicapped, needs the very best of us in terms of love and kindliness and all the other human values. Please be assured that I face this problem with you. May I suggest that you enjoy his presence as much as you find possible and see how the three of you get on with each other.

And so we learned about the groundbreaking discovery of a chromosome abnormality made by Dr. Jérôme Lejeune and his colleagues in 1959, the year of Andy's birth (see the appendix). In addition we received strong support of our decision to care for our baby and not to put him away.

Our hospital experience in 1959 of "leave him or take him" seems light years away from the situation that a young couple will encounter today. In addition to prenatal testing and associated choices, there are increasing prospects for family and child support. The following chapters will introduce two other Down syndrome children, Lindsay Yeager, born in 1980, and Blair Rodriguez, born in 1994. Descriptions of the services these families received will illustrate changes in attitudes at successive intervals of fifteen and twenty years after our time.

Steve and Lynn Rodriguez live in a picturesque town on the California coast. Like many women of her generation, Lynn has pursued a career. She had her first child, a daughter named Karley, at age thirty-two.

Because of the demands of balancing work and motherhood, Lynn delayed having a second child until she was thirty-six. Although she knew that her age put her at risk for a number of fetal abnormalities, she decided against any testing. Several of her friends had suffered through false positives after a prenatal blood test, and she wanted to avoid unnecessary medical intervention. Neither she nor her husband wanted to know the sex of their baby, and if a problem was identified, they would choose not to terminate the pregnancy. The Rodriguezes' doctor supported their decision to forgo testing.

In September 1994, Lynn went into labor four weeks before her due date. The delivery was straightforward and natural. Although Lynn was unaware of any conversation in the delivery room, Steve heard the doctor ask one of the attending nurses whether Lynn had had amniocentesis. At five pounds, five ounces, the baby girl looked tiny and strange. Both parents thought that something wasn't right, but no one said anything to them.

Steve went home and did some reading, and Lynn, her anticipated feeling of celebration thoroughly dampened, spent a restless night worrying about her new baby. The next day the Rodriguezes' family pediatrician saw the baby and said, "There is no point beating about the bush; I am pretty confident that your baby is Down syndrome, but we won't know for sure until we get the blood test results." The attending obstetrician said nothing, and the pediatric specialist was frustratingly evasive even though the baby had at least three of the indicators for Down syndrome. A nurse trainee, herself a parent of a Down syndrome child, had immediately noticed the telltale features, but she could not say anything because that responsibility lay with the doctor in charge. At least our doctor in Pennsylvania, in spite of his inexperience with Down syndrome, had the sense to advise Pete of the common custom of mongoloid abandonment before I even saw our baby.

Once the hospital staff knew that the Rodriguez parents had been told of their baby's disability, they surrounded them with support and advice. A nurse, who had an older child with Down syndrome, came and talked at length to Lynn. She said, "For the first year, just remember that this baby is just like any other baby; learn to know her and love her." After being notified of the birth by the hospital, a representative from Family First, the local family support group, came to see Lynn before she left the hospital, a caseworker from the Regional Center visited her soon after she returned home, and a nurse practitioner from the Health Net prenatal clinic called on her to see if she needed counseling.

Feelings of uncertainty create the biggest headache for parents. Once they know what the problem is, then they can begin to deal with it, although they will still feel overwhelmed with many unanswered questions: What does it mean to have a child with Down syndrome? Will they have medical problems? Will they be difficult to handle? Lynn remembered from her childhood the stereotypes of retarded people and recalled that the word *retarded* was always used in a negative way. She had never been around people with Down syndrome and knew nothing about the condition. Both she and Steve put a high value on intelligence. With an older sister who was exceptionally smart, how were they going to manage a child who was developmentally disabled? Coincidentally they decided to name their special baby by my maiden name, Blair.

Pete and I had faced the same questions. We also struggled not just as new parents but also as new parents of a handicapped child without support of any kind. The hospital had given us minimal information and did nothing to follow up after our departure; the doctor had given us a grim prognosis for the future, although he did his best to care for our immediate needs; our families lived in a remote country across the Atlantic Ocean; and our friends had doubts about our sanity.

Although we felt that we were undertaking our adventure alone, we learned later that we were part of a small group of pioneer parents who were daring to ignore their doctor's advice and keep their handicapped children at home. A local parents' association had been formed, but no one got in touch with us or told us about the group, probably because the doctor and the hospital didn't know of their existence.

To strengthen our coping mechanisms, we reminded ourselves that we had worked hard at making our first baby, and our task did not end with his birth; in fact, birth was just the beginning of a lifetime undertaking to bring our offspring through childhood to manhood. The fact that Andy would need more help to grow and develop made it even more essential that we should care for him. Why should we run away from this challenge and give the job to someone else? Surely we, as parents, were the best people to nurture him as an infant. I had planned to breast-feed all our babies, and I presumed that this would provide the best possible nourishment and help build up the immune system of our handicapped child. We felt that if we loved and cherished Andy, saw that he received his inoculations, and fed him the best possible food, he would have a good start on life.

In 1959 the small town of State College, home to the Pennsylvania State University, had one main thoroughfare and a few secondary shopping streets. We lived in a small, one-bedroom, furnished apartment next to the fire station near the center of town. The apartment building had minimal amenities, but the landlord, a sweet old man, did allow us to use a primitive washing machine and electric wringer in the basement where spiders lurked in the corners, cobwebs clung to the pipes, and odoriferous molds permeated the air. The wringer was moody and would frequently choose to revolve uncontrollably in wild circles, just when I was trying to put some delicate garment through its fearsome jaws. There was no dryer, so we hung our clothes on a line in the narrow garden.

Friends had given me a baby shower, and we were well equipped with a layette, diapers, and a borrowed bassinet to begin our new role as parents. Believing that a structured program would help our handicapped baby, I followed a careful routine of bathing, feeding, and sleeping. I used information that I had gleaned from a prenatal course given by the Red Cross. My class notebook contained lists of appropriate foods for the pregnant mother: two pints of milk a day, liver at least once a week, raw cabbage, and whole wheat cereals and breads; instructions for soaking and washing diapers; a long list of layette needs; and a longer list of bath equipment with bathing instruction given in minute detail.

The first few baths were done with these notes and a *Better Homes and Gardens* baby book propped nearby so I could bathe eyes, nose, ears, and genitals in the right order and with appropriately sterile Q-tips or cotton balls. I would have fussed over any new baby, but this one was special and I made an extra effort to do everything according to the book.

Although new mothers probably expect that their infant will be a model for a baby book illustration or a Gerber food commercial, many newborns are uncomely. Andy was uglier than most: his fat cheeks had lost some of the flabbiness so apparent in the hospital, but his watery eyes were small, with large puffs underneath, and what little hair there was on his flat head seemed to be falling out. After a few weeks his appearance improved, but we were constantly reminded that he was not normal. His muscle tone was poor and his head floppy. After our other children were married, I was mother's helper to our daughter when each of her four children was born and to our daughter-in-law when her two children arrived. These experiences recalled how strong most normal babies are and how quickly they are able to raise their heads or hold your finger tightly in their little fists.

Many new babies fuss and cry, but Andy was blessedly docile. He slept most of the time and hardly ever cried. I couldn't rely on him to let me know when he was hungry or needed changing. It was easy to let him go longer than the three- or four-hour schedule that was recommended in the baby books, and I had to force myself to wake him and stimulate his interest in nursing. Although I felt strongly that breast-feeding was important, it was a terrible struggle. In 1959 the common practice was bottle feeding; nature's best breasts were out of fashion. Because the doctor had suggested that we might not keep our baby, the hospital nurses avoided bringing him to me to feed. Instead they started him on a bottle in the nursery. I had to insist that I wanted to breast-feed him, but they still didn't let me start until my milk had come in, and so he missed suckling those important pre-milk nutrients.

When I did start nursing, my breasts were engorged. Sucking an overloaded breast is difficult for any baby but especially for one with weak sucking power. There seemed to be only one nurse on the maternity floor who knew anything about breast-feeding. She was helpful and kind, but the routine was far from established by the end of my six-day stay in the hospital. Each feeding took a long time, and Andy kept falling asleep. I worked at burping, changing his diaper, and switching sides, but it was still a slow process of forty-five minutes to an hour. I took to reading a book at the same time and felt guilty for not concentrating 100 percent on my baby. At night Pete would help by tickling Andy's feet to keep him awake and sucking.

At the end of a month, we went for Andy's first check-up. We were horrified to learn that he had lost weight. All new babies lose a few ounces in the first days but quickly gain it back and should put on two pounds or more above their birth weight by the age of one month. Again, I felt guilty and responsible for this innocent little baby. I thought I should give up the whole breast-feeding business, but the doctor and Pete encouraged me to continue. The doctor prescribed vitamins to increase Andy's appetite. To help the milk flow more readily, we propped pillows behind me to keep me upright or leaning slightly forward.

Our persistence paid off. In a week or two, Andy had started to gain weight and continued on a steady climb. His sucking improved, but the feeds still took a long time. I found the nursing relaxing and stopped feeling guilty about reading a book. Little did I know that only first babies allow you such luxury. By the time a mother tries to breast-feed her second baby, her first baby, already grown to a toddler, is the one demanding to be read a book.

In spite of hospitals and clinics now using lactation specialists to give new mothers advice on breast-feeding, no one seems to have found a magic potion to stimulate a baby with Down syndrome to suck a human nipple. As a result, only a small percentage of mothers of Down's children successfully persist in nursing. Lynn Rodriguez had breast-fed her first child, and she believed strongly in the importance of giving her special child the immunities provided in breast milk. But her experience was similar to ours. Blair was jaundiced, had little energy, seemed to lack any kind of rooting instinct, and had great difficulty sucking. Worrying that her baby would starve, Lynn pumped her milk, put it in a bottle with an enlarged preemie nipple, and virtually poured it into Blair's mouth. Lynn went through exercises similar to ours to wake and stimulate her lackadaisical baby. Occasionally Blair would show some interest, which gave Lynn hope to keep going. Finally after two weeks Blair started to respond, and the nursing improved. Lynn continued nursing until Blair was sixteen months old.

As Britishers, we believed in sleeping with our windows open. If it was very cold, we opened the window just a crack. One morning when it had snowed during the night, we found a layer of white fluff lining the inside of our window ledge. Andy's bassinet was near the window. When I went to pick him up for his early morning feed, I noticed his feet felt cold, and looking closer, I found that they were blue. Poor circulation is another characteristic of Down syndrome babies. Their skin often looks marbled and has patchy blue areas. We realized that we had to sacrifice our need for air for the sake of our baby. It was important to keep him wrapped up and in a warm room. We moved his bassinet to an inside corner and kept the window closed.

Initially our friends in Pennsylvania were at a loss as to how to respond to our tragedy. They were sympathetic and concerned, but they didn't know what to say. Some couples that might have given us presents for our new baby sent us flowers or notes of sympathy instead. I appreciated their kindness, but I had hoped for baby gifts. Even then I wanted Andy treated like everyone else. After all, he was just a baby with a funny face, fat tummy, and ten fingers and toes. He needed clothes, woollies, and blankets like other babies. In some ways this attitude might have been denial on my part that he was different, but the direction of this thinking proved to be beneficial later on. This was our first effort to treat him as much as possible as normal.

My best friend, Lois Fudali, was scared to come and see me in the hospital. She remembers dragging her feet down the corridor to my room wondering, *What am I going to say to her? Should I say I'm sorry?*

As she came into my room, I burst out, "Oh Lo, I feel so good; I just peed for the first time since the delivery." That broke the ice, and we both laughed.

As a young couple living in a small university town, we had an active social life. At first I had to force myself to go out because I felt shy about showing our odd-looking baby to people. I wasn't sure what they would think of him or how they would react. Would they see him as strange or freakish? Would they be embarrassed for our predicament? Would they hesitate to hold him because he was different?

As my pregnancy neared the end, I had looked forward to showing off our baby. I had anticipated the oohs and ahs of admiration, the cooing and sweet talk, the compliments and comments, "Oh he looks just like his father" or "He has his mother's eyes." Now I sensed emptiness in comments such as, "Isn't he sweet?" Instead I had to listen to remarks like, "Oh, he isn't so bad" or "He'll be all right. He'll grow out of it."

Then would come the question foremost in everyone's mind: "Are you going to keep him?" One husband asked me point blank, "How can you consider keeping him? He'll be such a burden to you. You'd be much better off placing him in an institution." Although his question seemed unnecessarily cruel and intrusive, he was simply voicing the prevalent opinion of the day and what most of our friends were thinking.

I reacted to such questions with feelings of hurt and anger, but I didn't want people to see me crying; so I quickly learned to become defensive, to explain our commitment to care for our child and our belief that we were the best candidates for the job. I began to realize that my role was to help other people sort out their reactions, understand the disability, and learn that we viewed our predicament as a challenge that we were determined to overcome.

Thirty-four years later, in addition to their concern over Blair's health, Lynn and Steve found it especially difficult to break the news to their family and friends. After the initial shock they themselves didn't view their situation as tragic, but they realized they needed to soften the blow for others. Although they didn't expect to deal with the queries we faced, their former general practitioner did ask, "Have you decided to keep the baby?" With the closing of state-run institutions or developmental centers, as they are now called, it is surprising that any person in the medical profession would expect a couple to have a choice. Or perhaps he thought that Lynn and Steve might put their new baby up for adoption, a process followed by parents who feel they cannot cope with a special-needs child. On the website of Rainbowkids.com, Martha Osborne reported in a 2008 article that there are long waiting lists of families wanting to adopt a child with Down syndrome.

Our baby was blissfully unaware of the tensions surrounding him. He slept through everything and seemed to enjoy being held and fussed over when he was awake. Our close friends, who saw him often, found it hard to resist the warmth and sweetness of an innocent child. As a mother breast-feeding my baby, it was easy for me to develop a bond of love.

Many times along the path of this new adventure, I recalled the "Hill standard" of my English boarding school. The private school was housed in red brick buildings aligned along the top of a hill outside Harrogate in Yorkshire. Each day at morning prayers we pronounced solemnly and firmly in unison, "To be the best I can be, being what I am, with the gifts I have got." The sound of the words and the chorus of the children still ring in my ears. I never dreamed that my early training would be put to this kind of test. During the years to come it was Andy himself who taught us how much truth lay in this guiding principle. My brother wrote, "This baby of yours is a challenge." Our youth was an advantage; it gave us more energy and patience to meet the challenge. All new parents fumble and muddle through the early months and call upon their mothers for advice; a vast ocean lay between our parents' counsel and us. We made mistakes, but we loved our baby and were trying to help him develop to his full potential.

Chapter 3:
Home to England

At three months, Andy was fairly well established in his routine and was gaining weight steadily. He was beginning to respond to our love and attention with recognition and smiles. Looking like a rag doll with floppy arms and legs, Andy would gurgle and laugh as his father held him high above his head.

The Fulbright travel grant, which had allowed Pete to do research in the United States, stipulated that we must return to England after three years. We had started out on the challenging adventure of looking after a disabled child without the support of our families. Now we looked forward to seeing them, but at the same time, we were nervous about their reactions. We had dealt with the responses of our friends, most of whom had been supportive once they accepted our determination to keep Andy at home. We expected more encouragement from our families, but would we get it? It is not only the parents of handicapped children who have to deal with the disappointment but the grandparents, brothers, sisters, uncles, aunts, and a conglomeration of cousins. Grandparents especially have a harder time changing their thinking and adjusting their dreams than the parents themselves who have the daily activities and close intimacy to further the baby bonding. Besides, grandparents have time to dwell on the problem, worrying about mother and baby.

In her 1987 essay *Kids Like These*, Emily Perl Kingsley likened the situation to a changed travel destination. An imaginary couple had planned an exciting holiday in Italy. They studied the guidebooks, learned some Italian, and looked forward to seeing art and architectural treasures. After months of anticipation, they arrive at the airport, board their plane, and sit back to enjoy the flight. When the plane lands, a stewardess announces, "Welcome to Holland." For some unexplained reason, the plane was rerouted. The dreams of seeing the gondolas of Venice, the Colosseum of Rome, and the works of Michelangelo were shattered.

The couple must stay in Holland and find out what this new and different country has to offer. They are bitterly disappointed and at first don't feel like exploring their unexpected surroundings. They have to find new guidebooks and learn a different language, but gradually they begin to realize that Holland isn't an unpleasant place; in fact, it is an interesting country. The pace of life seems slower, there is a lack of vibrancy; but they soon discover the tulips, windmills, and even world-famous paintings. The people are warm and welcoming, and some speak English. On their return home, they share vacation stories with friends. Although they have much to relate, they experience pangs of jealousy when their colleagues describe visits to Italy. The feeling of disappointment will always be with them, but they soon realize that dwelling on it will only inhibit their enjoyment of Holland.

Parents of a handicapped child have to go through the same process. Soon they begin to love their new baby, but they realize they must change their outlook and develop different dreams. Instead of visualizing their son as a successful student at an Ivy League university planning a career as a lawyer or doctor, or imagining their daughter as a ballerina or mother of several children, they have to lower their sights, adjust their course, and start to chart the unknown waters of a new ocean. They begin to live each day for what it has to offer and put different values on achievements. They begin to see success in the smallest of developments.

After the birth of a child with Down syndrome, some couples put off telling their parents because they are afraid of upsetting them, worry about their reactions, or want to protect them from the disappointment. Educational brochures, books, or videos are just as important for grandparents as for the parents. Simple information will help them provide emotional and physical support and share in the process of acceptance.

For both our mothers, the birth of their first grandchild promised to be a special event, and the news of his disability must have caused them great sadness. Even though my mother was just getting over the shock of her husband's death, we felt that it was important to tell our families immediately because we didn't want them to build up unrealistic dreams. Moreover, we needed their support and acceptance. Our mothers reacted with calm dignity. They sent cables and letters of sympathy and concern, but how did they really feel? Now it was time for them to hold their grandchild and to see what he was like.

We had sailed to America on the Cunard liner, the *Queen Mary*, and returned this time on the *Queen Elizabeth*. Pete and Andy remained immune to the vagaries of the ocean, but I was a bad sailor and spent most of the time moaning in my bunk or collapsed on deck nibbling dry crackers.

Pete had accepted a junior faculty position at Leeds University. Andy and I were to stay with my mother, who lived about fifty-five miles from Leeds, until Pete could find a house and make arrangements for our move. After World War II my parents, finding it a struggle to maintain their Georgian mansion, had moved to a modern house in a suburb of Hull. My younger brother, Bob, was living at home, and our former nanny (Nan), turned housekeeper, completed the household. Mother's friends and neighbors hid their curiosity behind polite expressions of sympathy and generous gifts of toys and clothes, but Nan, ignoring Andy's differences, talked and played with him as though he were just another of her babies. Reassured by her doctor son, George, Mother supported the decision to keep our child, expressed her admiration for our courage, and soon began to respond to Andy's sweet ways.

We settled quickly into a routine, and Andy loved all the extra attention. We bought him a pale blue crib with a bunny and ducklings painted on the inside. We hung a mobile over the crib and surrounded him with stuffed animals. My mother's doctor, a pragmatic Scottish lady with a distinctive Glasgow accent, commended us for this and urged us to provide as much stimulation as possible using color, sound, light, and touch.

From the time he was a few weeks old, we had laid Andy on his stomach to sleep. In spite of his weak muscle tone, he had soon learned to turn his head from side to side, and now he was able to push on his chubby arms and hold his head up to look around. His head, which seemed flattened out at first, had become round and was covered in blonde fuzz. His small, slanted eyes were still puffy and Mongolian-looking but he had such a sweet and cheery demeanor it was easy to love him.

On warm, sunny days we would lay Andy on a rug on the lawn surrounded by toys to encourage him to raise his head and push on his arms before flopping down again. These exercises reminded me of the lizards that run around our California patio, stopping every few seconds to puff out their chests and pump up and down before scampering on to a new location. We would put Andy on his back and exercise his legs and pull him up into a sitting position and help him down again. This was strengthening his arms and his stomach muscles. Sometimes we held him in a standing position on our laps to encourage him to feel his legs and push on his feet. It was the beginning of our self-designed stimulation program. Nobody had instructed us what to do; it just made sense to help him exercise and strengthen his muscles.

The original 1975 law in the United States mandating Education for All Handicapped Children (EAHCA) was renamed the Individuals with Disabilities Education Act (IDEA) in 1990 and has grown in scope and form over the years. In 1986 Part C of IDEA introduced a federal grant program that assists states in operating a comprehensive statewide program of early intervention services for infants and toddlers with disabilities, ages birth through two years.

Early intervention means that an adult intervenes between the child and the environment to provide appropriate stimulation and learning techniques and is based on collaboration among parents, caregivers, and service providers. Children who are experiencing developmental delays or who have been diagnosed with a condition that has a high probability of causing a delay are eligible. Parents are referred to the nearest early intervention center where an interdisciplinary team of professionals provides a comprehensive set of services from birth to three years. An individualized family service plan (IFSP) outlining the personal and social services needed by each member of the family is set up, and parents are encouraged to participate in all its phases. In addition, parents are urged to join the nearest branch of a Down Syndrome Association.

In 1994, before their baby was one week old, Lynn and Steve Rodriguez received a visit from a caseworker, herself the mother of a child with Down syndrome. After having their situation assessed at an intake interview by a knowledgeable doctor and case coordinator at the Tri-Counties Regional Center, an appropriate Early Start Program was arranged for Blair. For the first few months, two therapists came to the Rodriguez home for two hours each week. One therapist concentrated on developing fine and gross motor skills, helping Blair develop physically and teaching her how to roll over, sit up, crawl, creep, and eventually stand and walk. The other therapist used colorful toys of various shapes and sizes to teach Blair how to play and manipulate objects. She also introduced music and other types of stimuli.

In the second part of the program the visits were increased to four forty-five-minute sessions a week. Pre-speech therapy was added, as well as additional sensory, motor, and cognitive tasks to provide stimulation and encourage natural curiosity and learning. Steve or Lynn was always present at each therapy session so they could continue the program between sessions. Therapists will also work with children at daycare centers or at the home of a babysitter.

Current research has shown that in the first three years of life, a child's brain creates trillions of neural connections that either flourish or die in response to experience. It is obviously imperative to capture this growth period in all children but especially those who start life with a handicap. Our daughter-in-law, a special education teacher, told us that since the establishment of early intervention programs she had seen a marked improvement in the children with severe disabilities who attended her special elementary class in Utah. Some were already toilet-trained and most could communicate, though not necessarily with words. Our daughter, Lisa, now works as a special instructor for an agency in Pennsylvania that provides early intervention services. She says one of the most important aspects of her work is parent training. She helps mothers learn not to do everything for their child. In order to encourage a disabled child to communicate through sign language, it is essential for the parent to stop interpreting for the child. It also helps to reduce the clutter of toys so the child can focus on one toy at a time. These are just a few of the guidelines developed for early intervention programs.

After watching me struggle with soaking and boiling the diapers (I now had to learn to call them nappies) during our first few months in England, Pete decided to buy me a portable washing machine. Nan, who had always done the laundry by hand, regarded this newfangled machine with a mixture of envy and scorn. As the machine didn't dry the clothes, Mother's neatly manicured garden was frequently decorated with rows of nappies on a line flapping briskly in the breeze like a rope of white flags on an old sailing ship.

We had just become organized in this interim phase when Mother announced that she needed to have a lump on her breast diagnosed. The news hit us like a lightning bolt out of a blue sky. The lump had been there for some time, but Mother had delayed going to the doctor until after our return because she wanted to be at home to greet us. Within a few days, Mother was in the hospital. The surgery went well, but the prognosis was grim. Mother had cancer, a type that spread quickly, and she would require radiation treatment. When I went to visit her, she told me that she would need some kind of false brassiere. I was shocked, not realizing until then that her breast had been removed.

Never once did Mother speak of cancer, nor did we ever say anything to her friends and relatives. Except within the tight confines of the immediate family, such a serious illness was treated with hushed respect and total silence. That was the British way then, but how much better it would have been for her and her family if it had been brought out into the open and discussed.

When Mother came home, Nan was in charge of managing the house, and I had the job of looking after baby and grandmother. After giving Andy his morning bath and meal, I would help Mother take her bath. It was a terrible shock to see her dismembered body. Nursing Andy made me so conscious of breasts and their purpose. Besides, I was still adjusting to my role as a new mother, and here I was trying to look after and "mother" my own mother in her illness. I was afraid of what would happen. Would she die?

We put our mothers on pedestals. They are supposed to be invincible because they gave us life, and we expect them to be always there, strong and supportive. Now I had to use up some of my precious maternal energy and expend it on my mother, the figure in my life to whom I should be turning for emotional and physical support.

Friends drove Mother to the hospital for radiation treatments, which she endured without complaint. In time she regained her strength.

Chapter 4:
Leeds and a New Neighborhood

In September 1959 we moved to Leeds, a vibrant industrial city in the north of England, and bought our first home, a brand-new house costing £2,500 (about $7,000) in a small village on the outskirts of the city. It was a typical British tract development. All the houses were semi-detached redbrick boxes and except for orientation, were exactly the same.

As parents of a developmentally disabled child, we found the next few months to be the hardest and most challenging. Everything was new: Pete's job was new, our house was new, the neighborhood and its shops were new, and the neighbors were new. At least our area was a new development, and we were all moving into new houses at the same time. This gave us a certain new togetherness.

We greeted our neighbors and exchanged questions about our houses or information on the nearest grocery shop and delivery services. Many of the families were young and had small children; some had babies about the same age as Andy. I forced myself to meet the other mothers, but I found it terribly hard to explain that my baby was handicapped. We all like to meld into the crowd especially when we are young and inexperienced. We lack the courage to be different because we don't have the advantage of accumulated wisdom to help us develop confidence. However, having decided not to follow the usual course of action when our son was born, I had to continue to face the challenge of meeting new people and dealing with new reactions.

Sometimes I joined the other mothers taking their babies for a walk in prams around the neighborhood or to the shops. In those days the British pram (the word comes from "perambulator," meaning to stroll) was to a certain extent a status symbol, just like the car in America. Some people buy a Cadillac whether they can afford it or not because they think they need it as a symbol of wealth or success. Others, who don't believe in status symbols, are satisfied with a Chevy or a secondhand, beat-up jalopy.

In the daytime, winter and summer, rain or shine, British babies were put outside to sleep in their prams. In cold weather, they were well dressed in woollies from head to toe and wrapped in warm blankets with the pram hood up and rain cover and apron snapped in place. In summer, a decorative flowered fringed canopy took the place of the hood. The fresh air seemed to make the babies sleep well and gave them rosy cheeks.

Nevertheless, a matron of a school for retarded children warned of the dangers of exposing delicate mongol babies to extreme temperatures: "The notion that a baby should be out of doors in his pram in practically all weathers, and that the physical body should be hardened in order to be healthy, is so deeply rooted in the mind of the English mother that it is indeed most difficult for her to see things otherwise."

In her thoughtfulness for our special situation, Mother had given us an ordinary-looking navy-blue canvas pram, which could be converted into a pushchair (stroller) when Andy was older. She thought she was being practical. The pram would last longer and serve two purposes by helping us through the months or years it would take Andy to learn to walk.

However, this was definitely the Chevy of prams. Everyone else in the neighborhood had Cadillacs, beautifully designed prams with hard, bow-shaped bodies, sitting high and finely sprung on big wheels. They stood at least two feet above our humble, square-bodied canvas box. I forced myself to join the pram parade, but I felt miserable and humbled by my funny, floppy baby in his canvas cart alongside the neighbors' beautiful bouncing babies in their elegant carriages. Even though my baby was different, I would have given anything to put him in the best of English prams. I envied the other mothers their perambulators and most of all their beautiful babies.

Of course, I kept wishing we had not had a handicapped child and that this awful thing had not happened to us. But there was no going back: we had our baby, and we were not going to give him away. Moreover, I was determined to do the best for him and make the best of him. I dressed him in beautiful knitted outfits that my mother and I had made; I fitted our humble pram with beautiful blankets and hung colorful toys on the hood for Andy to watch.

As we became acquainted with the neighbors, I tried to explain the chromosome abnormality that was the cause of Andy's handicap. Acting as openly as possible about our situation seemed to help others respond and be more comfortable around us. Without exception people were accepting, and nobody avoided me because my baby was developmentally disabled.

We soon developed a tea group and met at least once a week at different houses. Tea, both as a drink and more especially as a meal, is the great healer and icebreaker in England. Even though it hurt to see how bright and active the other children of Andy's age were, I observed their progress closely because they provided a measure by which I could judge my child.

The following is an excerpt from a letter I wrote to friends in America on February 14, 1960, when Andy was ten months old:

It is a big responsibility to bring up a child, but it is an even greater one when your child is special. Most of all it is hard to know when to encourage and persuade a new development and when simply to be patient and not push too hard.

I am finding Andy's whole development most interesting. We are discovering that he is slow to learn something new of his own accord and often has to be shown how to do it first and then in time will copy us, but once he has learned, he doesn't forget and continues to enjoy his new discovery or lesson. For example, I have taught him to splash in his bath by splashing with my hand and then taking his and showing him the action of splashing. Now we have water everywhere and a wonderfully rewarding grin of sheer delight on his face.

When he was about seven and a half months old, I sat him, well supported by a cushion, in his high chair because he was trying so hard to pull himself into a sitting position when I held him on my knee to feed him. At first he was rather floppy, and I feared I was pushing him too fast, but in a couple of weeks he had learned to sit up nicely and now can sit for quite a while without support. He is beginning to feel his legs and loves his Daddy to pull him up into a standing position.

He hasn't learned to crawl yet, although he wriggles around a good deal on his tummy and reaches things he wants by a process of rolling and wriggling, but I am stuck how to teach him. He has learned, however, quite on his own, how to say Daddada and occasionally Mum and Babbaba.

He hasn't any teeth yet! The doctor tells me they are near and he chews everything available, the most popular being his socks, which he manages to pull off his feet in a very short time.

He is now a little over nine and half months and weighs eighteen pounds and twelve ounces, which is average. He has had one or two colds but otherwise seems pretty robust and healthy. He is learning to take his milk from a cup at breakfast but needs a good deal of persuading. He loves to be thrown around by Pete and adores pulling our hair and noses and anything he can get hold of. He is always full of smiles and laughs easily when tickled or thrown in the air.

I have always found it easier to follow a set routine, so I instinctively felt that it would help Andy understand what was expected of him if we followed the same program each day. From the time of his birth I had tried to feed him on a regular schedule and put him to sleep or pick him up according to the clock. As soon as he could sit with help, I started putting him on a potty every morning, hoping to give him a sense of its purpose and to catch his bowel movement. It worked quite frequently because, like many children with Down syndrome, he was regular. Although Andy wasn't fully toilet trained until he was four, this early introduction to the idea probably helped.

We took a break from our Leeds life to spend Christmas with my mother. She was recovering well from her surgery and radiation treatments. It was a traditional holiday in the setting of my parents' house, with fresh greenery decorating the polished antiques and aromas of roast turkey, Christmas pudding, and mince pies wafting from the kitchen. Nan did the cooking, and Mother and I fussed over setting the Jacobean dining table. The highly polished wood formed a perfect backdrop for linen placemats and napkins, cut-crystal wine glasses, and elegant silver reflecting the light from flickering candles.

At this time the class system was still an important thread in the fabric of British culture. I had been brought up as the daughter of a well-to-do surgeon, living in a Georgian mansion, with a nanny, live-in servants, gardeners, and a chauffeur. I had been to private boarding schools and to the University of St. Andrews with my father paying the bills and giving me an allowance. Pete's parents were from lower-middle-class families. His father was a cipher clerk with Shell Oil Company earning a steady salary, but the last few days before each paycheck were periods of financial caution. Nevertheless, family affections were strong, and the parents were extremely supportive of the children.

In his last year at a non-fee-paying state school, Pete won a scholarship to the university. In spite of being surrounded by wealthy students who had been educated in private schools, Pete's academic prowess earned him respect. Or perhaps his peers respected him because he was a former heavyweight-boxing champion of the Royal Air Force Scotland.

His family lived a few miles south of London's Heathrow airport. We drove there for the New Year and were welcomed into a warm environment, where Andy was the center of attention. He was accepted for just what he was: a small bundle of sunshine. Even the surly old part Border collie, for whom Pete and I were always strangers, adopted Andy as a member of the family.

Pete's mother had been devastated when she received our letter saying we had a retarded child. Then after seeing the first photos, she exclaimed, "Oh, he's not that bad. I just didn't know what to expect." She felt even better when she was able to hold Andy after our arrival from America in July. During this initial visit Pete's teenage sister, Susan, fifteen years his junior, happily intermingled her love for animals and babies. Proudly showing off several guinea pigs nestling in the pockets of her dress, she put out her arms to hold her new nephew. I cringed as those hands, which had just been touching guinea pigs, reached for my pristine baby. I whispered hurriedly to Pete to ask his sister if she would kindly wash her hands before touching our precious bundle. I was so concerned about cleanliness and felt that Andy must be shielded from any possible germs. By my second baby, I was happily picking up pacifiers from the floor, rinsing them under a faucet, and giving them back to the child; by the third and fourth, the dropped pacifiers were put straight back in the baby's mouth, and no one suffered any dire disease.

Our first break from the strain and responsibility of coping with a handicapped child came in August of 1960 when I went with Pete to the International Geological Congress in Copenhagen, leaving Andy with the Wyllie family in London. I worried unnecessarily that Mum and Sue wouldn't be able to keep our baby happy. But this was an ideal opportunity for both of them to participate in our special undertaking.

Sue recalls:

> Andy's cot was next to my bed. When I woke up, I would realize that this little face was looking at me, and as soon as I looked at him, his face would beam, "She's awake." He must have been staring at me for ages, just lying there waiting for me to wake up. Then he would haul himself up and peer at me through the bars. That was it, no more peace and quiet. He used to come into bed with me until it was time to get dressed.
>
> Every afternoon, whatever the weather, we walked him up the steep hill in Whitton. He used to play a game: he would put his head down on the apron of the pram and we would say, "Oh, we lost Andy, where has Andy gone?" And he would look up grinning. He played that game all the way up the hill and back again. The whole time we looked after him he never stopped smiling. He was just a grinner.

That was testament to a successful stay with an especially caring aunt and grandmother.

In November of 1959, the year that our son was born, an article was published in the *Ladies' Home Journal* referring to the mentally subnormal as "a subject for whispers and concealment." With this kind of attitude deterring research and inhibiting a better understanding of the retarded, warehousing was considered the only solution. Fortunately, a few forward-thinking professionals were beginning to develop a new philosophy, parents were beginning to defy the norm, and prominent people were beginning to lend their support. As a result, the plight of the mentally handicapped began to improve.

The Kennedy family became advocates of the retarded because a family member was handicapped and had been placed in a private school. In 1946, former Ambassador Kennedy established the Joseph P. Kennedy Jr. Foundation as a memorial to his eldest son, a naval aviator killed in action during World War II. Through this foundation scientific awards were given to investigators in behavioral and biological sciences; service awards were given to groups or individuals contributing to care, rehabilitation, or education programs; and leadership awards were given for activities on behalf of the mentally retarded that had awakened public awareness or increased individual and community efforts.

In 1960, President John F. Kennedy introduced important legislation that furthered the cause of the developmentally disabled in the United States. By talking about his sister, President Kennedy encouraged families to talk publicly about their handicapped children. His openness triggered a spate of articles in national magazines. Eager to gain knowledge after Andrew's birth in 1959, I read everything I could find. All the stories told of the pain suffered by parents on discovering that their baby was retarded or mongoloid. Invariably the medical advice was: "Place this child in an institution...do it now. The longer you wait, the harder it will be...the state institution is one place where he could get excellent care." In one instance a doctor told parents that they were cowards for not putting their child away. But these parents were telling their stories because they had the courage to defy their doctors' recommendations and keep their children.

In a June 1959 *Redbook* magazine article, "The Child We Weren't Supposed to Love," a specialist had told the parents of Wayne, who was Down syndrome, "He will have a ceiling on his intellect. He will never develop mentally beyond a little child. He will never go to school. He will never ride a bicycle. He will not be able to play with other children after his early years." A short time later, Wayne's parents were surprised to meet a Down syndrome child who could ride a bicycle and was learning to read and write. The head of the day school that he was attending said, "Those doctors should all be drawn and quartered."

In the December 1969 issue of *McCall's* magazine, S. I. Hayakawa, at that time president of San Francisco State College, wrote about his Down syndrome son born in 1949. In spite of a neurologist telling his wife, "Your husband is a professional man; you can't keep a child like this at home," they kept their son at home, sent him to a special school, and never hesitated to take him with them to public places.

We learned about current research and a different kind of thinking among professionals during our 1959 Christmas visit to London when we met with my brother's friend, Dr. Cyril (Chris) Williams at the Fountain Hospital for Children, one of the leading institutions in the field of retardation in England. He told us about new studies to examine the mental and physical development of developmentally disabled children in different settings, from a hospital or institutional setting to a small residential cottage. The conclusion was that children progressed much better in a cottage or group home facility.

Chris examined Andy thoroughly and gave us an encouraging report. He said that his muscle tone and reflexes were good and that he was developing extremely well. He commended us for our attitude, saying that we had good ideas and the right approach. Based on his present physical development and appearance, he felt that Andy was a "high grade type"—that he was probably in a high percentile of the intelligence range of Down syndrome. He told us that their intelligence quotient varied from twenty to thirty (severely retarded) to fifty to seventy (moderately retarded).

Chris's advice to us was, "Keep Andy at home, and treat him as much as possible as a normal child." He explained that as shown by new findings, all retarded children, Down syndrome in particular, develop far better in the home, provided the home surroundings are right and parents' attitudes helpful. In a hospital or institution, they become lost as individuals. They need love and respond better to close affection and individual attention. If they are taught in the right way, they can learn. The secret of teaching them is to find a point of interest from which to work. If Andy developed well, it might be possible to send him to the educational subnormal schools run by the state.

As this new philosophy became more widespread, many parents and professionals came to the realization that the retarded can do more than sit like sacks of potatoes in asylums. New medical treatments, home care, and specialized training have helped the handicapped become accepted into everyday life. Since the 1970s, radical changes in education and the introduction of early intervention programs have contributed to remarkable improvements in the intelligence of persons with Down syndrome. When our son was born, an IQ of fifty was considered the highest that a person with Down syndrome would attain. Now, insofar as IQ scores are any real indicator of ability, fifty is average, with many individuals reaching seventy-five to ninety. However, most articles make it clear that using normal standards to measure the IQ of people with Down syndrome is misleading because their skills vary a great deal and are not necessarily commensurate with their age or a standard test.

On the eve of 1960 we felt as though a bright light had started to break up the gloom of our child's life. We never forgot Chris's recommendation. His words became our slogan. Our goal to treat Andy as a normal person paid dividends beyond our dreams.

Chapter 5:
Andy's Progress

W e planned to space our children by two years, and I always managed to become pregnant the first month we stopped using birth control. In September 1960, we started our second baby. Fortunately, my pregnancy was easy, but we all had a bad dose of flu in the early months of 1961. While Andy recovered quickly, Pete and I were sick simultaneously. Feeling so ill that we could hardly move, we took turns dragging ourselves out of bed to care for Andy and wished we could ask someone to help. Somehow we made it through a nightmarish week and got better.

We had learned about the physical characteristics of Down syndrome from our doctor in Pennsylvania and from the sparse literature that Pete had found in the library. In our continuing search for information, we sent for the July 1960 copy of *Parents' Voice*, a quarterly journal published in England by The National Society for Mentally Handicapped Children. It contained information on meetings and conventions and on the latest developments in the provision of facilities for all types of retarded individuals, but it did not tell us what to do on a daily basis. Lacking the excellent resources and literature that are available to families today, we searched for a "how to" book on Down syndrome.

The only guidance we found was a booklet entitled *For the Parents of a Mongol Child* issued by Sunfield Children's Homes, Worcestershire, and reprinted in 1960 for the seventh time. Sunfield was established in the 1930s and to this day is a national British charity and residential special school for children ages six to nineteen with complex needs including autism (www.sunfield.org.uk). In 1946, the "matron of a home for backward children" (identified only as I. N.), unable to respond individually to the many letters she received, had decided to write a non-technical article addressed to the parents who were asking to place their mongol children in the Sunfield school. She dedicated her piece to "The most charming little people in the world." I shall refer to it as *The Matron's Report*, and I shall use the term "mongol" or "mongoloid" because those were the names commonly used by the matron and others at that time.

Matron described some of the physical maladies suffered by mongoloid children and warned parents about their poor circulation, suggesting that they be kept warmly dressed at all times, not exposed to extreme cold, and noting that they were susceptible to chilblains. *The Encyclopedia Britannica* describes chilblains as "capillary congestion of the skin of hands or feet, caused by cold." A small swelling or inflammation occurs on the skin, usually on extremities such as fingers or toes, like a minor form of frostbite. The inflammation burns or itches and can be treated with ointments. The best remedy is to improve the circulation or protect against the condition with warm wool socks and gloves.

At eighteen months Andy had finally progressed from a stomach-propelled frog leap to a proper crawl on hands and knees. During the winter months, he spent much time exploring the house at floor level. The English climate does not have the extremes of cold weather with subzero (Fahrenheit) temperatures that exist in parts of the United States. However, England is a small island surrounded by cold oceans. The weather is changeable and often raw and damp. In the 1960s most English houses were drafty, doors never fit snugly, and cold air blew around and under them. Double-glazing was unheard of, and only heavy curtains with linings helped shut out cold air at the windows.

Our new house in Leeds did not have central heating. In the morning we would turn on an electric heater in the bedroom to take the chill off until we were dressed, and similarly at night until we had crawled into bed with a hot water bottle. Downstairs we supplemented the one fireplace in the living room with electric convection heaters, which wafted heated air around inefficiently. None of these contraptions heated the corners or counteracted the drafts, and it was especially cold on the floor.

We had discovered that children with Down syndrome have poor circulation when Andy's feet turned blue as a tiny baby. Now, as predicted in *The Matron's Report,* he suffered with chilblains on his feet and fingers caused by all the cold air currents. We did our best to keep him warm without inhibiting his progress in locomotion.

In her article, Matron explained that some mongol children are susceptible to respiratory problems and heart complications; they have weak digestive systems and are inclined to have undeveloped tear ducts, causing their eyes to water or discharge. Fortunately, Andy had been born without a heart problem, and so far colds had not caused excessive wheezing or chest infections. I was always careful to bathe his eyes with sterilized water, and as he grew bigger and stronger, his watery eyes improved, although I noticed later that even as an adult he removed his glasses occasionally to wipe the corners of his eyes.

Unfortunately for Steve and Lynn Rodriguez, their baby was among the approximately 40 to 60 percent of children with Down syndrome who have defective hearts. Soon after Blair's birth in 1994, their pediatrician urged them to have all possible diagnostic tests. At three months an echocardiogram revealed a ventricular septal defect (large hole in the wall of the ventricles). The cardiologist told them that there was a possibility that the hole might close on its own. After a year of waiting, a more precise test was performed before further action was taken. By putting a catheter up the main vein of Blair's leg, the cardiologist was able to measure the size of the hole (9 millimeters) and the blood gas composition.

An operation was necessary, and the timing was critical. The surgery had to be delayed as long as possible to enable Blair to grow bigger and stronger, but it had to take place before too much damage had been done to her lungs. Last-minute delays—Blair had a cold, the pediatric anesthetist was out of town—added to the family's anxiety. Finally, when Blair was nineteen months, the surgery was performed. All went well until a serious complication developed two weeks after the operation. Blair, who hardly ever cries, wouldn't stop crying. She was obviously in pain. Eventually, when an ultrasound showed inflammation and swelling around the heart, the cardiologist concluded there was a build-up of fluid. High doses of aspirin for five weeks solved the problem and saved Blair's life.

The first successful pediatric cardiovascular surgery was performed in March 1956 at Salt Lake General Hospital on a normal four-year-old girl. In 1960 Lael Arnold, a five-year-old Down syndrome girl, who would become Andy's best friend, was only the third child in the country to survive open-heart surgery. But Lael's surgery was exceptional. If babies with Down syndrome were born with serious medical complications, doctors would suggest that parents let them die rather than undergo expensive and risky surgery. Why spend the money and valuable expertise on a child who was handicapped and was already a drain on society? In 1973 Public Law 93-112 was passed to prohibit discrimination on the basis of disability. Although the law was aimed at educational institutions, it applied also to medical practice. Now, aided by legislation and improved surgical techniques, a handicapped child with a life-threatening illness stands as good a chance as most children, and no doctor would dare suggest forgoing treatment.

In March 1995 advocacy groups supporting patients' rights bombarded the Stanford Medical Center with protests when they decided that a heart-lung transplant was not appropriate for a woman with Down syndrome, because she would not have the intelligence to cope with the post-operative regimen. In January 1996 the medical team reversed their decision. The report said, "Sandra Jensen, thirty-five, is believed to be the first seriously retarded person in the United States to receive a major transplant." Helped by her mother and a careful program of post-operative treatment, Sandra enjoyed another one and a half years of life before dying during surgery for the removal of a blood clot from a small lymphoma in her brain unrelated to the transplant.

As I re-read *The Matron's Report* for my current writing, I found the old booklet remarkably insightful. As well as explaining and suggesting remedial approaches for the physical maladies of the mongoloid, the author described some of their personality traits using descriptions of individual children in her care. This early account of what to expect in the way of behavior patterns and the typical characteristics of a Down's child proved especially valuable to us in understanding Andy's needs.

In the mode of the 1940s and '50s, Matron believed that mongol children were better off in a residential school or institution because she feared that parents would succumb too easily to the charms of their child, be afraid to exert discipline, or overindulge a child who was different. Many parents might have difficulty accepting the child's limitations and be inclined to expect him or her to be like their normal children. Because other children and their mothers might reject the mongol child, he or she would lack playmates, resulting in isolation, boredom, and loneliness.

Matron described how mongoloids grow up with complete confidence in other people. She wrote, "Unfortunately their confidence is often betrayed, their security shattered, their loving advances rejected, and their joy in life quelled because their actions are misinterpreted." Matron went on to explain that when their confidence is betrayed they are hurt and unable to understand the reason. She stated that although mongoloids have intelligence, they lack the ability to reason and are unable to comprehend or make use of logical arguments. This limitation frequently leads to behavior problems. Sometimes such children can be extremely obstinate and when thwarted, may withdraw into themselves, sulk, or behave badly. Matron feared that parents would fail to recognize and develop the "enormous wealth, inner warmth, and sympathy" of their mongol children. Their talents would be ignored; they would have nothing to do and would become dull, lazy, and sad.

Because mongol children have difficulty with speech and are unable to express themselves clearly, parents and teachers tend to underestimate their comprehension of what goes on around them. Matron recommends teaching mongol children as much as possible using all forms of stimulation because they are likely to absorb a great deal more than you would ever imagine. One day they may surprise you by doing something that you had no idea they had the knowledge or ability to accomplish. In conclusion she urged parents never to be ashamed of their children because they are different but to accept them for what they are, recognize their worth, and be thankful. From this pamphlet we learned that our child would teach us that intelligence is not everything; love and feelings can play an equally important role in life.

Matron was ahead of her time. Although she thought that children with Down syndrome were better off in a residential school where parents couldn't spoil them, she did believe, on the basis of her own observations, that such children were capable of learning.

In the sixty-five years since the first publication of *The Matron's Report*, exciting progress has been made in the area of special needs. During the past two decades, legislation has acknowledged the rights of the developmentally disabled and mandated a variety of programs and services. Public awareness and compassion have been raised by the integration of persons with special limitations into everyday life. Today's parents will read books reassuring them that their Down syndrome child should live at home and become an integral part of their family. Their special child will be able to do most of the same things as a normal child but at a slower pace. Most Down's children will be able to run and jump, ride a bicycle, play some sports, learn to read and write, love music, respond to discipline, have a great sense of humor, and love their parents unconditionally.

In 1960 we were glad to have found at least one helpful resource. We paid special attention to Matron's warning not to overindulge our son. Developing a program of discipline is difficult for any new parent of an active two-year-old, but it is especially challenging for the parents of special needs children. However, with patience and perseverance, these children can be disciplined and develop acceptable behavior patterns. Parents have to learn to judge their special child's behavior by developmental age instead of chronological age. A child with Down syndrome may be pleasantly placid at age two before becoming mischievous and obstinate at age three. It is also important to realize that in spite of possessing extra genetic material, inherited characteristics will influence their behavior patterns.

Organization had been instilled into me through the discipline of my home life and the regimen of boarding school. Also I had the advantage of being a stay-at-home mother, devoting myself to my first child full time. With the rhythm of a steady routine established during the first weeks of Andy's life and with Matron's warning imprinted on my mind, the next step was to introduce discipline. This took the form of picking up toys and saying no to naughtiness, even though it was hard to watch Andy's face, at one moment all grins and laughter, suddenly crumple into tears and howls. Lynn Rodriguez said about Blair, "She didn't listen very well and had to have numerous reminders or repeated instructions when she misbehaved. Amazingly, she responded quickly to requests for things she wanted to do."

As well as not succumbing to overindulgence, we had to learn to look for Andy's special gifts and develop his skills to the best of his and our ability. We needed to create an environment of opportunity in our home. We started with simple things. Andy was learning to play with his toys. Watching the activities of other children, I would show him how blocks could be stacked on top of each other and then knocked down; as with normal children, the knocking down part came quickly, the stacking more slowly. But he took great pride in making a tower of several bricks stay put for a few seconds before touching it and making it fall to the floor. I showed him how trucks could be pushed around and make a noise and how balls roll and bounce. *The Matron's Report* had told us that mongol children were good mimics, and we found that Andy soon started to copy what we showed him. In time he tried things on his own, especially if he thought we were watching and would tell him, "What a clever boy!"

During the spring of 1961, I wrote down a record of Andy's progress. It is reproduced here in the same chart form to give new mothers an idea of possible progress at this stage.

Andy at Twenty-One Months

Weight	Twenty-four pounds, eight ounces
Teeth	Seven teeth. They are still very slow in coming, but we think he is working on double ones.
General	General health very good, a few colds.
Bowels	Bowel training began at eight and a half months. By seventeen months, only occasional dirty nappies.

General Progress

Walking	He walked with help at eighteen months. Pushed baby walker on own at nineteen months. Now he is very confident with it. Walks around furniture on his own and with help walks across room. He can balance for a second but has no confidence.
	He can lower himself to pick up something without sitting down.
	He climbed upstairs unaided at seventeen months.
	He climbed downstairs unaided at twenty months.
	He climbs in and out of chairs, couch, etc., with ease and confidence.
	He crawled properly at eighteen months (changed method from frog leap on stomach to crawling with one knee and one foot)
Food	He is not good with meals. He eats minced meat but he is not keen on chopped vegetables or finely chopped stew meat.
	He is good with sweet things, puddings, apple, fruit, etc.
	He feeds himself when he feels like it.
	He started drinking from a cup at twenty-one months but is very uncontrolled and makes a game of it.

Andy at Twenty-One Months

Dressing	(Eighteen and nineteen months) He helps: he can take off socks and tries to put on socks and trousers. He puts his arms up for his shirts.
Communication	(Seventeen and eighteen months) He began to make himself understood when he wanted something. He would point and say "uh, uh."
	At eighteen months brings a book and asks us to read to him.
	At nineteen months he points to some pictures and animals when you say their name. Began to make a noise for pictures in a book. Sometimes says "p" for up.
	He looks at books on his own and makes various noises (not distinguishable); points to things. He is very interested in books. He sits in a chair on his own and looks at them.
	Newspaper: he holds the paper and pretends to read it.
Toys	He can put a stick through a hole in a brick.
	He threw a ball at nineteen months.
	Nineteen months: he can hold a pencil to paper and tries to scribble. He doesn't make much of a mark.
	He builds to about four or five bricks or cups.
	He plays peek-a-boo.
	He runs away and hides.
	He blows a horn, whistle, etc. He sets up Teddies in position.
	He plays drum and xylophone, and seems interested in music.

Speech, its development and clarity, presents one of the biggest hurdles for a child with Down syndrome. If we had been able to benefit from the kind of early intervention program available to Lynn and Steve

Rodriguez, Andy would probably have developed stronger oral motor skills and been able to talk more clearly as an adult.

The extra genetic coding of a person with Down syndrome causes a range of differences. In most children, small jawbones frame a small mouth, and a high arch in the middle of a flatter-than-normal roof restricts space needed for the tongue. Blocked nasal passages and floppy muscles in the jaw and tongue contribute to children keeping their mouths open and letting their tongues hang out. Although communicative skills had been blended with play therapy from the beginning of Blair's program, a speech therapist began introducing specific oral motor therapy just before her first birthday in 1995. During this pre-speech phase, the therapist, using a soft toothbrush, worked to stimulate and develop muscle tone in Blair's mouth and tongue. Peanut butter added to the brush stuck to the roof of her mouth, making Blair exercise her tongue to get it off. These exercises would also help her learn to hold her tongue back, an important habit to develop early in life.

In order to stimulate mouth movement and encourage taste, Lynn was instructed to introduce a variety of foods with different textures at an early age. Most mothers welcome the convenience and ease of pureed foods when their child begins to take solids. After tackling a variety of cereals and fruits, Lynn gave Blair pieces of bread and popcorn cake. Although she had no teeth, the foods encouraged her to chew with her gums, again exercising the muscles in her mouth. As soon as she was able to sit in a high chair, Lynn and Steve encouraged their daughter to feed herself. Cheerios were a good beginning and helped Blair exercise her pincer grip. Having been given such an early chance to develop different tastes and textures, Blair soon acquired an exciting and versatile diet.

As the time neared for the birth of our second baby, I encouraged Andy to climb up the stairs. He enjoyed coming down on his own because he could slide down feet first on his tummy, but going up took more effort. In my last months of pregnancy, he was getting heavy for me to carry. Although it required much patience and determination on my part to make him climb the stairs on his own, I usually held out because I knew he was capable of doing it.

The Matron's Report had said about her mongol charges, "With humor and calm determination one can lead them anywhere and obtain their complete cooperation." She suggested making games out of a difficult task or walking upstairs to the rhythm of a nursery tune. Hopefully as I marched up the stairs singing, "Jack and Jill went up the hill," Andy would be unaware that I had invented this game to make him do something he didn't want to do and would follow happily in my footsteps.

As time went by, we realized that exerting all the patience we could muster to encourage Andy to do something on his own was an essential part of our training program. It was so much easier and quicker to pick him up, but it was much better for him to learn to complete the task himself. We were not pushing him beyond his capability; we were just encouraging him to achieve his potential at this stage. It was his first physical attempt to go up a staircase; the achievement symbolizing the staircase of life.

Chapter 6:
Baby Jean

On June 24, 1961, I gave birth to our second child, a daughter. She was beautiful. We were overjoyed. We had managed to create a perfect baby. The delivery took place in Leeds General Hospital; the labor was short and the delivery easy.

Pete had driven me to the hospital but could stay only a short time; he had to return to our house to relieve a neighbor who was watching over a sleeping Andy. I had been alone in the labor room when suddenly my water broke and the contractions were stronger and closer together. I called the nurse on duty and told her that the baby was ready to come.

"Do you think you can manage to walk into the delivery room between contractions?" she asked. Deciding I was tough but feeling rather breathless, I moved carefully into the theater. With only seconds to spare, I climbed onto the delivery table as the sister in charge admonished the young nurse for allowing me to walk at such a critical moment.

Giving birth is an amazing experience: the will becomes subservient to the body as the body takes control, directing the muscles to work at full capacity in expelling their burden. The patient can only endure the pain and in some small way help the body do its job. It is like a kayak rider relinquishing control of her craft as she is swept through the rapids. She is tossed relentlessly from shore to shore and whirled in circles by the churning water until finally the raging river hurls her over a tumbling waterfall. Amazingly, the kayaker lands upright and glides into calmer waters, regaining control over herself and her boat.

The moment of birth is exhilarating. There is one final overpowering contraction, one enormous push, and then a great gush, a flow, a flood of warm, welcome relief as the baby emerges. The crowning joy is the sound of the new baby's cry.

As soon as the umbilical cord had been cut, the nurses wrapped up my newly born baby and gave her to me to nurse. I was amazed as this little precious bundle, so newly come into the world, sucked eagerly at my breast. The sucking instinct was automatic and spontaneous and so different from Andy's lackadaisical attempts to feed. It was such a beautiful experience to be sitting on the delivery table nursing my new baby only moments after the overwhelming exertion of the birth. The baby sucked contentedly as I drank a cup of tea—that enduring British comfort—which a nurse had thoughtfully brought me.

We named our daughter Elizabeth Jean and called her Jean. She looked like a piece of Dresden porcelain. She was perfectly formed, with a delicate-looking, fine-boned body and beautiful face. She had light brown hair and big blue eyes.

After a brief two-day stay in the hospital, I was sent home with my new baby. As part of the British Health Service maternity care program, I was allowed a home helper for two weeks to clean the house, look after Andy, bring me refreshments upstairs until I was allowed to come down, and cook our evening meal. Our lady was a pleasant, round-bodied woman who spent most of her time in the kitchen, hands in a bowl mixing pastry with flour creeping up her arms to her elbows. We were fed meat pies, fruit pies, and anything that could be bottomed or topped with pastry. During this pie binge, the red carpeting, which brightened our hall and staircase, looked as if it were covered with a light scattering of snow.

Nursing Andy had been a struggle until the second month; nursing Jean was a joy. I knew what to do: I had started the nursing process right after birth instead of waiting until my milk came in and my breasts were engorged; my nipples were tougher, and Jean was a hungry baby. However, she was not a placid, quiescent baby like Andy. If it is possible to accurately diagnose colic, she seemed to be a colicky baby. We had many rough nights when nothing seemed to comfort her. We worried about her crying disturbing the neighbors through our common wall, but they didn't complain. Her eager nursing was satisfying, but when I tried to burp her, she would often throw up a huge quantity of milk. It wasn't just a little spit up as many babies are inclined to do; it appeared to be the entire meal, and I would have to nurse her all over again.

I discussed the problem with the doctor and staff at the baby clinic. I was concerned that this was projectile vomiting, which can be a sign of a stomach problem or some obstruction in the digestive system, but Jean was gaining weight and the symptoms didn't quite fit. Nevertheless, I worried. All mothers worry about their babies, and after having had one setback, I was exceptionally eager to have a normal child with no problems.

Suppressing my concerns, I took the children outside as much as the English summer climate would allow. We had exchanged the detested canvas pram for a secondhand, fancier, hard-bodied carriage. It still wasn't a Cadillac, but it was better than the Chevy version and what is more important, I could attach a seat across it for Andy to use.

He was intrigued with his new baby sister and didn't exhibit as much jealousy as do some siblings. Andy, who was just over two years old, was now walking and liked to help me push the pram until he got too tired or our progress was too slow; then he could sit on his pram seat. Most of the time he played contentedly with his toys, took his nap, and went to bed without a fuss. He loved to please and be praised for his efforts. A big grin would stretch across his chubby face, and his narrow, slanted eyes would crease in pleasure.

The big chore was mealtimes. Persuading Andy to eat meat and vegetables took much time and patience; dessert in the form of fruit and puddings was easy. He had enough teeth to be able to chew ground meat or cut-up bologna, but he found it an effort because his muscles were weak. Remembering the Matron's advice, I invented a variety of games to get through the meat and vegetable course. I ran out of people for whom each mouthful was to be eaten, and thinking of rewards to offer could be challenging. I was determined to maintain a well-balanced diet and not allow him to live on sweets and crackers. It was probably worth all the patience and hard work. He always maintained a good physique and weight and never acquired the heaviness and roundness that is typical of many people with Down syndrome. As an adult he enjoyed a wide assortment of foods, but a program based on finger food and on a variety of textures like the one which Lynn Rodriguez followed with Blair when she was one would undoubtedly have improved both Andy's eating habits as a child, helped to strengthen his facial muscles, and assisted his speech development.

We had bought Andy a baby walker to help him learn to walk. It was a sturdy wooden cart on four wheels with an upright handle, which took the weight of a toddler without tipping. Andy had learned to use it first in the house, where he pushed it around the living room like a bumper-car ride at a fair. If he pushed the cart into a chair or table, he would get stuck and needed help to get going again. He didn't cry with frustration as many children do; he just sat down on the floor, looked unhappy, and put his thumb in his mouth, or gave up and crawled away to do something else. I had to encourage him to keep trying, to pull the cart away from the obstacle and push it in another direction.

As Andy found his balance and became more active, he started to lose his baby fat and was soon standing and walking with a good upright posture. He never developed the round shoulder-drooping head stance that typifies some children with Down syndrome and usually results from living in a non-challenging setting with few opportunities for exercise. Although Down's children frequently have flat feet, lack a sense of balance, and let their stomachs protrude, early physical therapy and ample opportunity to exercise should help them develop into reasonably active and coordinated adults.

As summer came into full bloom, Andy acquired more confidence and took great pride in pushing the cart up and down the sidewalk, his face beaming as we applauded his efforts. Of course, he would have kept going in whatever direction he was headed if we hadn't helped him turn the cart and return along the sidewalk to our house.

When we bought our house, the garden was a heap of dirt and the driveway a crude track. We had professionals pave the driveway, but Pete took on the garden landscaping. We began to enjoy the fruits of his labors by the second year. There was a green lawn at the back with clotheslines over it for hanging up the wash, a place to put Jean in her pram to sleep, and a spot for Andy to have a small, inflatable wading pool. In the spring, fragile white snowdrops and sturdy purple crocuses tentatively reared their heads among the rocks alongside the grass, verdant from the winter rains. Deep yellow daffodil buds opened up into wavy-edged cups. Red, yellow, and black tulips danced in the breeze and soon dropped their bell-shaped petals on the ground. As spring drifted into summer, daisies and dandelions fought to take over the lawn, and delphiniums and dahlias, pansies and peonies decorated the borders.

On summer afternoons, while Jean slept in her pram, we sat in striped canvas deck chairs on the back lawn. One of Andy's greatest delights was to play in his wading pool. He spent hours filling a bucket with water and pouring it out again, usually over the side of the pool onto the grass. He was happy to play in the water until his lips turned blue or his body was covered in goose pimples. All mothers should be aware that owing to their poor circulation Down's children get colder more quickly than normal children. Because Andy rebelled against coming out to get dry and warm, Pete played a game of picking him out of the water, and flying him through the air, squealing with laughter, to a big towel on my lap, where I wrapped him up tightly and rubbed him hard all over to stimulate his circulation and get the blood flowing again. As I dressed him, protests, sobs, and laughter all mingled together like a mélange of ingredients in a blender.

Our neighbors—an elderly aunt, unmarried son, and spinster niece—took a special interest in Andy's progress. The spinster niece babysat, and Henry, the son, gave Andy rides in his wheelbarrow. With bowed legs and flat feet, Andy toddled after Henry rather like a baby duck waddling in the shadow of its mother.

Our mothers had been thrilled when we phoned to say we had a healthy baby girl. Just before Jean's birth, my mother had moved to a smaller house with a more manageable garden and fewer responsibilities.

Andy had been christened in All Saints Church in North Ferriby, where Pete and I were married. The brief ceremony took place in October 1959 as soon as Mother had recovered sufficiently from her operation. Now that her health was better, we arranged a happier gathering for

Jean's christening in a small church near Mother's new home. Typical of many English villages, the church was built of gray stone with a square tower above the nave and a rounded arch framing the entry porch. For Mother it was both a happy and sad occasion. She rejoiced in our growing family, but she had to accept the fact that we were soon going to leave England.

Earlier in the year Pete had been offered an associate professorship at Penn State University, our former locale in the United States. The exciting proposition caused us a major dilemma. Having planned to live and work in England, we had put down roots by buying a house. We did not want to become part of the so-called brain drain, which was a fashionable topic in newspapers and magazines at the time. Although Pete was pleased to be a member of a flourishing Geology Department at Leeds University, he was disappointed when he was told that his salary for a position as Lecturer would be based solely on his age without regard to his experience and scientific reputation, in contrast with American policies.

With a list of all the pros and cons, we pondered diligently over the offer from Penn State; America won. Pete would have more opportunities for his research and would find encouragement and incentive to work hard; promotions and recompense would be clearly related to productivity; and he would earn a better salary, which would enable us to have a bigger home for our growing family.

It was with great sadness and trepidation that we broke the news to our families. It was hard on both our parents, but it seemed especially hard on Mother. She had lost her husband only two years earlier, her first grandchild was mentally handicapped, and now she was battling breast cancer. Penn State is about four thousand miles away across the Atlantic Ocean. Overseas telephone calls were an expensive luxury. We relied on written communications, but a letter is not the same as hearing a voice over a wire, or knowing that the family will come to visit for Christmas. We knew that Mother would not have the energy to come to America and Pete's mother would not have the money.

Once again we packed the eleven trunks and many additional boxes and arranged to have our belongings shipped in a large container to Pennsylvania. Mother gave Andy a big hug, held her new granddaughter for the last time, and blessed them both with tears in her eyes. We stayed a few days with Pete's family so that Granny Wyllie could say good-bye to her precious little ones. With heavy hearts, we prepared to leave England for good.

Chapter 7:
Return to America

On a sweltering August day in 1961, we arrived at New York airport to be greeted by warm-hearted friends offering practical help. We were driven the three hundred miles to State College where the Fudalis put us up for a few nights, the Smiths rented us a furnished house, and other families provided us with food, baby equipment, and guidance.

We had made a modest profit on the sale of our house in Leeds, having converted a raw shell on a mud patch into a polished home with terraced garden and paved driveway. This money, combined with Pete's salary as an associate professor, was sufficient to cover down payments on a car and a respectable home in State College. We found a brand-new, four-bedroom house on a quiet street in a recently developed area not far from a supermarket and a school. Standing on a half-acre lot, the white colonial house with shuttered windows seemed like a mansion after the intimacy of the semi-detached houses in Leeds.

Encouraged by a visit to a Junior Training Centre in Leeds for retarded children where we were impressed by how much could be done to help the children learn and lead as normal a life as possible, I had inquired about a new specialized program, which we understood had been opened on the Penn State campus. We wanted to get Andy into some kind of preschool setting as soon as possible because we felt it would help his development to be with other children.

Our original thought of keeping Andy only for a few months while we evaluated the situation soon developed into a strong commitment to make him part of our family. We were already learning to love him for what he was, a child who was cute and funny, a child of our making who was growing and learning like other children but at a slower pace. In a letter to Penn State asking about schooling I wrote, "Many ideas were put to us when Andrew was very small, but as we learned more about him and children like him, we have come to feel that he will always be happiest and do best living with us as a member of our family and attending (if possible) some specialized school or training center, so that he can learn what he can and perhaps play some small part in the life of the community."

It turned out that the campus school at Penn State was for older educable children, but in October 1961, soon after our arrival, the Centre County Chapter of the Pennsylvania Association for Retarded Children organized a playgroup where we enrolled Andy. It was called the Carousel Play Group and was for mentally and physically handicapped children three to eight years of age residing in Centre County. It met five mornings a week operating on the public school calendar. Six children attended initially, and by 1963 the number had grown to eight.

Mrs. Renée Stewart, the head teacher, had a special gift for organizing a program and working with handicapped children. A friend of ours called Becky was her assistant, along with two volunteer helpers. The objectives of Carousel were outlined as follows:

1. To provide the children with childhood companions and to instruct them in social living, both as individuals and as part of a group.

2. To prepare the children for day care training centers or special education classes when they reach public school age.

3. To aid them in muscular development.

4. To assist them in speech development.

5. To teach them acceptable habits of work and play.

6. To teach them to follow directions.

7. To bring each child up to that level of preparedness for simple academic work which he is capable of achieving.

8. To provide parents with some relief from the burden of twenty-four-hour care.

All the activities of the Centre County Chapter depended on funds raised in the local communities. They required Carousel parents to be members of the Pennsylvania Association with annual dues $2.50 for singles and $4 for families. In addition they asked the parents to contribute $5 a week for each child enrolled in Carousel, a remarkably low fee even in those days. If parents were unable to contribute, their child would not be turned away.

Several community service organizations provided support for the new playgroup. Donated equipment included a sturdy wooden jungle gym to help the children develop physical coordination and strength. It could be used inside the classroom as well as for outdoor activity in the summer. A photo was published in the local paper with Andy sitting cross-legged on the floor looking through the bars, while Mrs. Stewart helped another child climb the ladder to the top.

Gamma Sigma Sigma sorority offered babysitting with sessions to train high school students as sitters for special needs children or as companions for handicapped adults. Mrs. Stewart held a class at the school to teach the students how to entertain and work with developmentally disabled children and to make them aware of potential problems.

I gave a talk to the sorority describing the program at the school and noting how much it helped both the children and their parents. I explained that it was often hard for parents to acknowledge that their children were slower than average and needed special training. The act of sending a child to Carousel was the first step in acceptance of their child's handicap. The parents met other parents struggling with the same problems and saw children similar to their own. They received sympathy and understanding from the teacher and her assistants, all of which helped them feel less alone and gave them encouragement to face the world with more confidence. The teachers became surrogate parents and were able to introduce a training program lacking in the home. In trying to balance responsibilities to their other children, it was often difficult for parents to give extra time to the handicapped child, who most needed their attention; or the handicapped child would require too much of their time and the siblings were neglected. Most children can achieve much more than a parent expects. Families often think that it is not worth trying to teach their children a new skill, because they are developmentally disabled and won't be able to master it. They are usually mistaken, because with persistence and constant repetition most handicapped children, especially those with Down syndrome, are able to master many of the basic self-care skills.

At Carousel the children learned to become aware of each other and to play together. Toys could be shared with another child—never an easy lesson for any child to learn—and the phrase "wait your turn" would be repeated over and over. Some of the children adapted more quickly to mixing with others; some were too dysfunctional to be able to mingle, but the individual attention and classroom environment were of benefit and provided a necessary break for the parents.

Snack time provided an opportunity to teach the children to feed themselves, to drink from a cup, and to use a spoon or fork. Most importantly, toilet training was a major element of the daily routine; for some it was just a beginning, for others it completed a practice that had begun at home.

Every day Andy looked forward to school. He always responded eagerly, "Yes, yes" when we asked him if he wanted to go to school. He carried his school case, containing a snack and clean diaper, proudly swinging it as he walked to the car. He always responded excitedly when we asked him what he had done all day. He showed us new things that he had learned to do with his toys, how he could throw a ball, and how he was learning to dance. He had mastered the rungs of the ladder on the jungle gym and could slither down the slide.

He used to be shy with other children, retiring into a corner to suck his thumb. Now his natural friendliness had been developed into an outgoing boldness. Birthdays were always celebrated at school with great fanfare. Decorations, songs, special juice, and cupcakes made the occasions memorable. Andy knew what to expect for his third birthday in April 1962. He was excited that this time it was his turn to have a special occasion, and he was the one to blow out the candles on the cake.

As well as being a gifted teacher, Mrs. Stewart was active in the community. She spoke at meetings of the Centre County Chapter; she gave presentations to parents' associations of the local schools and attended state and national conventions on retardation. With the children she had a firm but kindly manner; with the parents she was always ready to give advice and encouragement. Thirteen years after we had left State College, Mrs. Stewart retired. She had devoted many years of her life to Carousel. Her former students were contacted and asked to write letters or send photos and drawings. Andy wrote:

Dear Mrs. Stewart,

This is your big student writing to you.

I just turn to nineteen on my birthday on April 21.

After I went to your school I went to Murray School and then I went to Ray School and then I went to Kenwood High School, and I'm going to graduate in June 8, 1978.

I've got a job now and I work at the Co-op supermarket and I work downstairs at produce department, I'm doing is package fruits and vegetables.

I'm helping around the house, like I clean room three times a week in my apartment house. That's my bedroom name.

I do other things around the house for my Mom.

I'm taking horseback riding, and I take the bus by myself to downtown.

I'm taking piano lessons on Thursdays.

Sign: Andrew Wyllie

We enclosed a photo and an article about his job at the supermarket in Chicago. Mrs. Stewart was the first formal outside influence on Andy's development. She must have felt so proud of the results of her early guidance and training. Andy had attended Carousel for three years, from the age of two and a half until he was five and a half, and we felt sure that he was one of Mrs. Stewart's star pupils.

The structure and discipline provided by the program had a strong impact on Andy's later development. His toilet training was completed, his coordination, including his gross and fine motor skills, improved, and he started to talk. He loved the individual attention of the teachers, and he learned to play with other children.

Since the legislation of 1986, early intervention and preschool programs for children with developmental disabilities are available to all families, as explained in chapter 3. The range of programs differs from state to state. Since her first week of life, thirty-five years after Andy's birth, Blair Rodriguez received excellent early intervention therapies and was well prepared for a preschool program. Lynn described her accomplishments with pride: "At the age of thirty-four months, Blair could walk, run, climb, feed herself, brush her teeth, communicate through sign language and some words, laugh, put simple puzzles together, identify some colors and numbers, dance, 'talk' on the phone, ride in her little cars and bikes, climb stairs, drink from a straw, use the potty (sometimes), follow many directions or instructions, and interact with different people." As it was for Andy, the next step would be learning to mix and play with other children.

When Blair turned three, she attended a special program in the regular preschool, which her sister Karley had attended. Unfortunately it was only offered for three hours a day, four days a week, so a working mother had to find additional day-care accommodations. Lynn managed to arrange for Blair to stay on at the preschool and join a regular class for the afternoon session. Part of this time was taken up by lunch and a nap, and Blair had no difficulty fitting in. She also had the advantage of experiencing both partial and full inclusion. Blair spent the one non-school day with the neighbor who was her regular babysitter.

— ★ —

Once we had settled into our new State College home in 1961, I was able to concentrate on the children. Jean seemed to be making good progress. It was such a joy to have a strong, healthy baby. Andy loved his little sister and would stand by the pram, thumb in his mouth, just looking at her. Perhaps he was urging her, in his simple mind, to hurry up and grow so he would have a play companion.

Pennsylvania winters were cold and dreary. For much of the time snow blanketed the countryside and weighed heavily on the tree branches, causing them to sink to the ground as though the lacy edges of a crinoline skirt were too cumbersome for the fabric, making it dangle and droop as the hoops swayed with the stately walk of its wearer. The rural scenery looked like an idyllic painting carefully prepared for a Christmas card.

Pete built Andy a snowman and showed him how to make snowballs, but it was hard to make him keep his gloves on. One day, all dressed up in his snow clothes and boots, he ventured into the deep powder and got stuck. He stood there and cried for us to rescue him from his predicament. We decided he was quite capable of walking back the way he had gone. We called encouragements and urged him to turn around and come toward us. He continued to stand there and cry, a little lone Eskimo in the middle of a snowfield. Eventually, with a supreme effort, he managed to stagger back to the house. It was hard to discipline ourselves not to rush to his rescue, but again, it was another lesson in teaching Andy that he was capable of doing something on his own if he tried.

Chapter 8:
Jean's Cancer

We had moved into our lovely new colonial-style house. We had new furniture. I had unpacked and organized our belongings. Pete had started his new job as an associate professor; he had classes to teach and a research laboratory to assemble. Andy was attending the new Carousel Play Group. I had found a weekly housekeeper to clean the house and keep an eye on the children while I went to the supermarket or the hairdresser unencumbered. We were beginning to feel settled and content.

In October of 1961, it was time for Jean's three-month checkup; she was actually three and a half months old. She had weighed six pounds fifteen ounces at birth and had now grown to a comfortable eleven and a half pounds. State College was a small rural town with a limited choice of doctors. We returned to Dr. Collins, our family doctor when Andy was born. He was a kindly man, easy to talk to, and I felt comfortable with him. Because he had given us such a grim outlook at the time of Andy's birth and suggested we not keep our mongol baby, I wanted to show him how wrong he was and let him see Andy's excellent progress. He was impressed, but he never mentioned that his earlier advice might have been inappropriate.

He examined Jean thoroughly and pronounced her progress satisfactory. As he prodded her stomach, feeling her different organs, he mentioned a tiny knob in her kidney area. He seemed to brush it aside as inconsequential and did not make a note of it on her chart. He said nothing at her next two visits, and I had turned a deaf ear to his statement and forgotten about it.

Andy was always happy. Jean was younger and still fussed at times.

She ate and slept well. I had nursed her until she was four months old, but I did not seem to have enough milk to satisfy her in the evenings, so I gradually weaned her to a bottle. She continued to gain weight steadily and enjoyed eating cereal. Between naps and meals, she seemed quite happy sitting in her baby chair or lying on her back in the playpen, but when I put her on her tummy to look at her toys, she always fussed.

On January 9, 1962, I took Jean to the doctor for her six-and-a-half-month checkup. After I had undressed her and had her weighed, Dr. Collins laid her down on the examining table and took a careful look at her stomach.

"Have you noticed that her tummy is lopsided?" the doctor said ponderously. "It seems to be bigger on one side than the other."

I had not noticed, but now that he pointed it out, I did see that it was bulging slightly on her left side. Because I changed her diaper several times a day and bathed her every morning, I immediately felt guilty for not seeing something abnormal. I did mention that she seemed to get fussy when lying on her stomach.

With studied calmness, Dr. Collins said, "I would like you to take her to the hospital in Bellefonte for some tests." He explained that a radiologist would put dye into her body and take pictures to find out what was causing the enlargement in her abdomen.

I was consumed with panic, fear, and confusion. As feelings of nausea washed over me, I thought I might throw up. What nightmare was about to overwhelm us now? I dressed my darling baby and drove home in a daze. I phoned Pete, who left his office immediately. He asked all kinds of questions that I could not answer. He arranged to take time off so he could come with me to the Bellefonte Hospital the next day.

The tests at the hospital seemed to take forever. I think we were there only half a day, but it seemed like a whole day. Jean was very fussy, and we were kept waiting in a cold and dreary room. The hospital employees were as unsympathetic as the room; nobody seemed to have much feeling for this sad little baby. Finally it was over, but the results had to be sent to the doctor, so we went home without knowing anything. Later Dr. Collins called and told us that things looked rather serious. There was a lump. It was probably benign (what did that word mean?), but he said it was necessary to see a specialist. We had already driven twelve miles to the hospital in Bellefonte; now we would have to drive thirty-five miles over the mountains to another hospital in Lewistown to see a specialist.

The next few days passed in a blur. We were experiencing the same numbness as we did when Andy was born. Nothing seemed real. We felt like robots mechanically moving our arms and legs to do what needed to be done. We called only our closest friends, the Fudalis, and asked them to look after Andy.

We did not want to put our worst fears into words. There was no point imagining more than what we had to cope with in the immediate present. It was January, and the weather was bitterly cold with snow on the roads. Jean had a runny nose and was cranky.

Dr. Morgan, the specialist in Lewistown, ordered more X-rays and recommended an exploratory operation to find out if the mass—it was now called a tumor—was benign or malignant. An operation sounded so ominous. I quickly learned that "benign" meant a growth without cancerous cells and that "malignant" meant cancerous. Cancerous? How could a little baby—our beautiful, normal, healthy daughter—have cancer? Only grown-ups and old people, like my mother, had cancer. Surely children did not have cancer. The doctor must be mistaken. How could we cope with anything more? Had not God punished us enough for whatever wrong we had done? This growth would certainly be benign. I prayed that it would be.

We had to leave Jean at the hospital for a few days so they could monitor her temperature and make sure she was well enough for anesthesia and surgery. It was such a wrench to leave her. I felt as though someone was tearing off part of my own body. The exploratory operation was delayed because Jean had a cold, but the doctors found in her groin a small swelling from which they extracted fluid for testing. The results confirmed our worst fears. She had a malignant growth, and the swollen lymph node showed that the cancer had already spread. Dr. Morgan told us that a growth in the abdominal area was called a Wilms' tumor.

With sadness and compassion, he told us that nothing could be done. "Take your daughter home and enjoy her for as long as she lives. It is God's will. I think He must need this baby more than you do." He did not hold out any hope, but if we chose to try to save our baby, we could take her to specialists in New York. He gave us the name of Dr. Dargeon at the Memorial Sloan-Kettering Cancer Center in New York City.

Parents face this kind of dilemma when their babies are born with a serious ailment or defect. Corrective surgery is an option, but the chances of survival are slim. The child may be mentally handicapped or have other problems, and there is no prospect of a normal life. The surgery or treatment will be costly and may require long stays in the hospital or complicated and expensive care at home. Other children and members of the family will be affected and suffer neglect. The parents will face years of high medical costs and serious debt just for a minuscule chance of survival and possible cure. What choice should they make? They listen to the advice of the experts and counselors, but only they can make the final decision. I feel there is no justification for right-to-life groups or courts of law to become involved in such cases, forcing countless years of expense and suffering on such vulnerable parents. It is the parents' personal choice alone; no one can, or should, make it for them.

Once again in our early parenting years we had an important choice to make. We could keep Jean at home, make her happy and comfortable, and watch her die—maybe slowly, maybe quickly. Or we could go to the best hospital and the best specialists in the country and ask them to treat her with the latest therapies and surgery. We could try for that small chance of survival and recovery.

Choice A would not cost anything and would signify our acceptance of the inevitable, but would it give us peace of mind? Would we feel that we had done the right thing? Would it be the best course for Jean? Choice B would be costly. We did have medical coverage, but for only 80 percent of the costs. The remaining 20 percent would quickly add up to more than we could afford. It would take a lot of time and effort, and Andy would be neglected; we would have to leave him for days at a time with sitters or friends. Pete had just taken a new position involving constant dedication to teaching and research; he would have to ask for some leave. According to Dr. Morgan, the chances of success were almost zero.

We chose B. It seemed obvious: we had to do everything in our power to save our baby's life. We had to give her that fractional chance of survival whatever the cost in time, energy, emotion, and money. We agreed without hesitation to go to New York.

In the 1960s there were no superhighways linking the center of Pennsylvania with cities to the west or east. We faced a long drive of six hours or more over winding roads through villages and towns before reaching the urban spread of New Jersey and entering New York City. We made the journey from State College to New York and back many times during the next few months. The first time was the worst; we had to find our way to the hospital negotiating the unfamiliar streets and traffic of New York City.

We arrived late on a Sunday afternoon. Dr. Morgan had telephoned the specialist and made arrangements with the hospital, but this did not make it easier. The hospital admitting staff would not accept the validity of our medical insurance because they were not familiar with the company. They asked for a large deposit, but we did not have the money. I sat holding Jean in my arms in the austere, high-ceilinged entrance hall. Were they really going to turn us away after driving six hours to this famous hospital, the only hope of survival for our desperately sick baby? I could not believe that the administrators would be so cruel. I sat trembling on the brink of tears and held Jean close. What could we do? It was Sunday, and the university offices were closed. Pete phoned his senior professor, who was able to persuade the hospital staff that Penn State's medical insurance was as reliable as the coverage carried by New York state universities. Finally, the paperwork was completed, and the hospital agreed to admit Jean.

Dr. Harold Dargeon was the specialist in charge of Jean. He examined her thoroughly and told us that the mass was a neuroblastoma tumor, a malignant tumor on her kidney. He didn't know if it was involved with or affecting the kidney. It is the most common cancer among infants. Although the cause is unknown, it appears to be an accidental growth that occurs during normal development of the sympathetic nervous system. It may have been present at birth. Apparently, in Jean's case it had grown from a tiny pea (which Dr. Collins had felt at three and a half months) to the size of a fist in a period of three months. This type of cancer is extremely difficult to treat and spreads quickly. However, with removal of the tumor or main site, there is sometimes a miraculous withdrawal and disappearance of other cancer cells. Surgery to remove the tumor was the only hope.

In order to increase the chances of an operation being successful, especially as there was no way of knowing how much the kidney or other vital organs were involved, it was advisable to reduce the size of the mass. Radiation treatment would have to be used. This would make Jean sick; she would have a difficult time maintaining her food intake, and she would have to stay at the hospital during the treatment.

We tried to listen carefully to everything Dr. Dargeon told us. He was kind and patient; he had witnessed many parents agonizing over decisions and struggling with frightening medical information. Without hesitation we agreed to follow his advice and program of treatment.

With great sadness and trepidation, we entrusted Jean to the nurse's care. We had to leave our little baby alone at the hospital and return to State College; Pete had to work, and Andy needed attention. After meeting the nurses and getting Jean settled in her hospital crib, we walked along the corridors of the pediatric wing. All the patients were cancer victims; all were children ranging in age from toddlers to teenagers, some hobbling on crutches with a missing leg, others in wheelchairs with intravenous drips. Jean was the youngest, although other small babies had been patients. In spite of the grim disease, an air of cheerfulness pervaded the area. Nurses chatted and joked with the children; bright pictures decorated the walls of a large dayroom; patients' drawings and paintings, toys, and games were scattered on low tables; and parents were visiting their loved ones. We were certainly not alone in our tragic predicament.

For the next several weeks Jean received radiation treatments. We drove to New York to visit her every weekend. We saw her becoming thinner and thinner until she looked like a child in a concentration camp. We feared that she would forget us, her parents. We worried that she would be unhappy and cry all the time or that she would throw up and have to be tied down in her crib with an intravenous needle in her arm. Our fears were unnecessary. She managed to tolerate the radiation well and was able to keep down sufficient nourishment so that intravenous feeding was unnecessary. She became the darling of the nurses and the mascot of the pediatric ward. She spent more time at the nurses' station or being carried around the hospital than in her crib or play area. She loved all the attention. The hospital staff called her Elizabeth or Lizzy (as this was her first name). She always had a smile on her face and was happy to see us.

After the course of treatment, we brought her home to nurture and nourish her for six weeks while the radiation took full effect. I handled my sweet baby as though she were a rosebud with petals about to unfold into a delicately layered flower. If I held the bud carelessly I might bruise the petals, blemishing the perfection of the full flower. Jean was so thin that the bones were visible through her skin. Her face, pale and gaunt, seemed overpowered by her big blue eyes, but she smiled easily, her muscles were strong, and she sat straight, with her head held high and her eyes sparkling. Her personality was developing, and there was a special sweetness, almost an ethereal quality, to her nature.

I was afraid she might be confused by the use of different names, but she adapted quickly to being Jean at home and Liz in the hospital. As I carried her downstairs in the morning, she looked around for more people; she missed all the different faces and attention she had received at Sloan-Kettering. She especially enjoyed Andy and always perked up when she heard his voice as he came in the house from school. She liked it when he brought toys to her crib or playpen and laughed when they had baths together.

It was hard work to persuade Jean to take more nourishment. She could only tolerate so much. But after a week or two, she was able to drink a full bottle of milk and take solid food. Gradually, her bones became less visible, and her cheeks began to fill out.

At the end of March 1962, we took Jean back to New York for the surgery. Dr. Dargeon was the principal specialist, but a cancer surgeon was an important part of the team. The doctors were satisfied with the shrinkage of the tumor and proceeded to operate. We stayed in New York for the event. The operation went well, and the surgeon was able to remove the entire tumor. The good news was that it had been resting on top of the kidney but had not grown into the kidney. It was possible that the pressure of the tumor might have damaged the kidney, but there was a chance that it was unharmed. The bad news was that the cancer had spread to the liver. We knew from the beginning that it had metastasized but hoped that it had remained in the lymph nodes. Cancer cells in such a vital organ as the liver are disastrous. The doctors recommended chemotherapy as the only course to follow. Now that the mother tumor had been removed, there was a remote possibility of a complete regression. Chemotherapy would help to fight and kill the spreading cancer cells.

Although high doses of intensive chemotherapy may give a neuroblastoma patient the best chance for recovery, the treatment may adversely affect other organs of the body. The bone marrow may stop producing infection-fighting white blood cells, making the patient especially susceptible to other infections. According to the Memorial Sloan-Kettering website (2011), a variety of treatments are now being used, depending on the stage of the cancer. These include stem cell transplants that destroy a patient's infected bone marrow and replace it with stem cells relatively free of cancer.

In 1961 no such procedure existed. Dr. Dargeon prescribed as high a dose as possible and told us we could give the chemotherapy course at home. He gave me instructions on how and when to give it: Jean was to receive one milligram of prednisone three times a day. The medicine was in powder form, and I mixed it in her formula or with solid food. Additionally, it was necessary to have a medical laboratory in State College take blood samples each week to monitor her hemoglobin and white cell count. I telephoned the results to Dr. Dargeon in New York and reported on Jean's food intake and weight gains. I kept a notebook and became a surrogate nurse. I recorded every dose, every meal, every bowel movement, and kept track of temperature and weight. In spite of keeping a careful watch on her white cell level, her condition made her prone to colds and virus infections, which gave us more to worry about. At first we had to take Jean back to New York to see Dr. Dargeon every week, then every other week, then every three weeks, and finally just once a month.

The three months following the first news of Jean's sickness had passed in nightmarish darkness. Similar to my reaction after Andy's birth, I kept

Loving Andrew

thinking I would wake up and find it had not really happened. It would be just another bad dream.

We were so focused on Jean that I felt sure our neglect of Andy would have repercussions. But Andy was such a happy, friendly child that he did not seem to suffer in spite of being constantly shuffled from one household to another when we went to New York. We tried to make his frequent visits to different places a special treat. He had his own overnight bag packed with his clothes and a few favorite toys. Hosts made him the center of attention, and often there were other children with whom he could play. When we came back, we took him out for ice cream, gave him special cuddles, and read him extra stories at bedtime. He was well established at Carousel and had the security of the daily school program giving continuity and structure to his life.

We could not have survived without our friends. As well as taking turns to have Andy for the weekends, they provided us with casseroles and salads, pies, and pastries to supplement the meager cooking our schedules allowed. A former exchange student at the University of St. Andrews was now married and living in Brooklyn. Their home, a second-floor apartment in a brownstone, became our New York base for our many trips in and out of the city, saving us the impossible cost of city hotels.

In spite of the chemotherapy treatment, Jean gradually gained weight. She began to lose her skeleton look, and her face and body became rounder. She was very pretty, a picture-perfect child with an engaging smile and delicate manner. She was crawling and starting to pull herself onto her feet. Andy liked to help her stand up and push the baby walker. Sometimes he held her hands and helped her take a few steps, grinning with pride as he aided his baby sister. Then, deciding he had done enough, he would casually push her down.

One day at the end of May when I had just finished changing Jean, Andy tried to grab a bowl of water from the table. I was holding Jean on my shoulder with one hand on her back. As I reached forward to save the bowl from Andy's grasp, Jean slipped over my shoulder and fell to the floor on her head. I was horrified. What had I done to this poor little baby who was already suffering so much? I picked her up, rocking and soothing her until her cries quieted down. Andy cried too, wondering what he had done.

I rushed Jean to the doctor, but he found no indication of any serious injury. He told me to watch for unconsciousness and warned me her eyes might show signs of bruising in the next few days. I ached with guilt, and my head split with the pain that Jean must have felt. I was angry with myself for being so careless and stupid. How does a broken bowl and puddle of water on the floor compare to the broken head of a sick baby? Jean did not seem to be any worse for the fall or show symptoms of a concussion, although she did have a black eye for a week.

When the weather was nice, I took the children for walks. I dressed Jean in beautiful dresses and a bonnet with a big lace-trimmed brim to keep the sun off her face. She looked like a model for a Reynolds painting. She also liked to crawl in the garden and explore the flower beds. She had a strong appetite for dirt and yellow marigolds. The artist's model soon became a grubby doll as she smiled at us with her soiled hands and blackened mouth.

On warm summer days we set up the wading pool near the back porch. Andy was now an experienced wader and enjoyed running across the grass and jumping in the pool with a big, clumsy splash. Jean, dressed in a slinky pink bathing suit, maneuvered around the grass on hands and feet to avoid the rough surface scratching her knees. She enjoyed playing in the water when her big brother was not commandeering the pool.

By the beginning of July, the doctors in New York gave us a promising report: the cancer appeared to be in remission, but it was essential to continue the chemotherapy.

We had hoped to have four normal children, but so far, our progress was not good. We had a child with Down syndrome and a child with cancer. We asked the doctors if there was any connection. Was there something wrong with us that we could not produce a normal, healthy child? Had the virus that I had when I was pregnant caused Jean's cancer? Was there any connection with my mother's cancer? Could there be a genetic cause? Was it safe to have more children?

Many of our friends already had one or two healthy children, and we were getting left behind. The doctors assured us there was no correlation between Down syndrome and cancer. However, they did suggest we all have chromosome studies done. This would tell us if Pete, Jean, and I had a normal chromosome count and confirm that we were not carriers of an extra chromosome. The 1959 discoveries had revealed that Down syndrome children have 47 chromosomes instead of the normal 46. In a few cases parents can be carriers of an extra chromosome, increasing the chances of having more than one Down syndrome offspring. We had these tests done at Syracuse University, one of the few places doing chromosome studies at that time.

The drive to Syracuse was a long 250-mile expedition through the Appalachian Mountains and skirting the Finger Lakes of Upper New York State. The tests necessitated drawing a large vial of blood from each of us. Both a doctor and a nurse made several attempts to jab the vicious needle into an elusive vein in Andy's arms before they finally succeeded. Poor Andy, who was usually so cheerful and placid, bawled loudly with fear and discomfort.

After several weeks, we received the results of the study: only Andy had the extra chromosome. The doctors told us there was no reason why we should not have a normal child. We should put our trust in God, along with biological science, and have more babies.

In early August some English friends invited us to spend a few days with them in the mountains. They had a son and twin daughters and had rented a cottage near a lake. It was one of those quiet retreats in the Allegheny Mountains where the breeze rustles through the tall pine trees, a chorus of birdsongs interrupts your morning dreams, and animals pad gently near the cabins looking for scraps. Andy loved digging up the beach and building sand castles with help from the twins while Jean enjoyed crawling around and splashing in the water. We tried to protect her from the sun, and I worried when she was carsick on the long drive to the mountains.

Soon after our return to State College, Jean took her first delicate, hesitant steps on her own. It was August 15, 1962. She was nearly fourteen months old and was small and fragile for her age, but she had come a long way in catching up. We still counted our blessings each day; we felt hopeful that perhaps a miracle had happened and she would recover completely, growing to live a normal life.

Five days later, Jean caught an intestinal virus. She had violent diarrhea and was running a temperature. I called Dr. Collins immediately and he told us to give her weak tea, Jell-O, and any plain liquids we could get into her. By evening, her condition worsened. I decided to spend the night in her room. I slept fitfully and was awakened by a banging noise in her crib. Jean was having convulsions. Her temperature was 105 degrees.

We called the doctor again; he told us to bathe her with cool water to bring the fever down. He did not offer to come to the house or suggest we take her to the hospital. If our own doctor would not come, it seemed inappropriate to call our neighbors, a lady doctor on one side and a nurse on the other. We hated to involve them in the middle of the night. The sponging brought down the fever a little, and the convulsions ceased. I dozed off once more and woke in the early hours to find Jean convulsing again. Her head was burning, but her feet were blue. I woke Pete and said we must go straight to the hospital. He called Dr. Collins and told him to meet us there. We were not going to wait for his advice. This was an emergency.

It was a Friday morning, and Lodi, our housekeeper, had just arrived. Hastily, we asked her to look after Andy. She understood our panic and helped us bundle Jean in blankets and get her into the car. Pete drove the long twelve miles to Bellefonte as fast as he dared. With my head spinning and my eyes blurring with tears, I cradled our baby in my arms.

Just before we reached the hospital, I looked at Jean's ashen face and knew that she was gone. Fearing that Pete might have an accident, I did not say anything until we stopped at the emergency door. Pete felt certain that something could be done to bring our baby back to life. The emergency personnel rushed her to a room and tried to revive her, but it was too late; her soul had already gone to heaven. She had joined God's band of littlest angels. He needed her and had a special role for her to play.

We asked the hospital to do an autopsy. It was seven months since the cancer had been discovered; we needed to know if it had been spreading in spite of the treatment and was the cause of her death. As always, I felt guilty. I thought I was to blame; I had not cared for her well enough; we had not done the right thing when she got sick with the virus; we should have taken her to the hospital sooner. The autopsy results showed that the cancer had spread extensively, even to the bones of her spine. If she had survived this virus, another one would have attacked her, and she would have died soon.

We had wanted to see and hold our baby one last time, but the hospital staff urged us to go home. Shaking, we hugged and held each other a long time. We could not believe that this was the end; one minute Jean was alive, and the next moment she was gone. Somehow we got in the car and drove back in silence. We felt drained. It seemed as though we had no tears left; our emotions were dried up. It was hard to break the news to Lodi, who had difficulty believing us. I was exhausted. I had hardly slept all night; I felt as though I had the same virus. I tried to rest but could not sleep.

A priest called at the house and offered prayers and comfort. Pete busied himself with the funeral arrangements. The Fudalis—Lois was Jean's godmother took care of Andy, brought food to the house, and drove us to the funeral ceremonies; they were always at our side, helping us through those difficult days.

I sent Jean's prettiest dress and bonnet to the funeral parlor. A private visitation time was arranged. I did not want to see her again, but at the last minute, I summoned the courage to go. There she lay, a Dresden doll so delicate and beautiful. Her head, framed by the lace edging of her bonnet, rested on a pillow of white satin in the tiny coffin. In spite of the autopsy, there were no signs of incisions. The mortician had prepared her well; gone was the gray pallor as she had lain dying in my arms. Now her skin was a delicate pink, the color of a blushed rose that never had a chance to unfold into full bloom. Why had God given us this baby and then taken her away again so soon? Why was she born, only to suffer pain and die?

A funeral service at St. Andrew's Episcopal Church in State College was brief and simple. The small, closed coffin stood at the front of the church with a single spray of flowers on top. We had asked for contributions to be made to the Centre County Cancer Society. Friends in the College of Mineral Industries raised money to pay for the funeral, and many came to lend moral support at the church. The service passed in a blur. We heard words and music, but nothing registered; everything blended into a numbing haze.

Jean was buried in the Centre County Memorial Park, a place of peace and tranquility, where dark green pines and scarlet trees frame a Carillon tower and cone-shaped shrubs dot the lawns. All the tombstones are simple plaques in the ground. She is buried in the Children's Garden. A bas-relief of little Bo-Peep and her sheep decorates a corner of the brass marker and the inscription reads:

Elizabeth Jean Wyllie
June 24, 1961
August 21, 1962

She died three days before her fourteenth month. We both wept and threw yellow marigolds on her coffin as it was lowered into the ground.

I saw her once more—
'Twas the day that she died;
Heaven's light was around her,
And God at her side;
No wants to distress her,
Nor fears to appall—
O then, I felt, then
She was fairest of all!
                    —H. F. Lyte

Chapter 9:
Life Goes On

Andy was our ray of sunshine, giving us hope and a sense of purpose in the midst of this dark storm. He was the constant element that kept us going, helping us realize that in spite of the tragic death of our daughter, life must go on.

He must have been aware of the gloom and sadness around him, but he carried on with his happy ways, seemingly unscathed by the trauma. He needed to be dressed and fed, he loved going to school, he took a nap when he came home, and he played happily with his toys without fussing. As yet, he was not very verbal, so he did not ask the questions that a normal three-year-old would have asked. With the extended stays at the hospital in New York, Jean had been in and out of Andy's life. Now we told him gently that she had gone away forever to become an angel in heaven. I am sure he missed her presence; there must have been emptiness in his life as there was in ours, but he did not cry. He had kissed and hugged his sister, and now when he saw small children like Jean, he went up to them and embraced them, perhaps hoping that they would be his sister. No doubt he expected Jean to appear again as she had before.

After her hospital ordeal, Jean had learned to crawl around the house and garden and had shared Andy's swimming pool; she had wanted the same toys and caused the occasional tussle; she had stood by his car and bicycle and pushed them but could not ride them. Andy had helped Jean walk, but when he tired of it, he just let her plunk down on the floor as though she was another toy with which he had finished playing. She had been too young to be an equal playmate. Soon we would think about having another baby to build our family and give Andy a companion. In the meantime, we bought him some new toys and tried to make up for the attention that he had lacked during the months of Jean's illness.

At school Andy was learning to play with his schoolmates, so we encouraged other children to visit and play with him at home. A brother and sister, who were about the same age as Andy, lived a few houses away. Their visits would usually result in tea parties in the garden with a miniature tea set at a small table with real cookies and juice. Andy loved to pour the "tea" carefully and precisely into the small cups. I taught him to serve his guests first before filling his own plate with cookies.

Since our families were so far away, we depended on our friends for practical help and moral support. Their children included Andy in their games as though he had no disability. Girls, in particular, liked to take a motherly role and make sure no one hurt him. We hoped it could always be this way, but we knew that he would often have to face ridicule, teasing, and prejudice.

On fine days we went for walks and visited a nearby park where there was a playground with swings and slides among the trees. Andy was eager to climb the ladder to the top of the slide but sometimes lacked the courage to sit down and slide to the bottom. From his high perch, it must have looked like a long way down. That did not matter if he was the lone user of the equipment, but other children, who were waiting their turn, could be impatient and pushy, sometimes saying, "What's wrong with you, dummy, just go."

What mother has escaped such a situation when her youngster, frozen at the top and out of reach of her helping hand, holds up a long line of eager kids? Will the other children be sympathetic to the fears of the timorous boy, or will they increase his fear by making fun of him? This was a situation that I had to tackle head-on. I would ask the children to be patient, explain that Andy needed more help and encouragement because he was slower to do things, and do my best to persuade Andy to come down the slide. With a little patience, it usually worked. After what seemed like an interminable delay, Andy would come whooshing down with a broad grin lighting up his face. I would tell him that he must be quicker another time to give the other children a turn. I did not say that he might get pushed because I had learned that the best results came from persuasive tactics rather than threatening ones.

Fortunately, Andy was not plagued with some of the health problems that other children with Down syndrome have to endure. Blair Rodriguez recovered well from surgery to correct a serious heart defect, but when her parents were preparing to send her to a preschool program, they faced the question of a hearing problem.

Approximately 60 to 80 percent of children with Down syndrome have mild to moderate hearing impairment. Several factors can be blamed: a small skull creates small ear canals and chambers, which get blocked more easily with accumulated wax; fluid sometimes fills the middle chamber; and small or abnormally shaped bones in the middle ear distort the transmission of sound from the eardrum to the inner ear.

Between two and three years of age, the brain is especially receptive to language; therefore it is essential to help a child whose verbal development may already be delayed. In her first year, tubes were inserted in Blair's ears to prevent the buildup of fluids and deter infections. But her speech had not progressed as well as might be hoped, leading her therapists to conclude that she might be failing to hear sounds in the high-frequency range. Children cannot learn to imitate sounds that they are not hearing; so, instead of trying to use their auditory senses, they will begin to rely on other sensory areas, such as sight.

Lynn described her struggle to get answers "as the most frustrating and most undefined road." The ENT (ear, nose, and throat) specialist and the audiologists were full of uncertainty, slow to give a diagnosis or suggest a solution. A proposed brain stem test had to be aborted because Blair did not respond to the required sedative; behavioral tests were inconclusive because Blair was too young to say whether she was hearing the different sounds. Eventually, the audiologist decided to base the results on the movement of Blair's head. The final conclusion: a mild hearing loss in high-frequency sounds. Blair was then fitted with $1,800 hearing aids, which were not covered by insurance. The aids were removed at night, but as with any nearly three-year-old, there was no guarantee that she would keep them in during the day. After learning that Blair hated wearing hats or sunglasses, I envisioned the traumatic scenario of high-priced hearing aids being lost down the toilet, thrown out of a window, or hidden among a jumble of toys.

— ★ —

Lynn and Steve have always been active in their local parents' organization. They have shared experiences and resources with other families and have benefited from personal recommendations for babysitters, schools, therapists, and medical specialists. In England we had felt isolated without a parents' group to give us support and information. However, during Andy's primary years we were drawn into the local chapter of the Pennsylvania Association of Retarded Children by a faculty couple at Penn State. Their daughter, Carol, had Down syndrome and attended Carousel at the same time as Andy.

In 1963 I was in charge of publicity for the Centre County Chapter. The organization, which had been in existence for ten years, comprised a small but active group of parents in State College and the surrounding communities. They had monthly meetings with speakers on different aspects of mental retardation. The meetings also gave the parents an opportunity to get to know each other, discuss problems, and share information on the latest research and federal activities regarding the handicapped.

The chapter raised funds to support a sheltered workshop for the handicapped, special activities for a girls' cottage at one of the state schools, and the newly established playgroup, Carousel. Monthly speakers covered a range of useful topics from the latest information on PKU testing (the full name, Phenylketonuria, has always been shortened because no two authorities can agree on the correct pronunciation) to speech therapy for the handicapped and counseling sessions for parents. Special education teachers from the State College schools came to a meeting to explain their programs, and the teachers of a day care training center for ages six to twenty described their operation. Using every available object and activity as a teaching tool, the day care center trained their students to learn within their individual limitations to become responsible and independent people. If it was not possible to educate their minds, then their aim was to educate their hearts.

The associate executive director of the Pennsylvania association reported that the number of state schools had increased, but they still had long waiting lists. A shortage of certified teachers and attendants was hindering the development of smaller schools near population centers. Paul Reed, president of the national association, told us that ten or twelve years earlier, parents were advised to put their retarded child away in an institution and forget about him or her. (We had received such a recommendation only four years previously.) But parents could not forget their children so easily.

Misery loves company, and parents started to bond together and become a force for change. An article in a 1959 issue of *Redbook* magazine described how local groups were growing into state organizations and an "army of parents" was spreading across the country to form a national association. Parents began to realize that all developmentally disabled children could be helped and taught something, and it was important to make professionals and politicians aware of this. The concept of independent living was established; disabled men and women might not be able to earn a living, but they could learn to take care of themselves in order to lessen their burden on the community. Work was progressing in the areas of parent counseling, day care centers, special classes, and sheltered workshops. But it all took money and the combined efforts of everyone. The most difficult task was to capture the interest of the average person who does not have a special needs child. Mr. Reed, stressing that the local chapters are the backbone of the organization, urged us to be bold, to tell the public about our problems and ask for help, and to let people know that we were not ashamed. The December 1963 minutes of our chapter stated: "There is a need for acceptance of handicapped children and adults by their contemporaries and by society."

After Jean's death, my youngest brother wrote: "I hope you have not been deterred from having any more children, although I wouldn't blame you if you have." We had certainly questioned our reproductive prospects, but after discussing the results of the chromosome tests with the specialists in New York, we were assured that there was no reason why we should not have a normal child. We were eager to provide Andy with playmates, and we felt it was important for him to grow up with brothers and sisters who could help him learn.

I gave birth to our third child on May 17, 1963. I do not think I could have continued to have more babies if the path to the parental summit had not been made so easy. This delivery was too fast for Dr. Collins; I had given birth by the time he reached the hospital. Nine months after Jean's death, we were blessed with another daughter. We named her Lisa Margaret; the Lisa was a derivative of Jean's first name, Elizabeth, and the name of one of our closest friends, Lisa Herzog.

After the birth, my tennis partner, Christine, wrote a letter, which I have kept in an album next to Lisa's birth photo and announcement:

> I write these words in great happiness because I know that little Lisa will fulfill all your hopes and expectations you once had for a little girl.
>
> She will be so very special because she was conceived with so much faith and courage at a time of great tragedy. You are two wonderful people, Romy and Peter!
>
> For a long time to come, Lisa will have a little white shadow you will only perceive with your hearts—but one day you will see that the little white shadow with the name of Jean has become one in the creation of Lisa.

Jean had been fine-boned and delicate; Lisa was round-faced and sturdy. She nursed eagerly and seldom spat up; she gained weight in leaps and bounds and was thoroughly normal and healthy.

Andy was happy to have another baby around and was always looking in her crib or baby carriage, perhaps to make sure she had not disappeared. He chatted constantly about "new baby Eesa." If he sat safely on the sofa, with a parent keeping a watchful eye, he was capable of holding her on his lap. He brought her stuffed toys or trucks to play with, hoping that she would grow quickly to become the playmate that he nearly had before.

The disruptions and strange occurrences at home did not seem to affect Andy's progress at school. A report card for the school year of 1963-64 gave Andy an almost perfect score for self-care, social adjustment, and music training. He still needed to improve in the areas of sharing toys and work materials and helping to keep the room and materials neat. Now four years old, his speech was improving. He made the correct sounds for most of the consonants, but still had difficulty with: b, t, ng, v, th, t, s, z, and ch. He could say single words but needed help with phrases and sentences, although he was able to repeat simple sentences after the teacher.

His physical development continued to improve; his walking, running, and general activities were more coordinated and his fine motor movements better. At the same time, he was growing fast and needed clothes. With a limited budget, I economized and used many of Jean's garments for Lisa. Occasionally, looking back at photographs, we are confused between pictures of Jean and Lisa, but from the moment of her birth, Lisa was her own person. Angel Jean watched over the new baby, but the little white shadow was transformed at once into Lisa.

One Friday morning in the spring of 1964, Lodi was busy cleaning and I was fixing lunch, having just returned from the supermarket. Andy was outside playing with the neighbor's children. Lisa was ten months old and was happy to maneuver herself around the first floor in a baby walker. She was in the kitchen as I warmed up a pot of mushroom soup on the stove. I had laid the table for lunch with soup bowls on top of flat plates. As I poured the soup into the bowls, Lisa reached up to the table, grabbing one of the plates and pulling the bowl of boiling hot soup over her head and face.

She screamed, I screamed, and Lodi came rushing into the kitchen. I did not know what to do; I grabbed Lisa out of her chair and put a kitchen towel over her head, thinking it best to keep the air off the burn. The doctor's line was busy, but somehow I had the presence of mind to call the operator and ask her to interrupt his call. Dr. Collins told me to bring Lisa to his office immediately. Why do I always think that doctors will come rushing to your house in such situations?

Lodi fetched Andy from the garden and came with me so she could hold Lisa in the car. The doctor acted fast, taking Lisa into a room and putting her on the examining table. He asked me to hold her still while he started scraping off some of the congealed soup. It was a terrible sight: my pretty, chubby-cheeked baby with her face and neck covered in burns. Globs of once beige-colored soup, now drying to a dirty gray, covered Lisa's forehead, nose, cheeks, and chin. One eye was already closed shut and horribly swollen, the other barely open. Pathetic whimpers came from her throat, and her body shivered with shock and fright. I felt dizzy and nauseated and was about to faint when the doctor saw me wavering and told me to sit down as he called the nurse to help him.

I experienced unremittable guilt. What had I done to this precious child? Had I ruined her looks for life? Would the burns become infected, and would she, too, die? Was this accident another threat to our chances of having a normal family? I cried silent screams for her pain and cursed myself for my carelessness. I had been too busy, too rushed to pay close attention to her movements. I should not have allowed her to be jumping around the kitchen in the baby walker. In sum: I was a bad mother.

After cleaning Lisa's face as much as possible, the doctor spread a new type of antiseptic cream liberally over the wounds and then carefully bandaged her poor head and neck, leaving only space for eyes, nose and mouth, making her look like an Egyptian mummy. Dr. Collins told me to give her baby aspirin for the pain and as much liquid as possible to offset the inevitable dehydration following a burn accident. The soup had splattered Lisa's eyelids, and we would not know for a few days whether it had penetrated her eyes and affected her sight.

Pete had cycled to work that day, but he came home as soon as he could and was calm and stalwart in his role as comforter. The next few days were crucial. The doctor changed the bandages each day and put on more cream. After a day or two the pain lessened, but as the burns began to scab and heal, the itching started and we had the challenge of keeping Lisa from scratching her face. We put gloves on her, but she kept taking them off, so we tied her hands into the sleeves of her sleeping bag. Following the doctor's orders, we gave Lisa lots of liquids, including a bottle whenever she woke in the night. This resulted in a regular night feed for several months to come.

Andy did not know what to make of all this melodrama. Standing by her chair sucking his thumb, he stared uncertainly at the ugly monster of a sister and must have wondered what would happen next. Only a portion of her face, covered in black and yellow scabs, was visible beneath the big white bandages. Amazingly, her eyes were spared injury, and in a few weeks the burns healed, leaving only some latent scabs and red marks. Eventually, the skin healed perfectly, and all the scars disappeared except for two or three tiny marks on her neck. The Egyptian mummy was reincarnated and grew into a beautiful young woman.

Chapter 10:
Kindergarten and Changing Attitudes

Although our plans for creating an evenly spaced ideal family had gone awry, we were still trying. The birth of a normal, healthy child had given a boost to our confidence, and we were beginning to feel like other families. We had hoped to have four children, a plan that now seemed untenable; but another child was certainly feasible.

Like many mothers, I felt I could cope with a new baby two years after Lisa's arrival. However, pregnancies sometimes happen unexpectedly, especially when you have been miserly with cream in a diaphragm, having deferred a replacement purchase until the last minute. This time the delay had significant repercussions: I became pregnant in April 1964. Lisa was eleven months old, making her twenty months when the baby would arrive. After we had gone through so much upheaval and tragedy, the thought of another baby so soon took my breath away. Lisa was developing well but was still a baby, and Andy, who attended school every morning and was one of the senior students at Carousel, still needed additional help and more watching than a normal child. To make matters worse, the children had been sick with German measles, and I caught the infection.

Clinically, German measles is called rubella. The popular name was spawned by detailed studies of the disease conducted in Germany in the nineteenth century. In 1941, an Australian ophthalmologist, N. M. Gregg, discovered that rubella early in pregnancy sometimes led to fetal defects, especially in the eyes and heart. The organs, tissues, and essential form of a baby are defined during the first eight weeks of its development. I was afraid to voice my concern because words might make the danger real. I finally said to Pete, "Darling, I'm worried; I think I may be pregnant, and I've just been sick with German measles."

As always, he responded calmly, "I'm sure there's nothing to worry about, but let's be certain and consult with the doctor immediately."

Dr. Collins examined me and confirmed that I was pregnant. He assured us, "There's nothing to worry about because German measles won't have affected the embryo at such an early stage."

The greatest number of defects result when the infection is caught between the third and sixth week of a pregnancy. In all probability I was sick during the first or second week of my pregnancy. However, to dismiss the danger so lightly was easier said than done. A termination was never considered, but the possibility of a defective baby remained an ominous shadow hovering over us through the next nine months.

Although our doctor brushed aside our fears, he may have been unaware of all the possible consequences. In the same year, 1964, a large epidemic occurred in the United States. The resulting studies showed that rubella was capable of causing extensive damage to almost any organ of an infant's body. Approximately 50 percent of cases result in babies being born with vision impairment, deafness, and mental retardation. Thanks to a vaccine developed in 1969, the congenital rubella syndrome has now become rare. Most women who lack immunity are vaccinated before they plan to become pregnant.

Three years had elapsed since we left England, and we had been hoping to combine a scientific trip for Pete with a visit to our families for the Christmas celebrations of 1964. Now we had to discard these exciting plans because I would be eight months pregnant in December, making flying out of the question.

We decided I should take the children and go home to England during the summer before my pregnancy was too advanced. I had to undertake this challenge alone because we could not afford two adult tickets. Besides the grandmothers' need to see their grandchildren, I needed to see my mother before her life ended, and she needed the support and rewards that our visit would provide. In her letters she complained of frequent colds and a persistent cough, causing me to suspect that her cancer had recurred and was weakening her immune system. Then came a letter from George confirming that the cancer had spread to Mother's lungs.

The journey, an eight-hour flight with two small children, was daunting. Although Andy and Lisa slept most of the way, when he was awake, Andy wanted to go to the bathroom every half hour, probably because he enjoyed flushing the toilet or playing with the soap dispenser. Overloaded with a child in one arm and a carry-on bag over my shoulder, I was terrified of losing Andy in the confusion of airports and train stations; to keep him safe, I used a harness, which we had bought previously in England.

Many parents have lost a child temporarily and are familiar with the desperation of the search. Andy's wanderlust had tested our nerves on several occasions. He had no fear of losing us, nor any idea that there was a potential danger if he left our side. Anytime we were in a store, park, or public place, he just wandered off, following whatever object or sound caught his fancy or enticed him away from the safety of his parents. One time Andy disappeared when we were shopping in a department store and we had each thought the other was watching him. We searched every corner of the floor we were on, looking under clothes racks, inside changing cubicles, and behind counters. Worried and embarrassed, we asked the store personnel to announce that a four-year-old boy was missing. Could he have gone to another floor? Surely he would not have climbed the stairs or found the elevator. He had climbed the stairs. A clerk found him on the floor above, happily playing in the toy department and blissfully unaware of being separated from his parents. At least he had the sense to find the toys.

The fact that godparents were chosen especially for him had always given Andy a feeling of ownership toward them. On this occasion, I told him that two uncles were meeting us at the airport, one of them being his godfather, Uncle George. Although he had not seen him for three years, Andy spotted him in the crowd of greeters as we came out of the customs hall. George was amazed when his godson shouted, "There's Unker Gor," and gave him an effusive greeting.

The first few days in England were spent with Pete's mother and sister. Mum had been especially devastated by Jean's illness and death because her third child, also a daughter named Jean, had died of pneumonia as an infant. Seeing our robust daughter brought her joy and relief.

Lisa, disturbed by the journey, strange places, and new faces, wanted only her mother to do things for her, but Andy remembered his grandmother and aunt and responded to them at once. They had not seen him for three years and were amazed at his progress. He had grown into a respectable-looking five-year-old. His height and weight were average, and except for a slight narrowing and puffiness around his eyes, his face was nicely molded and quite handsome. His hair was fine, so we kept it cut short. I always made sure that his clothes were of good quality and clean, and he took pride in dressing himself. His comprehension of what people said was excellent, and he worked hard to respond and make himself understood, which often involved repeated attempts to say a word clearly.

We went by rail to Mother's home in Yorkshire. She had arranged to meet us at Brough where the train stopped briefly before reaching Hull. At the same time as I was disembarking from the train, gathering up the children, and retrieving our luggage from a van far away from our compartment, I was searching for Mother. Finally, I realized that a frail old lady at the far end of the platform was my mother. I barely recognized her. Her face was pale and gaunt, her fine gray hair had become whiter, and her body seemed to have shriveled so that her clothes, always expensive and elegant, hung loosely on her bony frame. In addition to having to contend with her own illness, Mother had suffered with our suffering and carried a heavier burden because she was too far away to be able to do anything. We cope better with tragedies when we can act physically and are a real part of the drama.

I had not told Mother that I was expecting again because she would have worried about the journey and told me not to come. I planned to break the news over tea, an appropriate time for intimate conversation. At Mother's house, tea was always served on a large, double-tiered oak trolley in the study. The hinged edges unfolded to make a curved table covered by an embroidered tablecloth. The tea was in a silver teapot topped by a tea cozy. Hot crumpets, butter oozing from their cells, sat under the lid of a silver dish. Cucumber or scrambled egg sandwiches, homemade tarts (pastries) filled with lemon curd and jam, fruit buns, and a sponge cake completed the tasty offerings.

As we sipped our tea and spread raspberry jam on juicy crumpets, I delivered my news. Mother's reaction was one of shock. She exploded, "How could he (Pete) do this to you? I thought you were practicing this new family planning method."

"Well, Mother, it's not all Pete's fault," I replied. "Of course, he did participate. We both want another baby; it's just happening a little sooner than expected. You mustn't worry about me; I'll manage."

Without a husband to help, I found the four weeks with Mother exhausting. Everyone exclaimed over Andy's good behavior and progress. He became Nan's shadow, helping her dust and vacuum, watching her cook, or stirring some of the ingredients in the mixing bowls. But Lisa was a typically difficult fifteen-month-old. She fussed at bedtime and would wake in the night demanding a bottle.

In spite of the noise and activity of two small children, our visit lifted Mother's spirits and brought vitality and joy back into her life. Sometimes she joined us for walks along the country lanes or simply sat in the garden watching the children play. George wrote to us later: "Romy's visit was a tremendous contribution to Mother, and you can be very satisfied that all the effort and expense had a great effect on her spirit. You couldn't have done more."

The return flight to New York was in the daytime. The plane was full, so Lisa, without a paid ticket, had no seat. Both children constantly dropped their toys, books, and crayons on the floor, and I had to reach over my growing belly to retrieve them. Andy repeated his many visits to the bathroom, this time disturbing the occupant of the aisle seat, a young man who was on the second leg of a twenty-four-hour journey.

At the end of the trip, we were greeted enthusiastically by a different Pete; he had grown a mustache. In spite of his new appearance, Andy spotted him quickly and shouted, "Daddy, Daddy," but Lisa was unsure of her new-looking father. I was quite sure. I refused to kiss this man with his scrubby, tickly growth until he had shaved it off.

In September 1964, Andy entered kindergarten class in a regular school. This event was a milestone in his life and will be compared later in this

Loving Andrew

section with the corresponding experiences of Lindsay Yeager and Blair Rodriguez when they started kindergarten in 1985 and 1997 respectively. At birth we had been advised to "put him away" because our son's development would be so slow, making him only minimally trainable. Now, at five and a half years old, he had demonstrated that he was not only trainable but also educable.

What is really meant by the different terms used to identify children who are mentally handicapped? Changes in terminology during the twentieth century attempted to humanize the essential categorization of the retarded and to reflect the new attitudes of the general public, the professionals, and the politicians. In 1988, advocacy groups in the United States introduced the idea of people-first language, stressing the importance that someone is a person first and foremost whether he or she has a handicap or not. For instance, a "cripple" is a person with a physical disability; a mentally slow child is no longer a "retarded child" or even worse a "retard" but a child with a developmental disability; and a "Mongoloid" is a person with Down syndrome.

However, a fancy name does not alter that person's handicap, nor does tiptoeing around a sensitive subject make it go away. While we are busy glossing over reality with elaborate nomenclature, we need to question whether these cumbersome, tongue-tripping phrases have changed our preconceptions or influenced the real issues of acceptance and assimilation.

Until the second half of the 1900s, the mentally deficient, based on IQ, were divided into idiots, imbeciles, and morons, names that carry a cruel stigma today. The term *idiot* described a person who was severely handicapped, with an IQ of twenty-five or below. By the 1960s, those with IQs below twenty-five were called "profoundly retarded," and those with an IQ between twenty-five and thirty-nine were "severely retarded"; these groups are now referred to as "severely developmentally disabled." "Imbeciles" were moderately retarded, with IQs between forty and fifty-four, and were classified as trainable by the mid-1900s. These children could be taught to take care of their everyday needs and might be able to learn simple reading and writing. They are now referred to as "students who are moderately developmentally disabled." "Moron" is the Greek word for fool. Morons, who were defined as mildly retarded with IQs between fifty-five and sixty-nine, became the "educable mentally handicapped" of the 1960s. They are now called "persons who are semi-independent developmentally disabled."

By the 1960s, doctors and educators were beginning to realize that children with Down syndrome span a wide range of mental development, from severe abnormality to near-normal intelligence. Lindsay Yeager is an example of a person with Down syndrome who did not fit neatly into the developing classification. Lindsay was born in 1980, six weeks premature and weighing only four pounds, three ounces. In spite of being quite healthy and responsive for her small size, the doctors noticed that she had some of the indications of Down syndrome. Ten days later tests confirmed their suspicions but revealed that she was a Mosaic type. This means that not every cell in her body has an extra chromosome. These children (about one in every hundred cases of Down syndrome) have a better chance of developing to a high level. Although Lindsay's development may lag behind in some areas, in others she appears normal, which may give rise to unrealistic expectations. The majority of people with Down syndrome (with every cell having an extra chromosome) fall into the mild to moderate range, meaning that some will be educable.

When I met Lindsay in 1997 at the age of seventeen, she was termed "learning disabled" rather than "retarded" because her IQ was minimally subnormal. When asked to describe her disability, she said, "I suffer from *confusionization*. My mum sometimes has this problem when she has paid for an order at the supermarket and then walks out without her bag of groceries."

Although the subject of changing attitudes still had a long way to go, there were clear signs of improvement in 1964 when Mrs. Stewart felt that at age five and a half, Andy's progress at Carousel had reached a high enough level to make him eligible for a normal school classroom. The Corl Street Elementary School in State College agreed to admit Andy into the regular morning kindergarten class. An article in the local paper stated, "As evidence that mentally and physically handicapped children can be helped along the way to acquiring formal, public school education, Mrs. Stewart was proud to announce that seven children from

Carousel would enter public schools; five would attend a day-care training center, one would attend a primary special education class, and Andy Wyllie would attend kindergarten." A photograph of Andy accompanied the article.

In kindergarten the ability of a child with Down syndrome is unlikely to be over-stretched because any exposure to reading and writing will be through creative play activities. Nonetheless it seemed a big step for a developmentally disabled child in the 1960s when the terms *mainstreaming* and *inclusion* did not exist.

In 1975—a decade later—Public Law 94-142, Education for All Handicapped Children, established free, appropriate public education in the least restrictive environment for every child between the ages of three and twenty-one, meaning that each child should be educated with non-disabled peers to the maximum extent appropriate. Educators are required to assess each special education student and develop an Individual Education Program (IEP) to guide them in placing a student.

Lindsay Yeager was born six years before the introduction (1986) of early intervention services for children with disabilities from birth to age three (see chapter 3). Her mother, Carol, who is a schoolteacher, found that practicing a home therapy program and taking her baby to a weekly massage class helped her deal with the disappointment of Lindsay's birth by focusing on something positive. When her daughter was seven months old, she hired a private developmental therapist as well as enrolling her in a program for developmentally handicapped children, showing that she was well ahead of current practices.

Lindsay's progress was outstanding, far exceeding that of most children with Down syndrome. She started talking at age one and today speaks as clearly as a normal person. Unsure whether she could fit into a regular preschool program, her parents tried half time in a special class and half time in a regular class. In a regular class, Lindsay acted like a normal child; in a special class, she acted retarded, so the Yeagers decided to keep her fully included in regular classes.

Although her daughter was unusually bright, Carol felt that at age five Lindsay lacked the social skills necessary for a regular kindergarten class. Nor did she want her to spend two years in kindergarten in order to be ready for inclusion in a regular first grade. Unable to find a suitable special education class for one year, the Yeagers sent their daughter to a head start program before she joined a kindergarten class in the local elementary school.

Today the presence of a developmentally disabled child in kindergarten is taken for granted. Starting in 1997 at age three, Blair Rodriguez spent almost nine years at her neighborhood elementary school. Because of her hearing difficulties, Blair was eligible for a County Hard-of-Hearing Class, but for most of the time she was in regular elementary classes: one year in a pre-K class and two years in kindergarten. Andy, on the other hand, was breaking barriers in 1964. His classmates had no experience with a special needs child, but after a few queries and comments, they accepted him as just another kid. Andy responded well to his teacher, Dorothy Brown, and participated in the activities of her classroom, making wild and colorful finger paintings; collages of seeds, string, paper, and glue galore; and crayon scribbles, that rivaled a Jackson Pollock canvas.

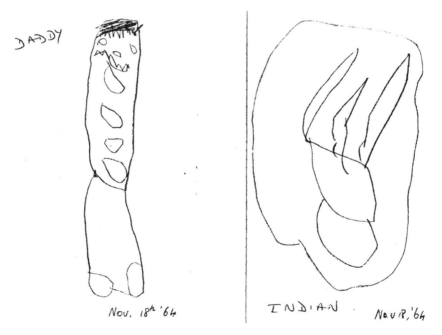

Figure 10.1: Andy's drawings at age five: Daddy and an Indian

In the playground his motor development and coordination fell behind the average, but it did not spoil his enjoyment of the games or use of the climbing equipment, swings, and bars. The jungle gym at Carousel had prepared him well, and he was happy to try anything.

As well as creating artwork at school, we encouraged Andy to draw at home. The development from the simple portraits on November 18 to the more complex compositions of December 3, 1964, is illustrated in figures 10.1 to 10.3. At the age of five and a half, his drawings began to have form and meaning. In figure 10.1, a portrait of "Daddy" has an armless body and head in one piece, with stick legs ending in stumpy feet. In spite of the lack of arms, the head has hair and the body a row of large buttons. On the same page, a feathered headdress inside a large circle represents an Indian. Figure 10.2 shows a collection of people: the boxy figure in the top center is armless; the two characters on the left and right have round heads with hair and charming faces complete with eyes, nose, mouth, and animal-like ears. Although the stick legs grow from the

Figure 10.2: A family group

head without a body, they end in stump feet and the stick arms end in fingers. The squat portrait in the bottom center is complete with head, hat, and arms, but the legs have become the body with circles at the end for feet. In Figure 10.3, Andy's drawings have developed into compositions. On the left, two suns shine above a house perched perilously on the crest of a hill. The house has a wavy roof, perhaps tiled, four windows, and a door. On the right side is a portrait of "Daddy on skis." A crowned head sits above a face with eyes and tooth-filled mouth. The one-piece face and body is legless and armless, but long skis sit alongside waiting for the action.

In a short period of time, the stimulation of a regular kindergarten class appeared to be adding measurably to Andy's abilities. In some of the following chapters, where appropriate, I will continue to compare Andy's opportunities and progress with those of Lindsay and Blair when they were at the same ages and stages as our son. The timing will be

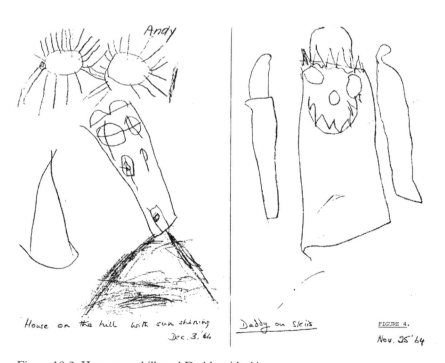

Figure 10.3: House on a hill, and Daddy with skis

approximately twenty and thirty years later, when social attitudes had changed radically.

— ★ —

While Andy was experiencing the challenges of kindergarten, we were facing a significant dilemma. In late September 1964, Pete was asked if he would consider a position as full professor at the University of Chicago. His immediate reaction was no. What person in his right mind would want to move from rural Pennsylvania to urban Chicago? We envisioned it as a grim, dirty city somewhere in the Midwest with an impossibly high crime rate and a miserable climate.

As November's chill set in and heavy clouds drifting across gray skies made snow look imminent, we left the children with friends and visited Chicago. The university wined and dined us, making us feel important. While Pete discussed science with the faculty, I visited the Hyde Park neighborhood and saw a variety of houses.

If we moved to Chicago, we would want to live adjacent to the university in the Hyde Park area, where 75 percent of the faculty lived. A renowned private school, connected to the university, would serve our normal children well, but special schooling for Andy was not so easily available.

Decisions relating to career moves are always hard to make. We were happy in the academic environment of Penn State set in a tidy, compact, safe, rural community. We had many friends, a lovely home, and an ideal setting for bringing up children. The size of Chicago and the variety of its resources awed us, but it was a tough city, where people double-bolted their doors day and night. However, at the age of thirty-four, it seemed foolish for Pete to reject this significant step up the academic ladder. So with a mixture of excitement and trepidation, we opened another door in the corridor of life and decided to go to Chicago. We would move in the summer of 1965, and by then we would be a family of five.

Meanwhile, the birth of our next child was imminent, and Pete had to fly to India to give a paper at the December 1964 meeting of the International Geological Congress. For every one of the six days of Pete's absence, the snow kept falling as though the angels in heaven had a sur-plus of fluffy white cotton balls and were discarding them over the small town of State College. One day when the snow was especially heavy, our resident helper, a high school senior, had a class and was unable to pick up Andy from school. Expecting to be gone only a short time, I left Lisa asleep in her crib. The narrow, winding road to the school was blocked, and I had to park the car far away and walk across a snow-covered field. An anxious Andy wondered why I was late. I wrapped a scarf around his face with his eyes peeking over the top, but the snow blew into our faces, making it hard to see and breathe. The snow in the field was too deep for Andy's little legs, but he was too heavy for me to carry, so we just had to keep plodding on, making slow progress. I was starting to panic, and Andy was crying. I tugged and urged him on, occasionally lifting him a step or two, fearing that we would never reach the road and that the car would not start. Would we ever get home, where, by now, Lisa was prob-ably awake and screaming her head off? Eventually we reached the car, it did start, and we did get home to find Lisa still sound asleep. I counted the days until Pete's return and wondered if I would stay sane.

Our baby was due the second week of January. By the end of Decem-ber, a bad case of heartburn was making me uncomfortable, and I was feeling unusually nervous, so Dr. Collins prescribed tranquilizers. The German measles threat still hung over me, and I was anxious to know that this baby was healthy.

On January 19, the doctor induced labor, and within a few hours I gave birth to a healthy seven-pound, fourteen-ounce boy. We named him John David. We were overjoyed to have a normal boy. He was a beautiful baby with a long, narrow face and dark hair. We sent telegrams to our mothers and felt relieved that all was well. After receiving the good news, Mother wrote:

You have now a lovely little family, and I hope really for your sake you will not have any more as you have done your bit and had four pregnancies…You have been also very brave, and many girls [I was now thirty-three] would never have attempted to go on having more children after your first two disappointments and tragedies.

I expected my anxiety to disappear with my extra weight, but neither was in a hurry to go away. Although John was a reasonably good baby, like all new babies he wanted to be fed on demand. Lisa, now twenty months, was jealous and difficult, especially at mealtimes, while Andy tolerated the upheaval and commotion without complaint and was delighted to have another baby in the house, especially because it was a boy like him.

We still had a housekeeper one day a week but no mothers to come and cook meals or take care of the other children, so Pete took time off from work to help. He was always willing to help out in the kitchen, having learned to cook during the British North Greenland Expedition (1952–54). He was the best of fathers and was especially playful and patient with Andy.

The following weeks became increasingly difficult, and I found out what insomnia really meant. I went to bed exhausted but could not sleep. Soon I had big black circles under my eyes. Even though I was nursing John, the doctor prescribed sleeping pills. If the medicine put me into a deep sleep, Pete could give John a bottle. After a few nights, I was able to take a pill, sleep for several hours, wake up for the 2:00 a.m. feed, and sleep again. In time I recovered my normal sleep pattern without the aid of medication.

On February 22, 1965, one month after John was born, my mother died. I was so thankful I had visited her in the summer and that she had lived to know of our baby's safe arrival. My brothers described Mother's last day when all three sons had been with her for Sunday lunch. Although she barely had the strength, she had made a great effort to get up and dress in a new suit for the occasion. She showed them a photograph of her new grandson and expressed satisfaction that he looked chubby. My brother said, "She seemed to have no idea of how ill she was...She died during the night without knowing anything."

I was unable to go home because I had just given birth and was nursing my baby. Letters describing the funeral helped me feel part of the occasion, but it was not the same as being there to say good-bye. Mother had borne her suffering with great courage and as a true Christian she would be received into God's care. Her ashes were scattered in the cemetery of the church where Jean was baptized.

Although Mother was so far away and had never been able to provide physical help for us, I had become dependent on her weekly letters. She was my mother, and I felt I could always share my own parental ups and downs with her. She adored our children and never failed to be interested in every detail of their lives. We are always children, and our parents are always people we look to for support and approval. Even as an adult Andrew would remind us that he was still "your little boy from the past." It is only when a parent dies that the umbilical tie is finally severed. Not long after Mother's death I had a dream that I had to sit at the head of the tea trolley and pour the tea now that I was the mother figure. I cried after hearing the news, and then my tears dried up and my emotions became frozen. I was depressed and started to fall apart.

Part II: Elementary
Ages Six to Fifteen

Chapter 11:
Chicago: The Big City

C hange, an essential part of progress, had already become an important element in our lives. After the birth of our first child, we learned to change our expectations for his future development; after resisting homesickness and succumbing to the brain drain, we adjusted to living in America; after cancer stole our second baby, we changed our original hopes for four children and now felt satisfied that Andy had two siblings.

After moving twice across the ocean, we should have become adept at changing our home base. We left Pennsylvania in July 1965 with Andy, aged six, Lisa, two, and John, six months, and arrived in Chicago to face a plethora of challenges. As always, everything was new: schooling, doctors, dentists, shopping, neighbors, colleagues, and friends. But the initial challenge was housing. We were persuaded to buy a brand-new townhouse within walking distance of Pete's office, schools for the children, shops, and public transportation. With assurances that construction would be completed in September, we put our furniture, household goods, and winter clothes into storage and rented a furnished house for July and August.

At the end of August, construction on the townhouses had not started, and the owners of our rented home were about to return. Feeling like gypsies with nowhere to live, we went to visit cousins in Florida, where we stayed for six weeks. Ground was finally broken for the townhouses in mid-September, the month we had hoped to occupy our new home. We lived in temporary housing for another four months and eventually moved into our own home in January 1966. On the day of the move, there was a heavy snowfall, the car had a flat tire, and the engine refused to start. It was a rough beginning to life in the big city.

Hyde Park, originally a village on the fringe of a teeming metropolis, had fallen into a serious decline after World War II. Ghetto families replaced wealthy whites, crime became rampant, and the University of Chicago considered moving. Legislation and a well-planned program of urban renewal eventually rehabilitated a shattered neighborhood. In time Hyde Park/Kenwood became the most successful interracial locality in Chicago.

In spite of the changing environment, our first winter in Hyde Park was miserable. Compared to the country cleanliness of State College, the city streets of Hyde Park were dull, dirty, and depressing. As I explored the neighborhood on our winter walks, vacant lots with half-hearted grass sprouting between pieces of broken asphalt and grass borders strewn with paper wrappings reminded me of the recent problems.

Because of the city's location on the edge of a large body of water, Chicagoans have to endure strong winter winds, adding intensity to the bitter cold. In our plain, temporary townhouse, I often felt imprisoned by the weather and the responsibilities of three small children. After Andy left for school in the morning, I would turn on television and exercise with "Gloria" while Lisa joined in and John watched on the sidelines from his playpen. Weather permitting, we went for walks in the afternoon, but it was a big chore to bundle up three children in snowsuits and boots, with Andy or Lisa invariably needing to go to the bathroom, or John requiring a diaper change, just as we were about to walk out through the door.

Moving from the all-white environment of rural Pennsylvania to the racially mixed urban setting of Chicago was a culture shock. I was as prejudiced about the black population as strangers were about our handicapped child. In time I learned to break down both barriers. I discovered how to help new acquaintances adjust to our son, and we learned to mingle comfortably with African Americans. Also I discovered that Midwesterners are exceptionally friendly and that the ethnic mix of Hyde Park gave a special character to the area. The black people whom we met in connection with Andy's training, education, and work accepted him unequivocally. In school the teachers were unfailingly supportive, and in his teenage years a black employee encouraged us to find him a place in regular employment.

— ★ —

Now that we were finally in our new home, the next challenge was finding appropriate schooling for Andy. Before leaving Pennsylvania, we had written to Elliot Knauer, the executive director of the Chicago Association for Retarded Children (CARC), to inquire about schools for Andy. His response was encouraging: the Chicago public schools had classes for both the trainable and educable mentally handicapped. The Chicago Association for Retarded Children ran day-care programs, schools, training centers, residential facilities, counseling, and referral services throughout the greater Chicago area, and a number of private schools offered a variety of day and residential care.

Soon after our arrival, we enrolled Andy in a summer day camp at the Southeast School of CARC. At the same time we started looking for appropriate schooling for the fall. Based on Andy's testing and schooling experience in Pennsylvania, the director of the Southeast School, Evelyn Nelson, agreed that he was too capable for their school and should be in a trainable or educable class in the public schools.

We wrote a letter to Dr. Melnick, the superintendent of our district, who directed us to the appropriate department to apply for a psychological test. We soon learned that children could not be placed in a special education class in the public schools unless a public school psychologist tested them. Our future experience with the testing procedure was about to test our patience, as well as Andy's ability.

On July 8, 1965, at age six, Andy was evaluated at the Hyde Park High School. Evidently, he lost interest in the test halfway through, and the psychologist rated him trainable. Since the trainable and educable classes did not start until age seven, the psychologist suggested Andy enter a kindergarten class. This did not happen because the public schools had no special education kindergarten classes and would not place Andy in a regular class, in spite of the fact that he had attended regular kindergarten in Pennsylvania.

We inquired about kindergarten classes in other schools in the area. The University of Chicago Laboratory School was a private school geared to the bright children of academic and professional families in Hyde Park and Chicago, and special education classes were not part of their program. A large Catholic Church and school stood on the edge of a park just across Fifty-Fifth Street from our townhouses. With great hopes that a parochial school would be eager to contribute to the needs of the developmentally disabled, we met with the sister in charge of education. Our expectations were quickly squashed when she told us they had no plans to accommodate special needs children.

The only alternative was the Southeast School, where Andy had spent the summer. It was located in Kenwood, and a bus service provided transportation. The school served children three to sixteen with learning disabilities and mental handicaps who had been excluded from the public school system. Andy was more advanced than most of the children, but it was the only viable program, and it provided a regular routine with educational activities. Mrs. Nelson, the director, was especially supportive of our situation, and a year later, in June 1966 (Andy had turned seven in April), she cooperated with Andy's teacher, Mrs. Elsa Hageman, in writing the following evaluation of his progress:

Physical Growth

There has been a noticeable change in the development of Andy's gross motor abilities. He has become confident of his capabilities, and his performances are not only more relaxed and flexible but are courageously executed. He walks and runs with good balance and alternates his feet on the stairs. He has good coordination in calisthenics. He operates the three-wheel tricycle and the little car with maneuverability, and hangs, suspended by his hands, from the parallel ladder. He assumes the position of hanging by his feet but as yet is reluctant to release his hands. He can roll, somersault, and hop with more ease and has done the intricate hopping in the game of sky blue or hop scotch. Creative construction of large wooden blocks is becoming a favorite free-play activity. He can inflate a balloon.

Andy is proficient in eye-hand coordination and is dexterous in all manipulative tasks. Right hand dominance is established, and he uses a thumb-finger grasp and release. Peg boards are filled in with a left to right sequence row by row, pastes and paints with brush application of proper amounts of materials, pencils and chalk are handled with natural ability, manipulates scissors following the lines of a design, and colors with even strokes and within limits. Andy uses multi-sensory avenues in learning and concept development.

Personal-Social Behavior

Andy has had excellent home training: he is meticulous in his personal appearance and in all areas of self-care. His wraps are hung up carefully on his assigned hook, and he can remove and put on coat and boots. He is completely independent at the toilet, and he washes and dries his hands, rolling up his sleeves before washing. His eating habits are good; he is proud that he now can peel an orange. He has recently learned how to start his jacket zipper and is learning the first step in tying his shoelaces. Andy has learned the social custom of the removing of his cap upon entering the building. This child is pleasant, happy, and cooperative. He is socially adjusted and always aware of the needs of others. He waits his turn and shares supplies and equipment willingly. If he senses that someone is taking advantage of him, Andy will defend and protect himself. In a group situation, he is showing signs of leadership and organization; he is a spectator as well as a participant. He sucks his thumb occasionally. This habit seems to be apparent when he is pleased with something he has created or when he is deep in thought. He makes a good transitional adjustment from one task to another and is self-sustaining. He is becoming more aware of social speech.

Speech and Language Development

Andy has excellent receptive and comprehensive language. He follows directive and casual commands. He sings off key but participates in the singing. He is not able to follow the rhythm band instrument. He can identify pictures and objects in response to varied commands: give me, show me, point, and identify pictures and functions. He uses short, intelligible sentences with some hesitation between words, "Andy—make—mistake" or "Andy—big—boy." He is an imaginative and interesting conversationalist. He attempts to correct his speech errors. Sounds are being stressed—the B is the current sound improvement.

Intellectual Growth

Andy has the incentive and the desire to learn. He has good recall and retention of new knowledge. His attention span is long, and he is able to complete a task without supervision. Form boards and inter-locking puzzles of several pieces are completed, and he has creative problem-solving ability. He traces accurately the children's names printed on a card and prints his first and last name. He can spontaneously draw a circle, square, triangle, and diamond. Andy can match, sort, and discriminate colors; the selection of colors by name is being developed. He identifies number symbols one through seven and draws them by rote, and his counting and grouping of objects is showing gradual progress.

This was probably the most comprehensive report that Andy ever received during his school years; moreover, it was written in clear language, and we, the parents, were allowed to read it. In Mrs. Nelson's view, there was no question about Andy's readiness for classes in the public schools. She expected that he would do well and test educable.

I had made inquiries about the next test in April of 1966. After being passed along a line of personnel at the Bureau of Child Study, I was told that the school principal in our area would ask the school psychologist to process the necessary forms for a test in the summer. After that Andy would be put on a waiting list for either trainable (TMH) or educable (EMH) classes, but we would not hear until fall if a space was available. If he tested at mental age four, he would be put in a TMH class or excused from school until he was eight. These responses did not encourage us. If there was no space available, was our child supposed to sit at home and waste this valuable, formative time?

The test took place on July 12 during lunch hour at the Hyde Park High School. The psychologist told us that Andy tested at mental age four. In her experience, children with Down syndrome usually tested at half their actual age; for Andy this would have been three and a half, so he had done well to reach four. He had good mechanical aptitude, but his coordination (unspecified) was poor, and he lacked "abstract" or reasoning ability. She said that at the present time he was not ready for an academic program, and it would probably be two years before he would test educable.

Disappointment was too mild a word to describe our reaction; we were angry. We felt we could not sit back and accept an inappropriate placement for Andy at this critical stage in his life. We wanted the best for him, and we felt he was ready for a more progressive program in the public school. Until now every educator who had worked with Andy had assured us that he was educable; he had spent a year in a regular kindergarten class in Pennsylvania; he had been accepted into an educable program at Penn State; and his teachers at the Southeast School had expected him to test educable. Was it possible that the Chicago public school standards were too high? How many normal five-year-olds (the educable standard) have reasoning ability? Was the psychologist prejudiced because Andy was Down syndrome and she believed he was probably not educable? Would Andy regress or vegetate in a trainable class, and would he even get into one? These questions filled our heads and helped to launch a long, drawn-out battle with the board of education.

We searched for information and answers in all possible directions. Everyone gave us a grim picture of TMH classes: they were overcrowded, understaffed, or staffed by caretakers and full of children with severe emotional problems. We consulted with an administrator at the Wood-lawn Mental Health Center; they provided us with a list of private schools in the Chicago area. We conferred with Mrs. Nelson and with Mr. Knauer, the executive director of the Chicago Association for Retarded Children. Mr. Knauer was interested in making our case a *cause célèbre* against the public school system if Andy was not given a place in the fall. Mrs. Nelson promised Andy a continuing place at the Southeast School. She could not run a separate "stream," but she would make sure that Andy progressed; she did not want him to mark time.

Of the half dozen or so alternate schools, only two were recommended. Shore School in Evanston was a day program, and the administrator expressed concern about the distance that Andy would have to travel—at least an hour each way. The Lt. Joseph P. Kennedy School ran a private boarding program in the western suburbs of Chicago. We visited the school and met with the principal. The setting was rural and pleasant, with abundant fresh air and opportunities for outdoor exercise and activities. We were impressed with the organization of the school. Its program and goals were aimed at helping high-functioning children develop to their fullest potential. We completed an application. Andy was accepted on a trial basis for a possible opening in their residential program at the beginning of 1967. However, if Andy attended this school, he would be living away from home and only visit us two weekends a month and for the holidays.

At the beginning of August, we had Andy tested by Dr. Ellen Rie, a psychologist in private practice, who had tested children for special education classes in Ohio and had been chief psychologist at the University of Chicago Laboratory School. Dr. Rie tested Andy using the Stanford-Binet Intelligence Scale, Form L-M. The results were: Chronological Age, seven years, three months; Mental Age, five years, four months; IQ, sixty-six. Dr. Rie's report stated:

> Andrew was extremely easy to examine. His attention span, ability to sit, and willingness to cooperate were optimum under the testing circumstance. Surprisingly enough he had no problem identifying and manipulating shapes, and he was able to draw the circle, square, and diamond with no difficulty at all. Consistent with this is his ability to write his name, forming the letters in a completely legible fashion.
>
> Andrew does have some difficulty with his speech. While his vocabulary is good, his speech is not always understandable. Speech therapy is recommended.
>
> Andrew is a mongoloid child whose level of adaptation is excellent. The prognosis for learning and further adaptations is good. I recommend that he be considered for an EMH class. The TMH classes will not meet his needs at the present time. Andrew has all the skills generally taught in the TMH classes, and there is very little to be gained by this placement. One should not put too much emphasis on his speech problem with respect to school placement (i.e., his speech will develop in time, and he should not be penalized for it now).

This report was consistent with the evaluation of the Southeast School and previous testing in Pennsylvania. Dr. Rie had obviously established a good rapport and seen the best side of Andy. When the school psychologist tested our son on July 12, Andy responded, "Don't know" with increasing vigor as the test progressed. He was probably annoyed because the test took place during his lunchtime, disrupting his accustomed routine.

With Dr. Rie's encouraging report in our hands, we felt we had some powerful ammunition with which to challenge the board of education. We thought wrongly. At the end of July, I had spoken to Mrs. Goddard of the Bureau of Child Study by telephone and been told that bureau's policy prevented them from divulging Andy's IQ or MA (mental age) scores. She reiterated once again that he was eligible only for TMH; these classes would probably be in Murray School, but they could not guarantee a place. I protested again, saying that we did not want our child cared for but educated to the best of his ability, and I was told rather curtly that all parents want the same. We arranged a meeting.

Our appointment was at 1:30 p.m. As we signed in, we were struck by the drabness of the offices with their regimented cubicles and rows of desks, behind which sat bespectacled gray-haired ladies or young girls with bouffant hairdos. Everyone was brusque, unfriendly, unsmiling, and uninterested in helping concerned parents. Eventually we were shown to the office of the specialist with whom we had an appointment. Mrs. Goddard was not in her office; thirty minutes later she came in. She was quite different from the ladies in the general office. She was smart, brisk, and professional but never uttered a word of apology for being late. We were probably naive to expect one; after all we were just parents.

In a pleasant and cooperative manner Mrs. Goddard listened to our case, seemed impressed with Dr. Rie's report, and said, "Yes, yes, this is all very informative, but we have a system and regulations by which we have to abide. The report from Pennsylvania and your private psychologist are not part of the Chicago Public School System. The school's test says that Andrew is trainable, not educable." However, she did agree with our concerns and promised to request a reevaluation. Pete responded, "We sincerely hope a different school psychologist is able to find out what Andy knows rather than what he does not know."

In a follow-up letter to the Bureau of Child Study requesting the reevaluation Pete wrote,

We recognize the danger of overextending Andrew and assure you that we would not wish for this; we just want him to be placed in the environment most

suitable for him to ensure that his interest is maintained during these important formative years. We have worked hard with this child to give him the best
opportunity to develop and feel most concerned at the prospect of having him
repeat TMH work, which he has been having in classes for the past four years.

Andy was re-tested on August 16 at the Black School. The result was
that he had a Mental Age of four to six. The psychologist felt that Andy
would be overextended in EMH and recommended a trial placement in
a pre-primary class, which was confirmed in a letter from the Director of
the Bureau of Child Study. At least our case was getting attention from
the top.

This was a slight improvement. However, there were few pre-primary
classes, and they all had long waiting lists and were located in culturally
deprived areas, not in Hyde Park. We were no further along. The choices
were a residential school in the suburbs or TMH in the public schools,
provided there was a place. The school psychologist who had tested
Andy on July 12 did not recommend the TMH classes; she thought Andy
should continue with private schooling. On learning that he had outgrown the range of the Southeast School, she urged us to consider the
Lt. Joseph P. Kennedy School, suggesting that we enroll him there as a
resident for a couple of years and then reappraise the options. This would
give us more time for our other children, which would be beneficial.

At a final meeting in the Southeast School, the director Evelyn Nelson
strongly recommended we keep Andy at home, thereby giving him the
chance of learning to cope with public and everyday life. He had already demonstrated his educability. She felt he would benefit more from
mixing with normal children in the neighborhood and being part of our
family life than from being away from home in a quality boarding school.
It was possible that TMH would be better than described, and once in
the school system, Andy would be observed by the teachers and could
be reevaluated in a year's time. We respected Mrs. Nelson's expertise and
agreed with her assessment of the situation. We had lost our battle and
had to accept the TMH designation.

Chapter 12:
The Mist Clears

Chicago became our home for the next eighteen years. Looking back on our first year there, I realize I had been looking at the world through a dark glass, as though everything was shrouded in mist and all the images were hazy and blurred. It was like driving through spectacular mountain scenery in bad weather. Unrelenting rain, mist, and clouds hover over the mountains, hiding the jagged peaks. Occasionally the rain eases up and the clouds drift down into the valleys, allowing the viewer a tantalizing glimpse of gray rock and snow-covered slopes, only to rise up and veil the edges once more. Finally, the rain ceases and white mountain peaks form a tooth-shaped outline against an azure vault.

After shedding tears over the news of Mother's death, my emotions froze and I became lifeless. Feeling like a mechanical toy, I managed to insert a key and wind myself up at the beginning of each day. Without zest or feeling, I performed the daily chores and cared for the children. But at night I wished I could sleep forever and not wake up to face another day.

Pete, realizing that I was seriously depressed, asked friends at the university to recommend professional help. The psychiatrist explained that emotions are like a deep well of water; each suffering drains away some of the water. In my case, the well had become totally dry so that any new experience was like a stone being thrown into the cavity. Since there was no water to break its fall, it hit bottom, sending painful reverberations around the walls. In time, with patience and careful treatment, the well would gradually fill up, and the emotional cushion would become more resilient. A year of therapy taught me how to deal with my failings and nurture my strengths. As I came out of my dark, shadowy world, life took on a new and exciting dimension.

Pete was delighted to be a member of the University of Chicago's stimulating Department of Geophysical Sciences. He was building a new research laboratory, and he found the teaching rewarding. I had joined a ladies' tennis group, found a reliable housekeeper, and begun to make new friends. Our new home, facing a street and connected to houses on either side, was part of a group of twenty-four award-winning town-houses. The three thousand–square-foot, three-story space had four bedrooms and was airy and well planned.

When spring came and it was possible to venture out of our winter hibernation, I let Andy and Lisa play with some of the neighboring children in the courtyards and alley adjacent to our house. One day Lisa came running into the house to tell me that the kids were teasing Andy, making him do bad things, like pulling his pants down, and calling him stupid and dummy. Although I hated doing it, I went at once and spoke to the children, explaining to them that Andy was handicapped, making his speech hard to understand and hindering him from doing the things they were good at. Trying to be kind but firm, I asked them to stop making him do things they knew were wrong and to let him join in their games.

Later Lisa asked me, "Mummy, why do the kids pick on him and call him names?"

She was not yet three years old but already was developing a protective, motherly attitude toward her brother. She herself did not notice that there was anything different about him, but the older children were immediately aware that he was slow and odd. A four-year-old had said to Lisa, "You shouldn't play with your brother Andy because he's an imbecile." His physical ability and behavior were not so different, but his speech was difficult to understand and made him obviously developmentally disabled.

I realized the time had come to give Lisa a simple explanation. I sat with her on my knee and told her:

Our bodies are very complex. They are made up of lots of different pieces, which have to fit together perfectly like a jigsaw puzzle to make a complete picture. If one piece has an extra knob on it, then the picture is incorrect. Andy's cells have an extra piece, called a chromosome, which distorts the final result. When the body has one part that isn't right, it affects the whole development of the person, so that he will be slower to learn, slower to talk, and slower to do physical things. You know many people have some kind of imperfection and need help in one form or another. Some people need to wear glasses to see well; others might have one leg shorter than another and need a special shoe to keep them balanced. Some children need a brace to help straighten a crooked foot. We're all going to try to help Andy do and learn as much as possible, and it's very helpful if you tell me when kids are being unkind to him.

Most professionals recommend that parents talk with their other children about a new special baby as soon as possible. It isn't easy to impart unhappy news to anyone, but it is especially hard to know what to say to your children. Dr. Cliff Cunningham (*Understanding Down Syndrome*) explains that parents worry that a child requiring extra care may affect their other children adversely. Lynn Rodriguez was concerned that her special child would inhibit family camping or that Karley would suffer from not having a typical sibling with whom to play.

Parents are afraid to prejudice their other children's feelings or burden them with worry. Most of all, they do not know how to break the news or explain the disability. However, the lack of any explanation can pose a greater danger. Children sense when something is wrong, especially if a conversation ceases when they enter a room or adults speak in whispers, using unfamiliar words. Observant older siblings will see for themselves differences in a new baby, or their friends will make comments or ask questions. In order to forestall possible misunderstanding or misinformation, Dr. Cunningham suggests finding a moment when the family is together. Explain the new phenomenon in as simple a language as possible without including unnecessary biological details, and avoid saying there is anything wrong with the new baby; he or she is just different. I found it helpful to explain that the extra genetic material of our special son, like an extra knob on a piece of a jigsaw puzzle, was affecting the overall picture and slowing the pace of his development. It is important to focus on the positive aspects. For instance, your family may find a new dimension of happiness as you form a team and work together to help the newest member overcome hurdles.

Because Andy was the eldest, I hadn't expected to say anything to Lisa until she was four or five, old enough to understand. Although Karley was five when Blair was born, Lynn Rodriguez decided to wait a year before explaining Blair's handicap. Since Karley is exceptionally smart, she could have told her sooner, but Lynn did not want to "cloud her relationship and feelings for her new sister." Having been the only child, it was important first for Karley to think of Blair as just a sibling without any additional complications. After becoming involved with Blair's therapies and observing obvious differences between Blair and her friends' siblings, Karley asked her mother, "Why is this happening?" Lynn explained, as simply as possible, that Blair would just be slower in her development.

After the birth of Lindsay, Carol and Neil Yeager decided not to say anything specifically to their older child, Adam, because at four years old they didn't expect he would understand. However, they did talk openly about their new baby's disability in the presence of Adam. When he was five, he surprised them by asking, "What is Down syndrome anyway?" They responded with a simple explanation. One day Adam said to his mother, "I wish I had Down syndrome." Like many siblings, he was envious of the attention being given to his special sister. On another occasion, a family with twin babies, one of whom had Down syndrome, was visiting. As everyone was commenting how alike the twins were, Adam pointed to one of them and said, "That baby has Down syndrome." It would seem that he was much more aware of the differences than his parents realized. Katie Yeager, who is two years younger than Lindsay, grew up knowing and accepting her sister's differences. It was not until children started teasing Lindsay in school that Katie became more aware of her sister's disability and felt the need to protect her.

In the eyes of our children and their friends, we tried to normalize Andy's handicap, to put it in perspective and lessen the impact, so that it became an everyday situation, not something extraordinary or monstrous of which they might be afraid. Although some of the neighborhood children had picked on Andy initially, they soon adjusted to his differences and usually included him in their games. A group often gathered in our backyard to play in the sandbox or crowd together in our inflatable wading pool. They sometimes had difficulty understanding what Andy said, but he was no more of a hindrance to their activities than a younger sibling.

We had a special routine at bedtime that included all three children having a bath together. As Pete and I washed them in turns, they enjoyed a collection of boats, jugs, and assorted bath toys. Everyone hated to come out; Pete and I usually dried Lisa and John at the same time and allowed Andy playtime on his own. In order to get him out, we emptied the bathtub. We had taught him how to rub a towel across his back and dry under his arms and between his legs. He took pride in being able to dress himself. To pull on his pajama bottoms, he sat on a chair, thrusting his feet into the pajamas, sometimes getting both feet into one leg, and then, laughing at his mistake, he managed to sort himself out and with a triumphant flourish, show that he could fasten the snap on the waistband and button up his top.

Storybooks were an essential part of the bedtime routine with all the children snuggling into a single bed and the reader balancing on the edge. All three children sucked their thumbs. Andy had such a hard time breaking the habit that he had permanent calluses on one thumb.

One way of bringing up a disabled child successfully is to make sure that the child becomes an integral part of the family. With this as our goal from the beginning, we now had a complete family in which to make Andy a fully involved member. We were always concerned about not making him the focus of our attentions, so we tried, as much as possible, to treat him the same as the others. With constant reminders, we worked hard to teach him good grooming and cleanliness, acceptable eating habits, and the ability to participate in family outings and social functions.

On winter weekends we explored a variety of exciting museums. One of the world's most famous, the Museum of Science and Industry, was nearby, located between a park and the lake on Fifty-Seventh Street. Its lively, easy-to-understand displays, which were all interactive and encouraged the viewer to press buttons, turn knobs, pull levers, or pick up phones, provided an endless source of stimulating activity. At Chicago's Field Museum, the children were awed by huge skeletons of prehistoric animals or intrigued with sparkling stones in their renowned gem collection. We could explore the planets and the heavens at the Adler Planetarium or look at hundreds of tropical fish at the adjacent Shedd Aquarium. In the spring we went to the zoos. Lincoln Park was on the near north side, easy to reach, and less overwhelming than the larger Brookfield zoo in the far western suburbs.

It was easy to lose a child in a museum or at the zoo, and Andy had not grown out of his wanderlust. He never seemed to worry about getting separated from his parents; he just did not think about it, and it was hard to instill in him the same kind of fear that kept Lisa and John from walking out of our sight. We took turns watching him and reminding him not to wander away. His attention span was shorter than that of other children of his age, and he would get tired or bored easily, occasionally plunking himself down on the floor and sucking his thumb. It was not always easy to persuade him to keep going—the promise of lunch, a snack, or an ice-cream treat usually prolonged his endurance. Nevertheless, we persisted in giving him the same experiences as the other children, hoping he would learn something new and develop more stamina for outings.

In the hot, humid days of Chicago's summer, we kept cool at the beaches where the children spent many happy hours building sand castles and paddling in the chill waters of Lake Michigan. Andy worked diligently at castle construction: he dug trenches, scooped up the sand, and patted walls into place; he filled his bucket with sand and water, carefully compressing the mixture before turning it over with equal diligence. He loved to wade in the water or lie in the shallow ripples until he was so cold that he had to be ordered out before he turned blue.

In 1967, an unexpected event changed our daily routine. Pete accepted the editorship of the *Journal of Geology*, but he needed a dependable person to manage the office and the daily routine of the journal's production.

He came home one evening and said, "Romy, how would you like a part-time job?"

"What do you mean, a job? I'm a full-time mother of three small children and couldn't possibly find time to work."

"I need an assistant with secretarial and management skills who is organized, can work independently, and is thoroughly reliable. You would be perfect," urged Pete.

"But I've forgotten all my office skills, I don't remember any shorthand, and I'm sure I can't type anymore. And anyway, who would look after John?" After six years of child rearing, my mind had turned to mush, and the idea of working in an office terrified me.

Pete was persuasive. "Well, think about it. It would be good for you to get out of the house. The position is part-time, and the hours are flexible. It would be something completely different and would take your mind off our family problems."

Andy was in school full time, and Lisa attended a nursery program in the mornings. We could ask our housekeeper to come two days a week to look after John, do laundry, and keep up the cleaning. All we had to do was find a babysitter for the other days. We were lucky and found a gem. Mrs. Glynn, a touch of Ireland still echoing in her lilting speech, became a surrogate grandmother to our children. She managed to be firm in the most warmhearted way; toys were picked up and put away before bedtime, and prayers recited before sleep.

For the next six years I was the managing editor of the *Journal of Geology*. Most of my income disappeared in taxes and babysitting fees, but I enjoyed the break from domesticity; the work boosted my morale and made me feel part of Pete's geological world.

From time to time, Chicago was subjected to huge snowstorms. One morning in 1967, during the second winter in our new home, we awoke to find so much snow piled up against our front door that we could not get out. The city had come to a standstill, schools and colleges were closed, and most people stayed home from work because there was no way to reach their offices. It was a week before we could dig our car out of the icy mess, so we walked to the store, bringing bags of supplies home by sleigh.

Finally the snow melted and winter gave way hesitatingly to spring, and the children could play outside again. Most kids learn to ride a two-wheel bicycle when they are six or seven years old. In spite of the initial warnings that our mongoloid child would never ride a bicycle, Andy had managed a tricycle without too much difficulty, and now for his eighth birthday in April, we felt he was ready to tackle a two-wheeler with training wheels.

He spent many hours riding his new vehicle competently along the paths between our houses, but it was a longer and harder struggle to get him to balance without the training wheels. During the spring and summer, Pete spent backbreaking hours bending over to help him balance on his bike as he wavered and wobbled around a school playground where there were no obstacles. Andy was determined but fearful. He lacked the delicate coordination and sense of balance necessary for the final launch, but with Pete's hard work and patience, he eventually mastered the art. He came home shouting with glee, "I did it, I did it." We all watched him ride shakily down the sidewalk to demonstrate his new achievement.

We made firm rules about staying on the sidewalks and within the vicinity of our townhouse complex; on no account were the children allowed to ride in the streets or go further afield unless they were with an adult. As well as the danger of heavily trafficked streets, we had to worry about tough teenagers stealing their bicycles.

In August 1968, Pete's decision to attend a scientific conference in Prague, Czechoslovakia, provided an opportunity for us all to visit England. Andy was nine, Lisa five, and John three.

A few weeks before leaving on our trip to England, we tried to prepare the children for visits with relatives. The first lesson was to tell them who Gran was and which aunts, uncles, and cousins they were going to meet. The second lesson was behavior acceptable to elderly relatives and in the public spaces of hotels. The third lesson was table manners that would stand the test of hotel dining rooms; in particular we decided it was time that Andy learned to cut up his own food. He found it hard to manipulate a knife and fork and relied on an adult to help him. However, he was now nine years old and big enough to fend for himself. He chose to be especially lazy and obstinate over this challenge. For several weeks, we struggled as much with our own determination to teach him as with his will to learn. We stressed the importance of being able to do the same as other children. Because of our refusal to give in, poor Andy went hungry for several meals until his obstinacy relaxed and he discovered that he could master the skill. His success garnered congratulations and smiles all around.

We rented a car and visited uncles, aunts, and cousins. In Yorkshire we stayed with friends Margaret and Bernard. Andy liked to help Margaret clear the table, but he also enjoyed being mischievous. When it was time for the next meal, Margaret could not find the linen napkins and cruets. Remembering that Andy had taken some things into the pantry and closed the door, pretending to play a game, she searched without success on the pantry shelves. Then, as she opened the refrigerator door to get some milk, she saw the missing items carefully stacked next to the butter and cheese.

The next morning Margaret and Bernard were awakened by a steady thudding downstairs. As they peeped around the door of the living room, they saw Andy marching back and forth to the steady beat of the song, "Seventy-Six Trombones." We had given them a record of *The Music Man*, and Andy had managed to turn on the record player, put the record in place, and set the needle on the disk.

On the way back to London, Andy was thrilled to meet his godmother, Mary. Her two boys had no difficulty accepting Andy and enjoyed introducing their American guests to a gentle form of cricket played on a carefully groomed green lawn framed by colorful herbaceous borders.

We stayed the next ten days with Pete's sister, Sue, the children's favorite aunt. Wherever we went there were animals: brother Bob had a lively collie, cousin Diana had a smoochy spaniel, friend Mary had two sloppy Labradors, and sister Sue had cats, rabbits, and a talking mynah bird. Andy especially enjoyed Sue's rabbits, which she allowed on the furniture. Sensing that this whole animal scene was giving the children ideas, I was not so enthusiastic about seeing white, black, and variegated rabbits everywhere.

The children were fascinated with Sue's husband, Mike, who was a professional rock musician. Dressed in purple bell-bottomed pants and lavender-colored satin shirt, he played guitar and led a group called *Jo Jo Gunne*. Mike could be tough and offhand at times, but he was always patient and gentle with Andy, who followed him everywhere trying to imitate his guitar playing. After our visit Andy played his own version of rock on a toy guitar and became an ardent fan of Elvis Presley. He also kept a poster of his uncle's group on his bedroom wall for many years.

While Pete was attending his geological meetings in Prague, Sue and I took the children to see the sights of London. We rode on the top of a red London bus from the palace to the Tower of London and took a riverboat to Westminster Bridge. At Buckingham Palace, nine-year-old Andy, looking like Christopher Robin, showed his toy soldier to a tall, helmeted policeman in charge of the gates. The burly man bent down to hear the small boy explain, "I'm Andy from America."

We watched the changing of the guard and thought of A. A. Milne's verse:

They're changing guard at Buckingham Palace—
Christopher Robin went down with Alice.
We saw a guard in a sentrybox.
'One of the sergeants looks after their socks,'
Says Alice.

Our preparations for the trip to our native land had paid off so that our relatives were impressed with the children's behavior and hotel stays were free of crises. Andy, Lisa, and John learned some English terminology and Cockney slang. They tried playing cricket and became immersed in the joy of animals. Although the significance of British history and the impact of the historical sites we visited were beyond their comprehension, they retained memories and impressions of certain events. Most of all, the trip gave the children a sense of family and of England. Although Andy never saw his godmother again, he wrote fond thank-you notes for the money she sent every Christmas.

Chapter 13:
Elementary School

In 1801, Jean-Marc-Gaspard Itard, a French doctor, introduced the concept of teaching the developmentally disabled in a publication *The Wild Boy of Aveyron,* where he described how he tamed and taught a boy he had found living with wolves. Following this, Édouard Séguin, a student of Itard, developed a teaching method using physical and sensory activities to develop mental processes. In the 1890s, an Italian pediatrician and educator, Maria Montessori, carried Séguin's work further. Using sensorimotor training on mentally handicapped children in Rome, she established a teaching method that today is the basis for many regular elementary schools.

In spite of this progress, the feebleminded continued to be shut away in state institutions or private residential schools until the mid-1900s. Author Edward Shorter wrote in his book *The Kennedy Family and the History of Mental Retardation* (2000) that in the United States, "No family has done more than the Kennedys to change negative attitudes about mental retardation." In 1962 Eunice Kennedy decided that it was time for her family to acknowledge and the world to learn that Rosemary, one of the Kennedy siblings, was retarded. Rosemary was only mildly mentally handicapped, but in 1941 her father, Joseph P. Kennedy Sr., thinking that a lobotomy would help her, authorized the operation. As a result, she spent the rest of her life in a private institution. Rosemary was a good athlete, and this gave Eunice the idea of promoting physical activity and showing that through sports the developmentally disabled could reach their potential. Through Eunice Kennedy Shriver's work, the Special Olympics program, founded in 1968, is now a worldwide organization with approximately 2.5 million people from 150 countries participating in hundreds of programs.

During his presidency, John F. Kennedy appointed a Commission on Mental Retardation and supported the use of federal funds to develop special education facilities and train teachers. Inspired by the Civil Rights Movement of the 1960s, which set an example for disadvantaged groups, parents became the motivators for education, training, and alternatives to state facilities. As well as establishing separate special schools, some states passed legislation forcing the public schools to provide classes for handicapped children. Illinois was one of the first states to pass a Mandatory Special Education Act (1965). It was four years before it became effective, and there were many problems with its implementation. The Chicago schools, for example, were desperately short of special classes and teachers. In September 1969, an article in the *Chicago Daily News* told the story of seven-year-old Ronald who was considered educable and longed to go to school.

"I'll be a good boy—see I can make Rs and Hs—let me stay," he said as he demonstrated his ability on the blackboard of his sister's first grade class in a Chicago elementary school. He was on the waiting list for a special education class, but the only available classes in his school district were full. Some developmentally disabled children were being deprived of special attention because the only space for them was in a regular classroom, which today many would consider to be ideal.

According to the same article, the Cook County assistant superintendent, Wendell Jones, estimated that only half of all mentally handicapped children in his area were in appropriate classes. It was reported that when her handicapped daughter was two years old, one mother started inquiring about special schools and was told her child was too young. "Now she is fourteen, and they tell me she is too old." Another mother went every semester to Schiller School to register her special needs son. Finally, a woman in the school office told her, "Get that child out of here. He belongs in an institution; he's crazy."

Our experience with the Chicago Board of Education in 1965–66, described in chapter 11, was similar to that experienced by Bette Ross in California. In her book, *Our Special Child*, she tells of an interview with the special education department of the district office where they had just moved. The interviewers told her that her son must be placed in a trainable class even though he had done well and been in an educable class in their previous location. The reason given was, "Children like yours always level off, and then they regress." Typically, no deviation from the set rules would be allowed. It was as though a large brick wall had been constructed to block the path of progress and the only way over or around it was to use the keys of the set rules to open the gate. That was the situation until the laws of the 1970s increased educational opportunities for the developmentally disabled.

Following the TMH evaluation for Andy, we lucked out and found a place for him in our school district. In the fall of 1966, he entered the TMH class at Murray School. At first Pete walked with him to school, but after the first year, he learned to walk the three blocks by himself, carefully obeying the crossing guard at the main street. In the afternoons I took Lisa and John with me and met him on his way home.

In spite of our misgivings over TMH, Andy's initial classroom placement turned out to be a rewarding experience. The teacher, Mrs. Williams, was a warm, loving black lady with a round, jolly face, her curly hair hidden under a blonde pixy-cut wig. She had a special charisma, which helped her control a bunch of unruly children. The students came in a variety of shapes, sizes, ages, and color. In the public schools of Hyde Park, black children made up 80 percent of the students; of the twenty-five students in Mrs. Williams' class, twenty-one were black. Their ages ranged from seven to approximately eleven or twelve. Andy was small, white, and insignificant; a young red-haired girl, four years older, kept him company. Her name was Lael, and she became his special friend for life.

At this time, Mrs. Williams had all the TMH children in her care. With one assistant, she somehow kept a disciplined room. Although her students were considered uneducable, she refused to be just a caretaker; she believed in stimulating all their senses and aimed to teach her students as much as they could learn. Her classroom was brightened with vibrant colors, pictures, and tables loaded with learning materials. She made large cutouts of the alphabet in sandpaper with the hope that tactile as

Loving Andrew

well as visual and auditory stimuli would help some of her students learn them. Through games and music, she began teaching numbers and pre-reading, as well as instructing her pupils in self-care skills.

At home Andy made a drawing of his family (fig. 13.1). The execution of the figures had advanced well beyond the tadpole stage; a space ship must have whisked us away to Mars, where we could view Earth as a tiny dotted object in the universe. "The Martians," one of Andy's favorite programs on television, probably inspired his drawing. Pete and the children were also loyal "Trekkies," and for many years Andy owned a large video collection of the *Star Trek* series.

Andy spent two years at Murray School. The second year the group had been split in two, and another teacher had taken some of the older children. Andy remained with Mrs. Williams. He was seldom absent, and his progress was graded as "doing his best." Although he gained little from the association with the other children, he benefited from the loving attention of a gifted teacher.

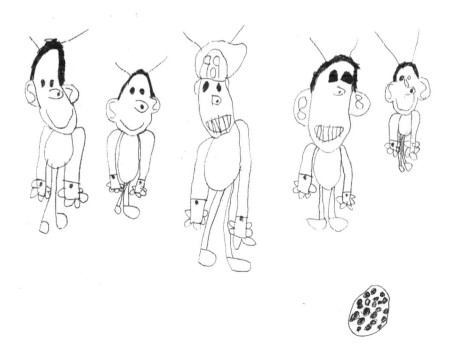

Figure 13.1: Andy's drawing of his family as Martians (age eight)

At the end of the summer term in 1968, Andy was re-tested by the district psychologist. This time he was rated educable. In the fall of 1968, he entered Ray School, one block away from home. On his way to work, Pete was able to walk Andy to school and see him safely into his classroom. We were so delighted that our son was finally entering an educable class, but our expectations sank when the principal explained that, owing to a shortage of qualified teachers, he had appointed Mr. Boyle, a regular classroom teacher, to manage the educable mentally handicapped group. Although Mr. Boyle had had no previous experience with special needs children, the principal was sure that he would be competent.

It turned into a very rough year for Andy. He was the only white child in a group of seven tough, older, black boys. At the start of school in September a temporary teacher, Mr. Guy, was in charge of the class and wrote the following note to us:

> When you send Andy with any type of equipment, regardless of how nominal the cost, please put his name on it. Several of the children do not have as much as you give to Andy. Consequently, they are jealous and act accordingly. There is virtually nothing I can do to control seven pairs of hands completely. When one of the other boys turns up with something that Andy claims belongs to him, it is one boy's word against another's. This puts the teacher in an impossible situation. We think that we have a goodly amount of equipment for the boys to use. We are appreciative when the parents supply equipment for their children, but please remember that this does lead to temptation.

We had provided Andy with a bag to carry his schoolbooks and lunch in, labeling everything carefully. We had also given him some pencils, which we had not labeled, so we presumed that these were causing the problem. Pete replied in writing, apologizing for adding to the disorder of an obviously complicated opening week and asked to have a meeting with the teacher so we could clarify what Andy should or should not bring to school.

Mr. Boyle was white and seemed afraid to show undue concern or any inkling of favoritism to the one white kid in his class. We sensed that confusion reigned in the classroom; one time Andy told us about a desk chair being thrown and broken. The kids were as much emotionally disturbed as developmentally disabled, with a variety of behavioral problems challenging the control of an inexperienced teacher.

Mr. Boyle's school report (undated) gave Andy a "good" in mathematics, listening, and physical education and "fair" in speaking, written language, and handwriting. In most areas, "He could work harder." Andy appeared to vegetate that year; he lacked brightness and did not seem to enjoy school, although he never complained.

One day, on his way home from school, Andy was pushed to the ground and roughed up. In nearly any school, whatever its population, teasing or picking on a kid who is different is inevitable. By being one of the first developmentally disabled students to be placed in a regular class in her school district, Lindsay Yeager was probably more subject to teasing in the school playground than if she had been in a separate class. Her sister, Katie, two years younger, came to her defense and reported the incidents to their mother. Lindsay's classroom teacher suggested to her mother that she visit some of the grades to explain her daughter's disability. Carol found this a challenging experience, but her visits did result in a marked improvement in the attitudes of the other students.

During Andy's school years (1966–1978) special education students were always placed in separate classes. As long as trained teachers were available, administrators believed that slow learners needed to be taught the basics of reading, writing, and arithmetic in a separate program. They were only integrated into regular classes if their learning or behavior problems had been corrected. At least Andy's classes were part of a regular school program where he and his classmates could mingle with other children in the corridors and playground.

We did not worry about Andy learning to socialize because we had planned a diverse program of extracurricular activities in the community. Moreover he was fully involved in our family life, and we made sure that our activities were rich and varied, from weekend outings around the city to vacation trips in different parts of the country and overseas.

As the twentieth century drew to a close, the debate over inclusion raged across the nation. Educators, who had spent years developing specialized methods for teaching special needs children to read and write at a pace appropriate for their ability, feared that their efforts might be wasted if school administrators were forced to fully include all disabled students into mainstream classes.

Special education encompasses a wide range of disabilities, from high-functioning children who can benefit from being included in a regular classroom setting to the severely disabled who need specialized training in a separate program. The concept of including all disabled children into regular classes is deceptive because it makes parents believe that their child is being normalized. It takes away the stigma of "special education," "disabled," or "retarded."

In reality inclusion is creating a nightmare for special education teachers concerned for their students' welfare and for mainstream teachers who lack training and experience to deal with the handicapped. Is a severely disabled child in a wheelchair really "included" in a regular classroom setting if he or she has to spend the day at the back of the room near the exit, ignored by a busy teacher trying to cope with twenty-nine normal, active students? Can children with Down syndrome learn and develop self-confidence as they struggle to keep pace with their contemporaries in a mainstream class? Instead of working with disabled children in a separate program, special education teachers are left to worry about their students learning the basic skills of life and reaching high school without being able to write a simple sentence or count money because an untrained aide did their homework for them.

Who will gain from the integration of all children regardless of physical or mental ability? Will the administrators be praised for their all-embracing policy? Will the school system save money? Will the parents feel less guilty? Will able children be more understanding? Will disabled children have their needs met? There are many variables. Developmentally disabled students should have their needs assessed individually and be placed in settings that will provide them with the best training for life.

After having her entry into regular kindergarten delayed until 1986 when she was six, Lindsay Yeager went on to participate in the regular first through third grades. However, in spite of being exceptionally advanced for a child with Down syndrome, she soon fell behind in reading. A resource specialist worked with her in school, and a tutor continued private coaching after school. When, by fourth grade, Lindsay was spending so much time with the resource specialist that she was missing out on socializing with her classmates, her parents decided she would benefit more from being in a special class.

In 1999, after spending two years in a regular kindergarten class, Blair Rodriguez continued in the same elementary school. She did not need a one-on-one aide as is sometimes necessary, but with the help of extra support, she was able to be fully included until third grade. After that her time was divided between hard-of-hearing classes and regular classes. At the beginning of sixth grade, as a result of medical challenges and behavioral issues, Blair spent most of the day in a special education class. Unfortunately, the teacher was terrible, so Blair's parents moved her to a junior high program where she divided her time between regular classes and a resource teacher.

Some schools have separate special classes for more severely disabled students or students with particular needs. However, the norm is now inclusion, along with the help of individual aides and a resource classroom where students can get instruction in academic subjects geared to their ability and pace. Our experience with Andy, and the Yeagers' experience with Lindsay reinforce my belief that higher-functioning children with Down syndrome will do better if they are placed in special classes for academic subjects (provided the teacher is good) instead of struggling to keep up with their peers in a regular classroom and spending much of their time in a pull-out program with a resource teacher.

For the next two years at Ray School, Andy had a Ms. J. Posey as his teacher. On November 6, 1969, she wrote this letter:

> It is thrilling to work with Andy. I enjoy every moment of it. He is improving tremendously in all phases of development (especially reading and oral language). He seems to enjoy each day thoroughly.... You have a darling little son.

The composition of the class was quite different. Although Andy was still the only white child, a smaller class size of only two other boys and five girls made the group easier to handle. Under Ms. Posey's caring attention, Andy blossomed. In the first year (age eleven), he was reading at first-grade level, and by 1971 (age twelve) his mathematics and reading skills had reached second-grade level. He read ploddingly but with great zeal and pride. The fact that he could read, write, and spell were well beyond our original expectations. His report cards were covered in an increasing number of Gs (good).

From 1972 to 1974, Mrs. Shelton was in charge of the EMH class at Ray School. Andy's reading ability climbed to 3.7 grade level and his math to second grade. Mrs. Shelton believed in helping her special class to not only learn about feelings but to find a way to express them. In his last year Andy brought home a carefully assembled book entitled *The Book of Feelings*. Each page listed an emotion and was illustrated with well-drawn and colorful people acting out the feeling.

Love is when you are with someone you like
Peace is when the world is quiet
Mad is when you are angry
Sad is when you are crying
Happy is when you are smiling with friends
Sleepy is when you are being tired
Lonely is when you are all alone by yourself
Hurt is when you are upset by something

For love, a boy and a girl, surrounded by six red hearts, are holding hands and saying to each other, "I love you" (fig. 13.2); for peace, Andy drew a large globe with different-colored areas separated by a shaded ocean; for mad, a boy and girl stand apart from each other with arms outstretched looking downcast; for sad, a single boy stands with tears rolling down his face; for happy, four alternating girls and boys stand in a row holding hands and smiling (fig. 13.3); for sleepy, a boy stands with his hand to his mouth yawning; for lonely, a boy in blue stands alone; for hurt, a boy stands alone saying, "No friend."

The class photo showed Andy with glasses wearing a dark blazer over

Figure 13.2: Love from *The Book of Feelings* (age fifteen)

Figure 13.3: Happy from *The Book of Feelings* (age fifteen)

a yellow shirt and matching tie. He was the tallest boy and the only blond in a class of seven students. In June 1974, at age fifteen, attired in a golden cap and gown, his face luminous with satisfaction, Andy graduated from elementary school. From the ranks of a rough beginning, he had developed into a confident and capable teenager.

While Andy suffered the vagaries of education in the public schools, Lisa and John enjoyed the special benefits of the University of Chicago Laboratory Schools, which followed Dewey's philosophy of hands-on teaching. Elementary classrooms were filled with cages of animals, tanks of fish, and jars of seeds and plants. The alphabet was taught phonetically, reading proceeded at a good pace, and foreign languages were introduced in third grade. It was said that students in the laboratory schools spent more time in physical education than in any other area except language arts. In high school, Lisa was a member of the field hockey and gymnastics teams; John was on the soccer and swim teams.

After refusing to allow John to practice chemistry at home, we discovered a bag of strange powder under his bed. John explained that it was food for his fruit flies but we shouldn't worry because he had anesthetized them in our freezer. How could we complain? Our son was responding to the lab school's teaching methods and was fascinated by science. It was a struggle to find good schooling for our developmentally disabled son, but our normal children were experiencing one of the best education programs in the country.

Chapter 14:
Achievements and Explorations

Birthdays are just as important to a child with Down syndrome as to any other child. Andy loved to be the center of attention, having learned about the excitement of birthdays in preschool. It was easy to invite a group for Lisa's and John's parties because their friends all lived nearby. Andy's classmates, on the other hand, lived on the fringes of Hyde Park or in the neighboring ghettos, so we rounded up neighbors, friends' children, and his special classmate, Lael Arnold, whom he had met at Murray School. I worried about keeping eight or ten children occupied for two hours, but with Pete's help, we organized party games: pin the tail on the donkey, musical chairs, pass the parcel, and mummy wrapping. All the children received prizes.

As a full-fledged member of our family, Andy was part of every party we hosted. At first I worried about the other children's reactions, but once Lisa's and John's friends had met Andy, they treated him like anyone else. Children can be cruel, but hopefully, if they see adults dealing naturally with a situation, they will also be accepting.

Arlette, the mother of Lisa's life-long best friend Bonnie, whom she met in nursery school, was an artist and my mentor and special friend. Having had little contact with Andy, she did not know how to relate to him until one day when he was visiting her house. Arlette had been writing invitations for her second marriage but could not remember if she had put the correct return address on all the envelopes. She was distraught at the thought of having to wade through the stack when she had other things to do.

"Can I help?" asked Andy, seeing that Arlette was upset.

How can a retarded boy help me with this problem? Arlette thought.

"Do you think you could look through these envelopes for me and see if I have put the number 229 on the return address?"

"Sure," said Andy. He did as he was instructed, sitting patiently with the box of invitations, going through each envelope as he repeated to himself over and over again, "Number 229." He found several without the number or the return address on them. Arlette was amazed at the ability and patience of this eleven-year-old mentally handicapped boy. He had rescued her from a tedious project. This incident showed how important it was for people to experience Andy's ability firsthand. Although they might have observed him relating to other adults or children and heard us singing his praises, fears or doubts could cloud their own attitude until they had an opportunity to work with him one-on-one.

We ourselves had to learn to trust Andy to do things on his own. By the time he was nine or ten, we thought he was probably capable of buying the Sunday paper. The money was not a problem because we always gave him the exact change, but the expedition involved crossing a street. The first few times we held our breath, hoping he would remember his instructions to look both ways and only cross if there were no cars coming. From the time he was eight, he had been walking to school on his own, but a crossing guard guided him at the street. He survived the paper purchase and was proud of his new job.

Occasionally Andy was taken advantage of by other children and got into trouble because he was gullible or enjoyed being the center of attention. One time a boy was bullying John and kicking him with his heavy shoes. Wanting to retaliate, John told Andy, "Pick up that rock and throw it at William. He's being mean to me."

Andy was proud to be asked to step in and help his younger brother. "OK, John, here goes," he said as he hurled a big stone at John's opponent. Although William escaped injury, he was frightened enough to run home and tell his parents what that big disabled boy had done.

William's father, who was a psychiatrist, phoned with an ominous tone to his voice and asked to meet with us. When he and his wife came over, we had a civil discussion about the incident. They were concerned that Andy would not understand what a serious thing he had done and that we would let him off without punishment. We assured them that Andy understood perfectly well what he had done and that he received exactly the same punishments and discipline as the other children. Many years later, John told me that he remembered the incident with an overwhelming sense of guilt for taking advantage of his brother.

Another time one of the neighbor children told Andy to pick up a bone, which was lying on the sidewalk, and throw it at a passing car. Andy did not stop to think whether the action was right or wrong. He was just pleased to be asked to do something, so he threw the bone and broke the car's windshield. The driver stopped, yelled at Andy, and asked to see his parents. We placated the man and promised to pay for the repair.

As he recalled this incident, Andy said, "You grounded me and locked me up in my room upstairs. It should have been the other kid who was grounded."

"You should have known that it was a bad thing to do," I replied.

"I guess the other boy was making fun of me," concluded Andy.

In addition to these learning experiences, Pete, who had grown up with hamsters and rabbits, persuaded me that animals would be good educational tools for our children, who had been begging for additional members to our household since our 1968 trip to England. Besides having something of their own to love, caring for animals would teach our youngsters about the mundane routines of feeding, cleaning cages, and exercising, as well as the more interesting aspects of mating and reproduction.

Chicago winters were too cold for pets to live in outdoor huts, so the basement became home for a succession of rabbits, guinea pigs, gerbils, and chinchillas. After encountering problems with rabbits dying, gerbils being sucked into the vacuum cleaner, and chinchillas failing to breed, we realized we needed a stable and lasting pet. In 1970, a neighbor's poodle had a litter of puppies. We chose a strong, healthy male and counted the days until we could bring the six-week-old black ball of curly fluff to our home. Andy had not shared Lisa's and John's enthusiasm for small animals, but he was thrilled to have a dog. When we asked him to select a name, he chose Poochy because we had told him that poodles originated in France and he thought the name sounded French. I made it Italian and more sophisticated by spelling it like the designer Emiliano Pucci.

A gentle poodle was at the opposite end of the spectrum from the fierce husky dogs that Pete had worked with on the Greenland expedition, but he took the training routine just as seriously. He walked Pucci around the neighborhood, patiently coaxing him to heel, stop, go, and come until he was a well-trained pet who only barked angrily when the mailman stuck letters through the front door.

Andy developed a great fondness for Pucci, regarding him primarily as his dog. He participated in the training routine and enjoyed walking him, making sure that he always sat at curbs before being given an OK to cross the street. He liked to talk to his dog as though he was a person. At least Pucci did not ask him to repeat words or have difficulty understanding his speech. Pucci also became an important participant in Andy's baseball practice. By the time he was ten years old, Andy had become an avid baseball fan. He followed the Chicago White Sox team and soon learned the names of the players and eventually the names of opposing teams and their chief players. His interest must have stemmed from seeing games on television because we had been brought up on cricket and soccer and never talked about baseball.

To help Andy develop physically and improve his hand and eye coordination, Pete established a regular weekend routine that involved taking Pucci for a walk and playing baseball with Andy in a nearby park. Pucci became a member of the team as Pete worked on disciplining him to stay, fetch, and give. The routine was as follows: Andy would stand in front of a fence, which acted as a backstop; Pete would find an imaginary pitcher's mound about ten yards away; and in another direction Pucci would sit bolt upright, quivering with eagerness. Commanding Pucci to sit until Andy had hit the ball, Pete would pitch as accurately as possible, trying to anticipate Andy's swing. Most of the time the bat failed to connect with the ball, which the fence caught, and if Andy could pick up the ball before Pucci retrieved it, he could try throwing it back to Pete. As Andy's performance improved, the ratio of hits to misses increased, giving Pucci a chance to dart across the grass to recover the ball and dutifully bring it back to Pete, who was especially appreciative of his fielding.

Sometimes Andy would play baseball on his own in the alley near our house, using his favorite players in imaginary positions around the field. He would talk to his hero, Tom Saver, as he practiced pitching the ball or throwing it up so he could hit it with his bat. Unfortunately, other children did not offer to join in, but Andy was happy to exercise his imagination and invent his own game.

Once a year Pete took all three children to see a White Sox game. When he moved away from home, Andy kept up his interest in sports and followed both the baseball and football leagues.

Many children with handicaps enjoy music. Piano, especially, is a wonderful exercise in hand, eye, and ear coordination. We enrolled all three children in private classes. Although we expected Andy to find piano a struggle, we decided it was worth trying to see how much he could learn. As with so many things that we dared to try for him, he surprised us. Evangeline Mendoza was a kind and patient teacher. Andy did struggle, but with the ever necessary persistence and patience, he learned to read music and play simple pieces. I supervised and helped with practice at home and enjoyed playing duets with the children as they progressed. John had such a good ear for music that he could not be bothered to learn to read the notes. Andy, on the other hand, practiced diligently and joined Lisa and John in recitals.

On a Sunday afternoon the Lehnhoff School recital room was filled with parents and children sitting on hard wooden chairs. When Andy's turn came, he walked to the piano carrying his music, which he laid carefully on the stand. Miss Mendoza sat nearby to encourage her special student. Andy looked around nervously and started to play, peering hard at the music and then at his hands to make sure his fingers were on the right keys. His playing was hesitant and unrhythmic, but he executed each note, murmuring, "One, two; one, two." He finished the piece and looked pleased as everyone applauded. I had been tense and anxious as Lisa and John played their pieces, but my hands were soaked in sweat by the time Andy had finished performing. I looked around the room at the audience and wondered what was in their minds as they observed this handicapped boy trying to play the piano. Did they think it was a waste of time, or were they admiring his efforts? For us it was yet another achievement to help Andy's general progress and add to his log of successes.

As with normal students, some Down's children have more musical ability than others. Lindsay Yeager took piano lessons for four years. Her repertoire included tunes from the Broadway shows, *Phantom of the Opera* and *Cats*. With her teacher's help she liked to "noodle around on the piano" creating New Age music. When I asked her to play something, she squirmed in her seat on the sofa and said she was too shy. After a while, as her mother and I talked, she went to the piano and played a competent and solid version of *Memory*. Lindsay also sang well enough to be a member of her school and church choirs. She performed in five musicals, one in middle school and four at church. Describing tours to distant cities, she said, "It is very fine to meet people wherever we go and see their culture."

Although Andy loved the sound of music and as a child would dance unabashedly, his body gyrating and contorting to the pulsating sound of a band, he failed to develop a sense of rhythm. However, this shortcoming never inhibited his dancing as an adult. When he was in his thirties, we took him to a faculty dinner dance where he approached several women (always the best-looking) and after politely introducing himself, asked them to dance. He became a member of a community choir, and when he attended church, he joined in all the hymns, singing enthusiastically out of tune and a few words behind; but he could read the words and recognize his favorite melodies. A Christmas ritual used to be Andy singing "Silent Night" accompanied by his mother on the piano.

Beginning in September of 1971, I enrolled in an evening program at the Harrington Institute of Interior Design. Although the classes took me away from the family, we tried to encourage the children to be proud of their student mother and take an interest in my studies. I explained the design projects and asked their opinions on color, fabrics, or choice of furniture.

After unsuccessfully trying to use a corner of Pete's office in the basement for my drafting table, I decided I needed a room of my own. Andy, who was now thirteen, agreed to move his bedroom to a larger space in the basement, and I converted his day-lit upstairs bedroom into a studio. Fortunately, Andy regarded the move as a privilege. He liked being in a different part of the house than his younger siblings and soon began calling the basement room his apartment. He was excited to help in the plan and decoration, and during his high school years, he rearranged the furniture several times, having learned from his mother the importance of making a drawing first. For his plans he imagined himself standing in the middle of the room and drew everything in a kind of perspective elevation on each plane. In a 1978 plan (Fig. 14.1), a cabinet with a radio and record player, two speakers with a connecting wire, and a desk and chair stand on one wall; Andy's bed with a picture above are against the second wall; a chest of drawers, couch, "pinbag" (Andy's version of beanbag),

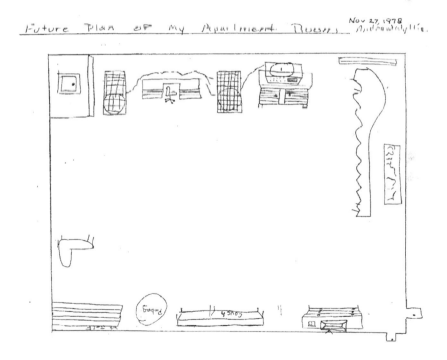

Figure 14.1: Andy's furniture plan for his apartment room at home (age nineteen)

and shelf unit are against the third wall; and a chair is on the fourth wall. His ideas for new arrangements were carefully thought out, and he kept his space neat and clean.

We had been trying to teach Andy to do things for himself and by himself. He was a skilled cyclist and was allowed to ride around our block. Occasionally we all went cycling along the lakefront where pedestrian paths took us safely through parkland and around the promontory jutting out into the lake at the end of Fifty-Fifth Street.

One day Andy decided to explore farther afield. Without telling anyone where he was going, he set off on his bicycle. He rode west along Fifty-Fifth Street toward Washington Park (nine blocks from our house), where he had attended a summer day camp. He told me later, "I was excited to be free of the family. You were always telling me I had to learn to be independent. But I was a little bit afraid that somebody might knock me down and steal my bike."

Confident that he knew his way, he rode past a large swimming pool, past shabby buildings surrounded by worn grass and overused play equipment, and along the winding paths of the park, expecting to find the street that led back in the direction of home. Instead he came to a different street bordered on both sides by shops, gas stations, and large buildings. Streams of cars and trucks rushed along, and all the people wandering in and out of the shops were black.

Andy recalled, "It did look different, but I was very careful and rode near the curb. I wanted to see how far I could go, but as I rode on, everything became stranger. I started to feel funny and scared. I didn't know what to do. Then I saw a gas station, and I remembered the gas men always talk nice to you when you fill up your car, so I thought the man would help me. I told the man, 'I don't know how to get home.'"

Realizing this young kid was handicapped and a long way from home, the attendant called the police. I was at home preparing food in the kitchen; Lisa and John were outside playing. None of us had been aware that Andy was on his bicycle and had left our townhouse complex. Just as I was about to put something in the oven, the doorbell rang. I opened the door and was surprised to find a policeman standing there. He asked me politely, "Are you Mrs. Wyllie, and do you have a son named Andy?"

"Yes, what's happened?"

"We have him in our patrol car, along with his bicycle," said the officer. We found him at Fifty-Fifth Street and Halsted, which is a long way from here."

I wasn't sure exactly how far away Halsted Street was, but the policeman went on to explain that it was several blocks west of the Dan Ryan Expressway, in the heart of the ghetto, and not a safe area for our son to be on his bicycle. Later, I looked it up on a map and found it was about two and half miles away.

The officer was very nice but continued in a firm tone: "You had better keep a closer eye on him. You shouldn't allow a boy like this to ride around the neighborhood on his own."

I felt guilty that I had let this happen. I had been engrossed in my design work and had not bothered to find out what Andy was doing. I was also angry with Andy for disobeying the family rules, but I had to admit to a feeling of admiration for his courage and sense of adventure. Maybe he had only meant to ride to Washington Park and back, but the park's circuitous tracks had confused him, and he had exited onto the wrong street. He had certainly demonstrated clear thinking by going to a gas station and saying he was lost.

Although Andy was embarrassed and did not want to talk about it anymore, we discussed the incident over supper. We talked about all the things that could have happened to him: he might have been knocked down by a car; his bike could have been stolen; he could have been beaten up by other kids; he could have ridden too far away for anyone to know where he lived. We all agreed it was a dangerous and stupid thing to do. Andy promised never to venture beyond our block again.

Our 1965 gypsy phase in Delray Beach, Florida, had introduced us to the delights of a seacoast holiday. For several summers, we rented houses near our cousins and the beach. Although the climate was always hot and humid, the skies were blue, the sea air fresh, and the beaches clean and uncrowded. Pete and I enjoyed the opportunity to focus on the children and introduce them to a variety of outdoor activities. As always, we made sure that Andy did exactly the same as the others; he had the same chores and the same opportunities to choose a movie or decide if we should go to the beach or the pool. If there were competitions, he participated; if there were group games with the cousins, he participated; but if there was something he really did not care for, like deep-sea fishing, I was happy to escape the adventure and find something else for the two of us to do.

My cousin Aileen and her husband, Landreth, had two children, Lolla and Lano, who were the same ages as Andy and Lisa. We spent every day by the ocean, at the municipal swimming pool, or at a private club. A buxom woman gave them swimming lessons. She helped her pupils overcome fear by instructing them to put their faces in the water and blow bubbles or curl up into a ball under the water and experience its buoyancy. She called herself Bobber, because as soon as her pupils could float, she took them to the big pool and encouraged them to jump off the diving board into the deep water, where she caught them and helped them paddle to the edge. On passing the test they received a bobber (like the ones used for fishing) to attach to their costumes. After this they soon learned to swim the dog paddle and then more elegant strokes.

Lisa and Andy learned at the same pace. However, when it was time for Andy to jump off the diving board, he froze. He looked as though he was being forced to walk the plank of an old sailing ship. He shuffled to the edge of the board and turned around as if to go back; then he faced the water but could not bring himself to jump. Pete and I were watching from the side of the pool and trying not to say anything except to encourage him and tell him it would be all right because Bobber would catch him. I agonized for him as a line of children stood waiting behind him. I was embarrassed by his slowness and acutely aware of his disability.

Finally, we said, "Andy, if you're not going to jump, you'd better leave the board and let the other children have a turn. You can try again later."

But a young girl behind him said, "No, it's OK, we'll wait. We know what it's like; we've all been through this."

I was overwhelmed by this mature and sensitive response from a young child. She knew that Andy was handicapped and needed some extra time and patience. After a few more minutes and with the girl's words of

Loving Andrew

encouragement in his mind, Andy finally jumped. Bobber caught him as he surfaced, and everyone at the pool cheered and applauded. Andy was overjoyed. During the next couple of weeks, he quickly gained more confidence and learned to swim back and forth across the pool. The swimming triumph and the outdoor life of Florida were reflected in his general development. His body became toned and stronger, and his speech improved with his increasing self-confidence.

One year we rented a charming one-story house with a large garden and smile-shaped swimming pool, where our children and their cousins spent many happy hours jumping, diving, splashing—in fact, doing anything that didn't involve straightforward swimming. An inflatable canoe, which we had bought for use on camping expeditions in Illinois, made a great vehicle for a variety of games. Our visits to Florida established an easy rapport between the cousins, and no one treated Andy differently. If he did not understand what he was supposed to do, someone repeated the instructions to him or showed him the maneuvers of the game.

With each successive summer, the children became better swimmers. They all participated in competitions at our cousins' private club but found it hard to beat their Florida competitors, who had the opportunity to swim all year. They especially enjoyed jumping off the diving boards, gradually gaining the courage to climb up the long stairs to the high board. Andy was a strong swimmer and just as capable and daring as his siblings and cousins, but he did admit that his tummy felt strange when he jumped.

In the fall of 1970, we enrolled Andy in a weekly class at the Hyde Park YMCA. As well as finding the classes enjoyable, it boosted Andy's confidence to be doing something successfully with normal children. It also provided him with an after-school activity, just as his younger sister went to dancing classes. However, unlike his sister, who occasionally played hooky, Andy was always in attendance at his classes.

Whatever the level, swimming is an excellent sport for children with Down syndrome. Without requiring the hand and eye coordination of a ball sport, swimming develops and strengthens muscles, tones the body, and builds stamina. It can also provide the camaraderie of team membership. In spite of being developmentally disabled, Lindsay Yeager was recruited for her high school swim team and was named athlete of the month for her performance. She liked the coach because "he understood my problems." Although she does not attend the full practice program, Blair Rodriguez is on her high school swim team and has the full support of the coach and fellow team members.

Many Florida children learn tennis, so we enrolled our children in classes for a month. At the end of the course, they participated in a competition and were rewarded with ribbons for their efforts. Andy competed with kids his own age in swimming, but tennis revealed his lack of co-ordination. Unfortunately, we did not continue the lessons in Chicago, but Andy took up the sport again when he moved away from home and regularly won medals in Special Olympics tennis tournaments.

In addition to vacations, Pete and I agreed that it would be educational for the children to do some weekend camping. For several summers we made excursions to explore the Illinois countryside. Our Sudanese friend, Amir Nour, and his Scottish wife, Ann Morrison, sometimes came with us. When we met Amir, he was teaching art in the Chicago City Colleges and creating sculptures. He was a big tease, and the children, with easy familiarity, treated him as though he were a favorite uncle. He had first met Andy when he and Ann came to our house for a New Year's Eve party. Amir didn't realize Andy was handicapped; he just remembered him looking so handsome as he stood at the top of the stairs dressed in a red paisley dressing gown, saying, "Hello, come up here and I'll put your coat away."

Andy thrived on attention paid to him by adults, and Ann and Amir treated him exactly as they would treat any other young adult, always including him in conversation and encouraging him to be part of the group. Their complete acceptance of him as a normal person helped us to include him in adult gatherings, urging other people to treat him in the same natural manner.

Our camping expeditions were well organized because Pete, using his experience in Greenland, took care of planning our provisions and packing all our gear. We had bought a large family tent to house two adults, three children, and a dog. It had a triple frame on the outside and a dividing curtain inside, allowing the children to sleep in one half, and

Pete and me, with the dog at our feet, in the other half. We called the tent "The Wyllie Hotel."

Work permitting, we tried to leave on a Friday afternoon and beat the weekend traffic rush out of Chicago. A two- to four-hour drive west, north, or south took us into farming areas, lakes, and river canyon country. The children fought about who would have to sit in the middle of the back seat. Andy claimed that because he was the eldest and tallest, he should sit on the outside, but Lisa and John would not let him have his way and Andy objected loudly. We solved the problem by ordering everyone to take it in turns.

I chose the campsite and fussed about the layout, and Pete supervised pitching the hotel. It was essential to put all the poles together in the correct order; otherwise raising the tent and staking the frame did not work. Each child had a roll-up foam mattress and sleeping bag. Andy was particular about rolling out his mattress and untying his sleeping bag in his special spot in the tent. Pete and I used unreliable air mattresses, which sometimes left us vulnerable to the bumpy ground before the night was over. The children each had a small suitcase in which they packed their pajamas and a change of clothes.

Although he grumbled and sometimes pretended he could not do something, Andy was expected to perform the same rotation of camp chores as Lisa and John. This might involve collecting firewood, cleaning up the tent, or washing dishes. He enjoyed taking special responsibility for Pucci. He put out his food at suppertime and made sure he had a bowl of water under the picnic table. Andy took his dog for walks to explore the campsite and areas nearby. We reminded him to keep Pucci on the leash for fear that our well-trained dog would cast obedience aside and chase after tempting whiffs of rabbits or rodents.

With Pucci in tow, we went on several nature trails and climbed up and down ravines. Andy walked in a clumping, flat-footed fashion and complained when the path was especially steep, but we managed to persuade him to keep plodding along. While we cooked supper, the children enjoyed fishing and searching in the mud for frogs and tadpoles. On arriving home after one camping trip, I discovered that John had brought back several frogs.

"How did you manage to sneak those slimy things into the car?" I asked.

"Oh, I packed them in the suitcase with my dirty clothes," said John. After that I took extra care in sorting the laundry.

I breathed a sigh of relief when our camping period came to an end, but the country experience proved to be good preparation for the group camps, which all the children attended later, as well as for Lisa's and John's extended backpacking adventures.

Chapter 15:
Family Graduations

Nineteen seventy-four was our year of graduations. After six years in Ray School, Andy (aged fifteen) graduated from the educable mentally handicapped program. At the ceremony he looked just like the other graduates, all of them bedecked in golden gowns and matching caps. Radiant with pride, he carried his certificate home and showed it to his brother and sister. They both tried on his robe to see how it would feel when they finished middle school. We took his photo in the back garden with Pucci at his side. As Pucci looked up to him, Andy turned to his beloved pet and said, "Well, I did it, Pucci. Aren't you proud of me? Now I am going to high school."

Andy could read and write, swim, play the piano, ride a bicycle (sometimes too far afield), and find his way around the neighborhood on his own. In the last two years he had grown unknown inches and spanned several sizes in clothes. He wore glasses and always kept his clothes and hair neat. He was polite and friendly and made sure people understood what he said, sometimes spelling a word if he could not pronounce it clearly. He might have received better instruction in academic subjects at the Lt. Joseph P. Kennedy private boarding school, but he had become proficient in the basic skills of life. By sending him to the nearby public school and making him a fully participating member of our family, we had succeeded in helping him become integrated into the regular life of the community.

I graduated from Harrington Institute of Interior Design and felt satisfied that I had worked hard and achieved my diploma. I took the summer off before accepting a job with an interior design firm in the city. Our most exciting graduation was a ceremony at our alma mater, the University of St. Andrews, Scotland, where Pete was awarded an honorary doctorate of science.

We flew to Scotland and stayed in a small hotel in Edinburgh so the children could meet their great-aunt Florence, who was my father's youngest sister and the last of eleven children. She had been a schoolteacher and always took an interest in the lives of her nephews and nieces and their families. After our trip she wrote, "I remember how surprised I was that Andy's writing and spelling were so good when I read his diary."

Before leaving Chicago, we had repeated our previous rehearsals for appropriate behavior in hotels and people's homes. We had shown Andy how to put his knife and fork together when he had finished eating. One evening in the hotel dining room, Andy had put his knife and fork down on his plate but not together because he still had vegetables (his favorite peas) to finish. Before Andy could pick them up again, an energetic waiter whisked his plate away.

A frantic Andy protested vociferously, "Hey, I haven't finished. Why did you take my plate away?" He had remembered our instructions and done the right thing, but now his food had disappeared. By the time Pete went to the kitchen to retrieve Andy's plate, the peas had been thrown away. We tried to placate a frantic Andy. Eventually, he calmed down when an apologetic waiter brought him a second serving.

After Pete had received his honorary degree, we spent a few days in St. Andrews, a city of gray stone, mystical ruins, and a history that spans more than twelve centuries. A papal bull established the university in 1411, making it one of the oldest academic institutions in the world. Until recently, students wore scarlet gowns to classes, creating a splash of color as they hurried through the colonnaded cloisters or paraded along the pier after Sunday services.

Satiated with sentimental memories of our student lives, we drove to England. In order to stay in touch with our relatives and to continue the children's contact with their aunts, uncles, and cousins, we had been trying to make trips home every three years. Whenever we travelled or were in public places, we worried about Andy's behavior and were unnecessarily conscious of any aberrations. John remembers that Andy's differences did not matter because all three of them had Yankee accents, strange vocabulary, and different clothes and haircuts. They were "those weird Americans" to most English children. Family and close friends had become used to Andy's ways and related to him with ease.

Our special child was now a full-blown adolescent who had developed sexually and was attracted to girls and young women. This is a difficult time for any teenager but more so for young men or women with Down syndrome. They change physically, and their hormones switch into high gear at the same time as normal children. They have the same social and sexual needs, but they do not always understand the physical changes or know how to handle the sexual awakening. A young child with Down syndrome who is attractive and cute can be forgiven for inappropriate behavior, but a tall, gangling teenager can become obnoxious if unknowingly he tries to express his feelings to an innocent friend, or even stranger, with a big hug or kiss that has sexual undertones.

Dr. Sigfried Pueschel writes about the dangers of leaving this developmental stage to "incidental learning." Young adults with Down syndrome need specific instruction on how to deal with puberty. Girls can be taught the correct procedures and hygiene during menstruation; boys can be reassured that wet dreams are normal and masturbation should be practiced in private. Most of all, it is essential to teach youngsters appropriate social behavior and skills. No touching of private parts of the body in public, no spontaneous hugs or kisses to unsuspecting friends or acquaintances, no inappropriate love notes or invitations to marry. Proper behavior and conversation can be practiced at home with frequent reminders and reinforcement in public.

Kellan Kight Sarles, in an essay entitled "Ready or Not" for the *Down Syndrome News*, explained that she had always been able to find help and answers for the medical and educational needs of her Down syndrome son, Ben, until he became a teenager and started to ask for a girlfriend: "I not have a girlfriend...I'm ready for it." Lacking specific guidelines, the author found that there were no easy answers, nor could she conjure up a suitable or willing girlfriend. Ben rejected the suggestion of a girl like him: "I don't date Down syndrome girls. I want real girls." Kellan realized that her companionship as a mother was no longer enough; Ben was breaking away. Nor could she act for Ben; it was necessary for him to find his own girlfriend. All she could do was practice with him how to ask a girl for a date, just as they had practiced ordering in a restaurant or using the telephone. Another boy had already asked the one girl in school who he thought was available. His mother urged patience; he was only fourteen, and there was plenty of time.

Lindsay Yeager said, "I started dating in sixth grade." Her mother tempered this statement by explaining that at age twelve Lindsay and a regular seventh grader, an especially gifted boy, shared an interest in acting and became good friends. On several occasions, one or other of the mothers accompanied them on a special outing. At the first meeting, Lindsay said, "We discussed our feelings of nervousness." After a few months Lindsay ended the relationship because the boy was a "computer bug." She said, "I could see it now: I am married to him, my water breaks, and he won't leave his computer." She told me her second boyfriend was Rudy, "a sweet guy" whom she met through a regional occupation program. He attended a special education school and helped her get on and off the bus after she had broken her toe. She went to movies and lunch with him but stopped seeing him after he "hugged her too tight." Lindsay had the sense to recognize that this young man was a little too physical, something with which she was not comfortable. Before Lindsay would go out on a date, she would lay down the ground rules: "I am warning you I don't kiss on the first date." She would also ask the boy, "Are you very sensitive? Are you open?" If only all teenagers could think along these lines.

As we did the rounds of our British relatives and friends, fifteen-year-old Andy was like a chameleon. He could acquire a different demeanor depending on whether he was visiting young cousins or socializing with an attractive girl or woman. With Uncle Bob's young twin girls he played easily at their level, riding their tricycle in and out of the trees, pretending to be the owner of an unused doghouse, and sharing their toys. But at Uncle John's house he left Lisa and John to play with the two- and three-year-old cousins while he focused on their live-in nanny, for whom he developed a crush. Other teenagers would be too shy to reveal their passion in front of others, but Andy expressed his feelings openly, oblivious to the reactions of others. With his long hair smoothed down to one side, he held the nanny's hand and followed her everywhere like an ador-ing puppy. The nanny was mature enough to take it in stride, but other girls might have been embarrassed or offended by such behavior. It takes subtle sensitivity to be able to respond warmly to such overtures while at the same time discouraging excessive physical contact or unacceptable behavior.

Uncle George, now living in Wales, had married Marilyn, a pretty and petite young dancer who had modeled for some of his sculptures. She became another subject for Andy's burgeoning love. Although we reminded him that Marilyn was his godfather's wife, he hovered around her as she prepared the meals or sat with her in the garden where vines of climbing roses in red and pink framed the whitewashed walls. She man-aged to put his adoration to good use, getting him to pick and wash the vegetables or set the table.

From Wales we drove to London to see Pete's family. We took Pete's mother with us on our expeditions to parks and country estates. Gran had a special soft spot for Andy, who showed off his learning skills by reading books to Auntie Sue's little girls. On an outing to a park, he chased his cousins with a frog in a bucket and then made up for his teas-ing by picking a bunch of flowers for their mother. During tea parties in the garden, Lisa presided and Andy passed the cookies, making sure there was a big stack left for him. The neighborhood children soon ad-justed to the American visitors and did not treat the odd-looking big kid any differently.

However, Andy did not always meld into the crowd. During a visit to Stonehenge, our children were enjoying climbing on the large stones and exploring the Druid ruins when two young boys started to snicker and point to Andy, whispering, "What's wrong with him? He's weird."

Andy shut them up quickly by saying, "Don't laugh at me. I can't help it; I'm handicapped."

In their innocence and ignorance, children can be unkind. Like rela-tives of other disabled persons, I would struggle with myself whether to say something or just ignore the stares and comments. Now it seemed that Andy was mature enough to handle the situation himself.

Part III: High School and College
Ages Fifteen to Twenty

Chapter 16:
High School

Kenwood High School, serving the Hyde Park/Kenwood area, was situated about two miles north of our house. None of the schools in the area provided bus service, so Andy joined other high school students who used public transportation. Pete went with him a few times until he was sure Andy knew exactly which buses to take and how to pay the fare. It was the beginning of Andy's public transportation education; he became more proficient on Chicago's buses, trains, and elevated rail than anyone else in the family.

Andy's introduction to high school in September 1974 held a great deal more promise than the beginning of Ray School in 1968. When we met the principal, Elizabeth Jochner, we learned that she had refused to open a special education program until she discovered the right teacher to run it. Celeste Pharr had retired from teaching physical education and retrained in special education. In spite of appearing gentle and soft-spoken, Mrs. Pharr was perfectly capable of controlling a room full of boisterous developmentally disabled young adults. The special education class was composed of young black men and women of mixed abilities who would prefer to talk or play than learn the skills necessary for possible employment. All the students came from the Hyde Park area, and Andy found a few familiar faces from his classes in Ray School. For many of the students, a regular high school program was beyond their capability owing to lack of preparation at home or in elementary school. Other students had emotional problems and needed the structure of a special class.

Mrs. Pharr was in charge of the work-study program, and Pamela Hashimoto taught Andrew the basics: English, math, science, and social studies. As yet no teacher or administrator had introduced the concept of including special education students in regular classes for all parts of the curriculum. However, since Education for All Handicapped Children had become law, students were mainstreamed (included in a regular class) for art, music, and gym. One year Andy sat in on a French class. A partial mainstreaming program would help our son acquire the social skills necessary to find a place in the working world, but he still had the advantage of instruction in academic subjects tailored to his pace and ability.

Andy was proud to be a high school student. He went eagerly to school each day and did his homework dutifully. Martin, a school guard, kept a fatherly eye on him, recovering Andrew's watch, which was stolen by some kids in the playground. He also saved Andy a reprimand for tardiness by opening the school door, which a group of boys had locked at the end of the lunch break. Another time a student demanded to know the combination number of Andy's locker. Andy dealt with the bully by calling to his teacher, "Miss Hashimoto, Miss Hashimoto, help me." She came quickly and rescued him.

The regular physical education classes, which Andy attended with other students from his special class, included instruction in driving and preparation for the written test, "The Rules of the Road." Andy had turned sixteen in April 1975 and was eligible for driving lessons. We wrote a letter to the teacher expressing our concern that some of the information was more than Andy could handle. Mr. Davis replied on November 21, 1975:

> I received your letter and understand your concern perfectly.
>
> The standard set for driver's ed is done by the state of Illinois, not by the PE department at Kenwood.
>
> I, too, feel Andy is a fine young man. I wish that he were able to perform on the level of his peers. To make special adjustments for him just isn't possible at this time.
>
> To us at Kenwood—or I should say in driver's ed—he is considered another student. I think he understands and likes it that way. I do take into consideration his handicap when his assignments are turned in.

Although some of his classmates kept failing the written test, Andy managed to pass after two attempts. A year later came the challenging question of whether he should be allowed to drive a car. The physical education teacher felt that Andy was capable of driving and asked for our opinion. We decided quickly that driving a car on Chicago streets and expressways was not for people like Andy. Without a doubt he was capable of operating a vehicle in an open parking lot or on a quiet country lane, but dense, unpredictable traffic could test the skills of the most experienced and reliable drivers. We felt confident that he would not be able to make split-second decisions when a situation demanded one. Many normal people avoid stressful driving, and too many inexperienced people do drive, adding to the dangers.

One of Lindsay's Yeager's ambitions was to drive a car. When her mother said, "I don't think so," Lindsay responded with an obstinate note in her voice, "Muuuum, I have to. I can learn like everyone else." After high school Lindsay was hoping to attend a nearby city college, and driving was the only way to get there. Like us, Carol thought her daughter might cope with driving on quiet side streets but would find major highways too confusing and dangerous. Fortunately, by the time Lindsay graduated in 1998, she was able to use Access Services, which provides vouchers for disabled people to take cabs, so the need and desire to drive dissipated.

Andy expressed his disappointment at our decision. "Why can't I learn to drive like everyone else? I know I could drive a car; I watch what you and Dad do."

We were firm: "Andy, you are capable of doing many things, but you have to accept certain limitations because you are handicapped."

From an age when Andy could understand, he had known that he was handicapped, developmentally disabled, different, or special, depending on which adjective suited his idea of a situation.

"Instead of driving a car, you are learning to ride a horse, and there are many people who can't ride."

We should have anticipated his response to this remark: "When I'm good at riding, can I have a horse of my own then?"

"Well, that's not very practical in Hyde Park. We don't have anywhere to keep a horse. Besides, like cars, they cost a lot of money and are very expensive to look after."

In the fall of 1995, while gathering material for this book, I arranged a meeting with Pamela Hashimoto, Andy's homeroom teacher at Kenwood. In the seventeen years following Andy's graduation she had been head of the Special Education Department prior to becoming a guidance counselor.

Before our meeting Pam wrote, "I always smile when I think of Andy. He was a remarkable young man."

Our review of Andy's years in high school opened another window onto his life. "Why was Andy so special to you?" I asked Pam.

"He was special because he brought such a unique element to the special education classroom. His attitude was consistent with what he'd been taught at home. He understood he had limitations and that people were not always kind to him. But he also knew there was a lot he could do, and he almost always did his very best and took a lot of pride in his work. His level of acceptance of himself and others took many people by surprise. He was straightforward and always gave you an honest answer. He didn't dwell on what he couldn't do or didn't have. He just went about the tasks that he needed to do. A lot of kids and teachers were in awe of the way he was able to do what he did. To Andy it wasn't any big deal; he was just being himself."

"How did the other kids in your class accept him?" I asked.

"They were torn. At first they resented him for being there because they were trying to blend in with the regular kids, and here was this different-looking boy in their class, making their task more difficult." During Pam's tenure at Kenwood, Andy was one of only two students with Down syndrome who participated in the special education program.

"But they also came to respect him for what he was," continued Pam. "Many of the students learned from him. Observing him helped them become more self-aware and even wiser in how they viewed things. A few said they wouldn't want to trade places with him, but they almost wistfully wanted their life to be as simple as his, uncomplicated by difficult decisions in their peer group, at home, and in the future."

"How well did he cope with the academic work?" I inquired.

"Oh, sometimes he would grumble and say he didn't want to do something. His frankness would surprise the other kids, and his honesty was refreshing in a way. But he knew what was expected of him, so after some initial grumbling, he would get on and do it."

"Did he get frustrated at things he couldn't do?"

"Just like any kids," Pam assured me. "But I could usually persuade him that he could do it."

"What level of reading and writing did he reach?"

"About an eight-year-old level. But when I think of his being able to carry on a conversation, it's higher than that. I hate to think of limitations set by a reading and writing level. There's so much more to living."

"I think he manages very well socially," I added.

"He doesn't get burdened by a lot of the things that burden us," said Pam.

"Right. He seems able to cut through a lot of the complexities of a situation. Did he have many friends?"

"I think Andy was kind of a loner in his way," explained Pam. "He did get along real well with Edith. Both of them had a real freshness about them. She wasn't bogged down by any adjustment stuff."

Edith had been in Andy's class in Ray School. She was a black Muslim and wore the traditional head covering.

"But mostly he would come to school, do what he needed to do, and go home," continued Pam. "He didn't feel the need to become involved with a lot of social activities. He was quite independent."

In summing up her memories of Andy, Pam said, "He was kind of a catalyst. He left everyone richer for his being there, not as much because of what he did but because of who he was and how he carried himself and an awareness he brought about in others."

Andy was fortunate to have such a skilled and understanding teacher. When Andy connected strongly to someone, his devotion was absolute. In return, Pam and the other teachers in the special education program contributed a great deal to furthering Andy's sense of self as well as his preparation for the working world.

In spite of the current push for total inclusion, Lindsay Yeager's high school remained sensibly conservative. In 1997, Lindsay's placement was similar to Andy's except that her situation was twenty years later. Lindsay was mainstreamed for art, music, and physical education and received the help of a resource specialist for academic subjects. Perhaps because she was a girl, she was more socially orientated than Andy. Many of her friends were from regular classes, which may result from today's greater integration of students with developmental disabilities. Also Lindsay's differences were minimal. Her speech was fluent, the physical features typical of a person with Down syndrome were hardly apparent, and she was just a delightful, warm-hearted young woman willing to be a faithful and trusting friend.

While updating this book in 2011, I learned that Blair Rodriguez is now sixteen and a sophomore in high school. As would be expected for a student with Down syndrome, Blair is not able to participate with her peers in subjects such as algebra and science, and she requires significant modification for core academic subjects. She does have a special education homeroom but moves around to different classrooms according to her schedule. Blair is included in regular or resource-level classes for world history, ceramics, and reading, with pull-out time for speech and other services. Blair loves reading, and the program is self-paced with the help of student teacher assistants. Socially Blair participates in "The Friendship Club," a mix of regular and special education students who meet once a week for outings, activities, and talent shows.

In Andy's second year of high school, a student could obtain credit for after-school employment. Mrs. Pharr's class in work skills helped to prepare the students, and teachers observed their performance at the job site. We hoped that Andy could participate in this program, but where in the neighborhood could we find an employer who would want to hire a teenager with Down syndrome?

We had established a regime at home to teach the children about work and responsibilities. Everyone had small chores to do: washing the dishes, walking the dog, collecting and putting out the garbage, and tidying up rooms. Andy did his share, grumbling as much as the others, especially if someone missed walking Pucci and he had to take their turn.

I had always done our grocery shopping at the Hyde Park Co-op supermarket. Andy sometimes came with me and enjoyed pushing the cart or finding the groceries. The store personnel were a congenial group, and I had made a few special friends, especially in the produce department, where a young African American named Ron was in charge of stocking the shelves. He was an indiscriminate flirt, joshing young and old, black and white, with unfailing pleasantness and humor. I had always responded to his warmth and often stopped for a chat. He knew the children and was especially friendly with Andy.

One day in the spring of 1976 Ron said to me, "You know, you should get that son of yours a job here. There's no reason he couldn't work in this store."

It was an exciting idea. I had never thought of trying to get Andy a job in a supermarket, but with Ron's words in my mind, I started to think more about it and discussed it with Pete.

Ron warned me, "You may have a battle with the manager because he's never hired a retarded or handicapped person. But many of these people come from foreign countries and can't speak English well, so why shouldn't Andy, who can speak English (though not always clearly), be able to get a job here?"

As Ron had predicted, the manager, Harvey Asher, was not receptive to the idea: "Oh I don't think we could hire someone who is retarded. It's out of the question."

I was persistent and persuasive, citing Ron's suggestion and the fact that the school had a work program. "Andy would be able to earn credits for the time he spends at the Co-op, and his teacher would take an interest in his job. You could hire him for a trial period, and I will stay in touch with you and Andy's boss and coordinate the schedule."

"All right, we'll give him a chance, but there's no commitment until we see how he does." Mr. Asher decided to assign Andy to the care of Masao (Mas) Yukawa, who managed the produce department.

Andy was placed in the basement, where he was taught how to clean up in the vegetable preparation area, sweeping and mopping the floor at the end of the day. It was quite a triumph to have obtained a job for him in regular employment; the big question was whether he could keep it. It was significant that the store placed him out of sight of their customers. They had dared to employ a handicapped person, but they were not ready to publicize the fact; nor was Andy ready to work in the public eye.

The first three months did not go well. Andy had to learn that this was a job, and a job required a person to work all the time. Andy kept saying he was tired and needed to sit down, take a break, or go to the bathroom. He probably did find the work exhausting because he was not used to doing constant physical labor. He also found it boring, which made him feel tired.

As soon as I realized that he was slacking off, we talked about it at home: "Andy, you know you have a real job now. You have to do what the boss tells you to do, and you have to keep working at your task until it's done. You can't just decide you are tired or thirsty or hungry and need a break. You have to follow the rules and take your break at the times they tell you; and you don't need to go to the bathroom all the time, you just think you do. You have to hold it and wait until your break time. You've done very well to get a job, and now you have to show them that you can work like everyone else does. Think about your paycheck and what you can do with the money you are earning. Do you understand?"

Listening reluctantly to this long lecture, Andy replied, "OK, Mum, I'll try."

At first the other employees did not understand how to respond to Andy; they treated him as a child, teasing him and giving him rides on a trolley. When Ron told me about the playing routine, I spoke to Mas, explaining that he must instruct his workers to treat Andy as a normal adult with a job to do and not as a handicapped child. Mas was kind, patient, and solicitous and responded well to my suggestions. He also received advice and information from his daughter, who was a special education teacher.

Andy had improved sufficiently by the end of the three-month probation period that the manager, Mr. Asher, agreed to keep him. He worked several days a week after school and for eight hours on Saturdays.

Two years later the Co-op published an article on Andy's employment in a December 1978 issue of the *Hyde Park Herald*. It was a two-page spread captioned with a photo of Andy and the title, "I want to work here all my life." The text was interspersed with photographs of Andy mopping the floors and working on wrapping vegetables with Mas. The store was now eager to publicize their success in hiring their first handicapped employee. The following is an excerpt from the article:

It took lots of his time, Mas admits, and sometimes he lost his patience. But it was worth it, he says. "Andy is a real gain to the produce department. Everyone likes him. He is so pleasant and agreeable, so willing to work and do his job well. And he has lots of friends upstairs; many of the baggers were his schoolmates at Kenwood." Mas's affection for Andy is very apparent.

Gradually there was improvement. First he began to take an interest in his tasks. Then he wanted to try all sorts of tasks. He learned to weigh merchandise, bag oranges, and put tape around bananas. He learned to trim lettuce.

As he grew physically stronger, his mental adjustment improved also. Now he wanted to do more difficult things each day.

Finally there was a great step forward. Andy began to initiate tasks. "Now he comes to work and sees what needs to be done," Mas said with satisfaction. "And he does a very good job."

He turned to Andy. "How do you like working at the Co-op?"

Andy beamed. "It feels great," he said. "Everyone is so friendly. I have lots of friends. I want to work here the rest of my life."

When Mas asked Andy why he liked working in the produce department, Andy replied, "Because I achieve." As well as this sense of pride in achievement, Andy brought home a paycheck and was able to buy some of his own clothes and have his own bank account. Ron of the produce department had started the idea, Harvey Asher, the manager, had the courage to respond to my persuasive tactics, and Mas Yukawa had the patience to train Andy to work. We had hoped to find a nominal job for our handicapped son, but having him established in regular employment far exceeded our earlier expectations. Whenever Andy went shopping with me, I saw the genuine friendliness with which the employees greeted him. It must have been an educational experience for them as well, to learn that a developmentally disabled person was not all that different.

The Co-op was like one big family; they held a Christmas party every year in the grand ballroom of one of Hyde Park's oldest hotels, the Windermere. Ron had encouraged me to go to the party with Andy. Everyone sat at large round tables, mostly grouped by age or department. Supper was served, a band played for dancing, and door prizes were awarded. Andy, dressed up in his maroon blazer, dark shirt, and checked tie, helped hand out the prizes and showed that as well as being able to perform a job he could dance as energetically if not as skillfully as anyone else.

In addition to finding work, we looked for recreational opportunities for Andy. In the summer of 1976, the same year as he obtained his first job, Andy began horseback riding lessons. Therapeutic riding was developed in England after the polio epidemic of the 1950s. In 1969, a regulatory body was formed in the United States to oversee about fifty riding associations. The programs have expanded and therapeutic riding is now known as Hippotherapy.

Frances Perkins, an elderly lady and veteran horsewoman, established Friends of Handicapped Riders for the Chicago area in 1971. With untiring devotion, she organized the program, which was based at the Acorn Hill Equestrian Center in Naperville. Teachers and horses also traveled to the South Shore Country Club near Hyde Park and the Chicago Avenue Armory in the downtown area. Riding experts selected docile and easily trainable horses and instructed volunteers to help students who had physical, mental, and emotional disabilities. Lessons incorporated exercises and games, which could be adapted to therapeutic programs practiced by other agencies. For the physically handicapped, the warmth and movement of the horse stimulated unused muscles, improved balance and coordination, and most of all gave each disabled rider a boost in self-esteem.

I was especially moved when I watched a physically disabled couple walk across the large arena of the armory holding hands and dragging their legs and feet, which splayed out awkwardly as they moved. As soon as they mounted the horses their muscles relaxed; feeling safer on the horse's four legs than on their own two, they sat up straight, looking like proud commanders of their newfound territory. In the Friends of Handicapped Riders' brochure, a student is quoted as saying, "Horseback riding allows me to experience the sensation of freedom that cerebral palsy rarely permits…it excites me to control my body and my horse in a smooth, rhythmic gait…The horse responds to me as he would to any rider. Often it is hard to receive such a natural response from a person."

Andy had none of the physical difficulties experienced by the victims of cerebral palsy and muscular disabilities. He sat on the horse with ease and quickly showed that he was a natural rider. He responded to the instruction, learning to control his steed in walking, trotting, and turning movements. Each season he improved until he was able to control the horse over low jumps.

By 1979 he had become so expert that Fran Perkins said to us, "I think he should participate in a dressage show at Acorn Hill." She wanted him to demonstrate the ability of a developmentally disabled person to anticipate, control, and handle a horse according to the requirements of a strict routine. Although these horses were docile, they still had minds of their own.

I expressed my concern: "Are you sure Andy can do dressage? It seems to require such precision."

"Oh yes, I'm quite sure he can. He's very good at following my instructions."

Dressage is the French word for "schooling." Riding horses are trained to carry out a wide range of maneuvers to a tight standard with the aim being to make the horse respond willingly to the demands of the rider. The military began using this type of methodical training in the early sixteenth century. The international rules are based on the traditions of the best riding schools in the world. Routines range from the *campagne* or elementary level (which would be Andrew's class) to *haute école*. The Vienna school, using white Lipizzaner horses, are famous for their demonstrations of the haute école in which the movements become so elaborate and precise that the horse seems to be dancing.

On the day of the show in Naperville, we watched the finely dressed riders from all over the Chicago area perform their intricate routines at different levels. It was hard to tell which had been more carefully groomed, rider or horse. Many of the riders had tailored jackets and elaborate hats with fancy scarves trailing on their necks; the horses' coats glistened from hours of brushing, and their manes and tails were plaited and threaded with ribbons.

Andy's horse was not so well groomed because it had been relegated to a paddock to make space in the stable for a visiting animal, but Andy looked as fine as many of the riders. Fran, dressed in riding clothes herself, rehearsed Andy in one of the paddocks.

As the time for his routine approached, Pete and I took our places on the benches of an indoor arena. Part of me wanted many people to witness this special performance, but in case Andy or his horse muffed their exhibition, I was relieved to see a small audience. I sat fidgeting nervously on the hard seat, my hands clammy with sweat. I was glad the event was indoors so there would be fewer distractions for both horse and rider.

Finally the moment arrived, and our son, outfitted in beige jodhpurs, a black jacket over a white shirt and cravat, and a black velvet riding cap, rode into the arena looking a little stiff as he whispered a few words to his horse. No doubt both of them were nervous.

The purpose of the level-one test was described on the scoring sheet: "To determine that the correct foundation is being laid for successful training of the riding horse, that the horse moves freely forward in a relaxed manner and with rhythm, its spine always parallel to the track of the prescribed movement; that it accepts the bit and obeys simple aids of the rider."

Andy entered at a working trot, stopped, and saluted; as a man called out the order of the program, he directed his horse to track to the right, make a serpentine movement in three loops, and turn in small circles, all the while keeping the horse at a gentle trot and rising rhythmically in the saddle. Then he repeated the circuit at a canter, changing to a trot between figures, before completing the diagonals and circles of the routine with a final ride down the center line, ending with a halt and salute. As he turned to leave, he looked our way, his happy face reflecting his sense of achievement. The judge graded him the same as any of the other riders, giving him a total of 127 points, which was a 60 percent score, and a comment of, "Nice ride."

Andy was awarded a silver plate with the inscription: "Acorn Hill Dressage Show." We thought that he performed magnificently; was this really our child with Down syndrome whom we had been advised to place in an institution at birth? It did not seem possible that he had developed the mental and physical ability to execute the intricacies of such a precise discipline. We reviewed Andy's achievement with a deep sense of satisfaction and likened him to a Greek hero overcoming the challenges of life as he soared through the air on Pegasus, his winged horse.

In spite of this triumph, or maybe because of it, Andy did not always succeed in his tasks. His expertise in riding had involved him in helping with the other handicapped riders. For some reason, he failed to respond to the riding director's requirements. In July 1979, the coordinator of the South Shore program sent us a letter enclosing the instructor's evaluation on Andy:

> We have been having quite a bit of trouble getting Andy to behave and follow directions. He seems to feel that he is given a special place in life because of his handicap. The effort he puts in is at best minimal. At this point, we have asked him not to come to volunteer, but only to ride.

We had already learned to discourage Andy from thinking that he was too special. In any class or work situation, he had to learn to follow directions, conform to the rules, and do his job when he was assigned a task, whether he was being paid for it or not. Parents are constantly reciting these guidelines to their teenagers, whether they are normal or disabled. Andy may not have been given enough specific direction for helping the other handicapped riding students. Perhaps he was just expected to see what needed to be done; we were not there to witness the problem. A similar situation had occurred when he first started working at the Co-op supermarket and would probably occur again in other employment situations. Andy was bright enough to make use of his disability status when he wanted to avoid the effort required to work hard at something he did not particularly enjoy.

It was important to help Andy develop a work ethic and learn to behave appropriately in public. Even though he was different, he had to learn to fit into society. His riding training and success had added immeasurably to his self-esteem, but now, like other teenagers, he wanted to stretch his wings and test the limits of his role in society. We began to talk about socially appropriate behavior, giving the phrase the acronym of SAB.

Chapter 17:
Summer Camps and New Horizons

During the summers of 1975 and 1976, we sent all three children to Camp Martin Johnson, which was run by the YMCA at Big Bass Lake in the Manistee National Forest of northern Michigan. Several of Lisa's and John's friends attended the camp, and after some thought, we decided that Andy, now aged sixteen, could benefit from the experience. While he was at Ray School, he had attended a Chicago Park District summer day camp for the mentally handicapped a short distance from our home. Although camp was not a completely new experience for him, spending four weeks away from home might be a hardship.

We knew it was a gamble. Would Andy fit in? Would the other children treat him fairly? Would he be an extra burden for the counselors? Would our children feel imposed upon because they might be embarrassed by or held responsible for his behavior? The counselors were required to write reports to the parents, and at the end of the first year, Andy's counselor sent us the following letter:

From my talk with you on Visitor's Day, Mr. Wyllie, it seemed that there had been some question as to whether Andy was ready for an extended overnight camp experience. From my observations, Andy was perfectly ready for the experience and suffered no more discomfort than any other youngster spending his first summer away from home. It did help that your letters to him were frequent, as he looked forward to receiving one every day.

The other campers, from the very start, tried to treat him as though he were no different, even though Andy constantly pointed out that he was "special" and that he was "handicapped."

I tried as hard as possible to be firm with him but found it hard to do so. I couldn't quite play the roles of both friend and foe. My CIT (counselor-in-training) gradually fell into the role of foe, while I became friend. This only resulted in Andy's alienation of the CIT.

Since Andy didn't see very much of John or Lisa while he was here, he came to me exclusively for comfort, attention, and affection. Maybe you can see how I couldn't constantly be firm. I really hadn't the heart.

I was away for a week in the middle of the session, and when I returned, Andy threw himself upon me, crying, holding me. It took all the restraint I had to keep from crying also. I wish so strongly that I had had the time, patience, and energy necessary to do the job I would have like to have done.

He's one of the most special people I have ever met. He has so much love to give that I was constantly amazed. If you ever have the opportunity to watch him swim, I strongly suggest you do so, as he enjoys it so thoroughly.

I believe that the whole experience this summer has been good for him, and I hope that if he is able to return next year, he do so. I enjoyed him very much and am glad to have had the opportunity to have been his counselor.

We gave each child several stamped, addressed postcards and envelopes to encourage them to write letters home. In turn we wrote to them frequently. John's letters were usually scribbled untidily in pencil; he was anxious to know if we had been watering his plants and feeding his animals and fish. Lisa wrote clearly in pen telling us about her cabin-mates and activities. She always had a list of requests: clothes, fruit, and candy.

In high school Andy was reading and writing at about fifth-grade level. Camp gave him an opportunity to learn to communicate through letters. His ability to express himself clearly and logically, to recount and describe his activities, was astonishing. All his letters were neatly written in pen and are reproduced here exactly as he wrote them. In every letter he told us how much he missed Pucci and asked if we would please bring his dog to visit because animals were allowed at the camp.

July 1: I want you to bring Pucci up here to the camp…I'm advanced swimmer in the camp and I take canoeing class and I take boating class and horseback riding and I take photography class and I take art and craft.

In the handicapped riding program Andy was using an English saddle, and he had learned to post and direct the horse by pulling on the reins in the direction he wanted the horse to turn. At camp he adjusted to riding western without posting, and he learned to turn the horse by putting the reins on one side of the horse's neck or the other. He told us:

> July 3: I ride Brandy the horse and I do it western way, like I turn him with my left hand and my other hand on my leg and I youss my feet to make the horse to go and we play games with the horse. Then I go to swim...and swimming teacher name is Suezy and she gives us six warm ups to do it. I have sunborn on my shoulders.

Along with Lisa and John, he qualified for the white level (advanced) swimming group and did well in distance swimming, demonstrating strength and stamina in a race to an island and back.

> July 17: I miss you and Pucci and Ann and Amir too. I have a good time in the camp with friends. I go swimming in the evening then we put our clothes on after we dry up then we go back to the cabin and we change in our other clothes for bed time and get in bed and I writhe this note under the sleepy bag.

On a postcard he told us about playing with matches.

> July 17: One day I go to the Washroom from my cabin Tamarack then so I finish the washroom so I go back to the cabin of Tamarack and I find the match box then I feel the ache to lit the match then I put it in the garbage and it go off like a flame then I get a towel then go to washroom to have a shower then Rick my CIT come up to the washroom. I get out of the shower and dry off then I get dress in my clothes then Rick take me to Dennis. The man talk to me and he expect my abology for the fire so he promise me never to it again.

We wrote a stern letter to him in reply, and he managed to stay out of trouble.

One or two evenings a week the camp organized social events with dancing. Lisa wrote that, to her dismay, all the ugliest boys asked her to dance. John didn't know how to dance, so he didn't ask anyone. However, he did tell us that Andy asked many girls to dance, but most of them refused, so he got mad and upset.

Andy's cabin sometimes played rough games: they made a rope noose and hung it over a beam and played at "hanging" Andy, making him stand on a chair with the rope around his neck and then threatening to kick the chair away from under him. John discovered what they were doing and reported it to the counselors, who put a quick stop to such a dangerous game. We were shocked when we learned about it and worried that we had done the wrong thing in sending Andy to the camp, but normal children have to endure similar games, and they survive to tell the story.

The second year all three children had a more enjoyable time at the camp. Lisa and John had more friends there, and Andy said he was in a nicer cabin:

July 14, 1976.
I miss you and I miss Pucci.
I have a great time at the camp.
I am in a nice cabin this year.
This cabin is called Menominee and it is the best one then Tamarack.

The camp gave the children their first experience of being away from home; it taught them independence as well as how to share cabins and get along with other kids. They excelled in the sports activities, and they enjoyed crafts, games, and outdoor adventures. John collected frogs and snakes but managed to leave them behind before returning home. Andy fitted in better than we expected, and his participation probably provided an additional and different challenge for the counselors so that they and the other campers benefited as well.

As a young couple trying to build a family, we had learned to adjust our expectations for Andy and were amazed at how much he had achieved. Having changed our outlook for our eldest child, we were especially appreciative of the successes of our other children. Lisa, who was suffering through orthodontic work and learning to cope with contact lenses, excelled in gymnastics and sports and had a wonderful circle of friends.

Andy loved music but had no sense of rhythm and sang with tuneless gusto. In compensation, our youngest child excelled in music. As well as playing the trombone and later the tuba in the school band, John's fifth-grade teacher had discovered that he could sing. The teacher encouraged him to join the Chicago Children's Choir, whose director, Christopher Moore, used a blend of girls' and boys' voices to produce music in the tradition of European boys' choirs. An inner part of my soul has always been stirred by the sound of boy sopranos, so I was especially thrilled when John became a soloist. One day when the choir was performing in one of the campus courtyards, I heard the pure, high, unaccompanied sound of my son's voice echoing across the open space as he sang the Negro spiritual, "Give Me Jesus." I listened with tears rolling down my cheeks.

We continued to make vacations an opportunity to broaden our children's outlook on life and expand Andy's horizons. For the next few summers, our adventures took us to the tropics: a dreamlike villa on a rocky cliff in Jamaica with car, cook, gardener, and private pool; a Club Med at Cancun on the Yucatan peninsula in Mexico, where Andy became an expert snorkeler and practiced socializing with the club's young attendants; and back to Jamaica for two weeks at an ocean-side resort.

During our 1978 visit to Christopher Columbus's "fairest isle that eyes have beheld," Andy decided he was old enough to socialize on his own. As the steel band took over from the rock group, we realized that Andy had disappeared. We checked the dance floor, the room he was sharing with John, and the game room. Eventually, we found him in the bar. He was sitting drinking beer with a young couple, obviously honeymooners. They said, "Oh, he's not bothering us; we're having a nice chat." They were being warm and hospitable to him but probably would have preferred to be on their own. Mustering all our powers of persuasion, we said, "Andy, you've had a really nice visit with these good people, but it's time to leave them on their own. Come along and join in the dancing and limbo competition."

Andy replied indignantly, "I don't want to come with you parents. I'm old enough to do what I want and choose my own friends. I'm nineteen and can drink a beer if I want to."

It was difficult to explain to him that newlyweds may not want to be bothered by an overly friendly, developmentally disabled young man.

With Andy in a better mood, we enjoyed climbing up the waterfalls at Ocho Rios, river rafting, and horseback riding. Andy was especially pleased because the stables used English saddles on the horses, and he was able to show off his superior knowledge. One day, as they cantered along the beach, a tree branch suddenly blocked their way. Experienced Andy steered his horse around it, but inexperienced John, expecting that his horse would follow, was knocked off his steed. When Andy saw what had happened, he came to John's help and held his horse until John was able to re-mount.

At home in Hyde Park, Andy was developing other interests. He had always enjoyed playing with hair. When he was nine years old, we had visited the Herzogs in State College, Pennsylvania, and Andy discovered that Heather, who was two years younger and had long, thick, wavy hair would allow him to brush it, put it in braids, or pin it on top of her head.

During his adolescent years, he became obsessed with hair. We thought he might want to become a hairdresser or that playing with women's hair was part of his sexual development; perhaps the texture and smell of hair made him feel close to a woman. Whenever women friends with long hair visited us, they became Andy's clients. He brushed and combed their tresses as long as they had the patience to let him. Ann Morrison, one of his more faithful models, went home to Scotland for several, months and Andy missed her. In November 1976, he wrote:

Dear Ann,

I miss you so much because I like you so much.

Please come back to Chicago to stay here because I need you here, Ann, and I don't want you to go away from Chicago.

Ann I will miss you hair because remember I all ways to something with it.

Amir wants you to stay here in Chicago and he will miss you so much and my parents will too.

Lisa and John will miss you that much.

I know why, because we like to have Christmas presents from you and Amir.

from your best friend, Andy Wyllie.

Andy always said exactly what he meant. His perceptions were uncluttered by frills and false compliments. In this letter he said truthfully that he and his siblings missed Ann because she was responsible for buying them gifts at Christmas.

When he was at a loss to find a model for his hairdressing efforts, he borrowed my curlers or hairpieces and fixed his own hair. Sometimes he came to dinner with strangely puffed-up hair in a new style. After I had rescued my hairpieces and hidden them, Andy (he was fourteen at the time) found a catalog of hair products and without anyone's knowledge, ordered a wig. Evidently it was a cash-on-delivery order, which he had to collect at the post office. Without the knowledge of anyone in the house, he had managed to find the telephone number of a taxi service, order a cab to come to the house, tell the driver to go to the post office, and ask him to wait while he paid for his package. When Pete opened the door, he was surprised to see a taxi driver returning Andy to the house and asking for money. Andy had enough cash to pay for the package but had forgotten about the cab fare.

"Where have you been, and what have you been doing?" said Pete in a shocked voice.

"It's none of your business; I don't want to tell you."

Andy was upset at being discovered. Even though we were worried about him leaving the house and going somewhere on his own, we had to admire his initiative. His only mistake was to miscalculate how much money it would all cost, a failure to which many normal adults have succumbed.

Recalling events for this story, we asked Andy, "Why, as a teenager, did you have such a fixation with hair?"

"I was always jealous of ladies having pretty hair," he replied.

At the time his sister had thick, wavy blonde hair, which she wore long and full; his brother had thick, dark hair, which had become wavy and curly as he entered his teens. Andy's hair, typical of many persons with Down syndrome, was stringy, straight, and lacking in volume. As an adolescent, he wanted to see what it felt like to have nice hair, so he tried everything he could think of, from curlers to hairpieces to wigs. Starting in the 1970s fashion has allowed men to have permanent waves and color treatments. After leaving home and being free of parental control, Andy went to hair salons and tried Afro perms, softer curls, and finally a nice straight cut, which we all preferred. He always shampooed his hair every day and took excellent care of it.

As Andy struggled to become an independent adult, his parents pursued their careers. After graduating from Harrington Institute, I spent nearly three years learning the intricacies of interior design at a firm in downtown Chicago. Then, wanting to be independent and based at home, I established my own company Intekton, Inc. Evidently my preoccupation with design work had some repercussions at home. In a 1977 letter addressed to his father, Andy expressed his feelings about his parents arguing:

Dear Dad,

When Mommy ask you to do something, obey her and don't be mad at her, because I don't like that at all, because you are being lazy to her.

I don't like you and Mom fighting like that, so please stop it for good. And start a new life together and do things to make your family happy about our parents.

Andrew J. Wyllie

P.S. And God says that too.

Evidently what we considered mild arguments reverberated with at least one of our children as fights.

We had always allowed the children to watch cartoons, especially on Saturday mornings, because it gave us a chance to sleep late or read the paper in bed. Although we encouraged Andy to do other things and always made him come with us for outings, we never stopped him watching his favorite shows: *Star Trek*, soap operas, game shows, and religious programs. Just as people who live on their own relate to characters in soap operas or find friends through chat rooms on the Internet, Andy made television a substitute for the friends, social life, and sports activities Lisa and John enjoyed.

I found it comforting to compare Andy's recreational activities as a teenager with those of other Down syndrome people when they were the same age. Lindsay Yeager was more gregarious than Andy, but her favorite occupation also was watching television. She told me, "I like to have some peace and quiet; too much noise gives me a headache." However, she was perfectly capable of keeping herself occupied with creative activities: she kept a journal, wrote poetry and lyrics, drew designs for clothes, and liked singing, dancing, and acting. At age sixteen, Blair Rodriguez also loves dancing and performing. In this web-crazy age, she has excellent computer skills and spends hours watching videos of *Hannah Montana*, Michael Jackson, and other teen programs on YouTube.

As a family we often discussed religious festivals and attended services at Easter and Christmas, but we did not belong to a church. Lacking a religious focus, Andy had become enthralled by televangelism and was especially susceptible to the appeals of charismatic preachers. Without our knowledge, he had been writing to Reverend Rex Humbard of the Prayer Key Family in Akron, Ohio, and receiving small gifts of crosses and religious literature.

Pete began to miss money from his wallet, which he often left in his jacket in the hall closet. Suspecting that his loss might be a preacher's gain, he asked Andy, "How have you managed to get these crosses and pamphlets about God? Have you, by any chance, taken money from my wallet to send to the Reverend Humbard?"

Andy did not answer at first. Pete continued, "Andy, answer me. If you've been taking my money, you will have to pay me back out of your own pocket money. Just think about it and tell me. God wants you to tell the truth."

When Andy had done something wrong, or when he was upset for being disciplined, he went sulking to his room, shut the door, and thought about it. Occasionally he came out and said he was sorry; sometimes he wrote us a note about it. This time he gave us his confession in writing and owned up to taking more than one $5 bill:

Dear Dad,

As you will take $5 out of my money, also take $10 out of my money because I take $10 from your wallet and I pray to God and he forgive doing that to you. And I'm sorry I did that and I try not to it again if I don't think of stilling money again.

From your Andrew Wyllie

P.S. Please don't disturb me. I try to get some sleep. You may talk about to-morrow night.

This was a serious misdemeanor, and Andy was severely reprimanded and punished. His excuse was that God needed the money. We explained that one of the Ten Commandments stated, "Thou shall not steal," and stealing or borrowing without permission was a serious offense and God would not like it. We stopped his allowance for several weeks and kept a close watch on any mail that Andy sent or received.

Andy now regarded his basement room as his own apartment. In response to our urging about the importance of work, he took his responsibilities at home and at his Co-op job seriously. We also lectured Andy about the need to do things on his own and for him to learn to be independent. If the children had problems, we encouraged them to talk about them. Andy chose to express his frustration in writing. On April 9, 1977, he wrote:

Dear Parents,

I like to have things change around here with my big responsibility.

Would you please tell John not to be smartalick and boss me around, but I want him to be nice all the way and I will be nice to him.

And I like to have our Mom to change too, like not to scream and yelled and cry out.

And I want Daddy to change too, like, not to take my allwance away.

I am old enough to be myself and I don't need help because I help myself please don't take care of me because I can take care of myself, so I won't get no more prombles here at home again, but I try to prove myself without family around me.

Sign by Andy Wyllie

P.S. I like to have things new around here.

In spite of our strict rules about never letting strangers into the house, we came home one day to find Andy entertaining a group of young men in the living room. They looked remarkably smart in dark suits, with smoothed-back hair and clean-shaven, freckled faces. They seemed to be holding books on their laps.

When Andy saw us, he said, "Oh hi, Mum and Dad, these people have asked me to join their church and go with them to a meeting."

The young men were Mormons going door to door to enroll new members. Andy was ready to join the Mormon Church immediately and looked forward to the social opportunities that the young disciples offered.

He had also been succumbing to the hypnotic preaching of the Reverend Robert Schuller in his *Hour of Power*. One evening, as we were enjoying our regular family dinner, Andy said, with an angelic smile on his face, "Dad, can I have a check for $500?"

"What for?" asked a surprised Pete.

"I want to buy a star to hang in the Crystal Cathedral. God needs my help."

"How do you know God needs your help?"

"Reverend Schuller told me."

In the early 1950s, the Reverend Robert Schuller left the farmlands of Iowa and began preaching his Christian message in Southern California. He spoke from the roof of a snack bar to a congregation sitting in their cars at the Orange Drive-In Theater. By 1959 his swelling automobile congregation had outgrown the parking area and needed a church.

The first Garden Grove Community Church, designed by Richard Neutra, was an elegant linear structure of wood, steel, glass, and stone bordered by a reflecting pool. By 1975 the congregation had outgrown the Neutra church, and Reverend Schuller hired renowned architect Philip

Johnson to design a larger building. Responding to his client's concept of a church that would "awaken the senses, uplift the spirit, and allow the individual to see the heavens above," Johnson designed a glass cathedral, a great, soaring volume with a lacelike framework of steel trusses inside walls of mirror-glass. Its $16 million cost was covered by contributions from an enormous congregation. By now Schuller had taken his preaching beyond his Southern California community to the greater congregation of the American public through the medium of radio and television. His faithful followers, responding to mesmeric messages, willingly subsidized commemorative windows, "pillars of steel," pews, and Mylar stars.

It was for a Mylar star to be hung from the roof of the cathedral that Andy wanted to give his name and money. It was hard to convince him that even small contributions of $5 or $10 to Rex Humbard or Robert Schuller, let alone $500 for a Mylar star, were more than he should give. We did not want to discourage his interest in religion, but we suggested he restrict his contributions to an occasional $1 out of his own pocket money. He followed our advice and in November 1979 wrote to Reverend Rex:

Dear Rex,

　　I like you to help my best friend, Amir Nour to stop smoking for his health in life once again. I try to send you some money as I can to do it. I will send $1 and thats all for now.

　　Andrew J. Wyllie

　　PS. God love you so do I to keep him in your heart and in your life.

During one of Andy's vacations at our present home in Pasadena, California, we took him to a Sunday-morning service in Schuller's great crystal edifice. The experience will stay in all our minds for a long time. We joined several hundred worshippers sitting in individual seats upholstered in gold-colored fabric. The service opened with a resounding organ voluntary that filled the glass-enclosed space. As three ministers took their places on a rose-colored marble dais behind banks of potted ferns, two ninety-foot-tall glass doors opened inward while fountains outside shot up arcs of water. Light, representing the spirit of God, flooded the cathedral as the service was projected to parishioners sitting in their cars in the parking lot.

In order for everyone in the huge space to see the minister, his face was projected on a large video screen. The simple Protestant service was supplemented with superb music provided by choir, organ, and a full orchestra. Afterward the ministers circulated among the congregation, and a young preacher, Dr. Tino Ballesteros, conversed with Andy, reassuring him that God would be always at his side.

We asked an usher why no stars hung from the roof. The original stars, which were to be made of crystal, were never fabricated because they might have fallen onto the heads of the congregation during an earthquake. After the fire department prohibited the use of Mylar stars, parishioners contributed star-shaped plaques set in the walkways around the building.

We took photographs and asked Andy what he thought of the cathedral and the service. He said, "It was very special. I really felt God was there."

Chapter 18:
College

Andy graduated on June 8, 1978, after four years at Kenwood High School. Of the eight students in the special education division, he was the only one on the principal's honor roll.

The ceremony was held in Chicago's Auditorium Theater, a magnificent building designed by Adler and Sullivan in 1887. The coarse masonry walls and rough-cut granite piers of the exterior stand in contrast to the richness of the interior design. The hall's perfect acoustics are achieved through a series of ellipses from the arcs of the ceiling to curves formed by the tops of the velvet-covered seats. Small lights, glittering like stars in a midnight sky, accentuate the elliptical shape of the ceiling arches. A hum of anticipation emanated from the audience of families and friends as the nervous blue-gowned graduates fidgeted in their seats.

Finally the faculty and officials took their place on the stage and the ceremony began. A variety of loud whoops and cheers hailed the less-orthodox students; resounding applause greeted the special education students as they received their diplomas. Andy walked sedately up the steps to the stage, holding his head high and grinning from ear to ear. He shook hands politely with the principal and holding firmly to his diploma, embraced his teacher; he then turned toward the audience to make sure we had witnessed this great moment of his life.

I had to keep dabbing my eyes as I remembered the time of his birth and the prognosis that he would never learn to read or write or develop into a self-sufficient adult. Now our nineteen-year-old son with Down syndrome was actually graduating from high school. We never dreamed that one day he would be among the many seniors in this sea of pale blue caps and gowns, tassels carefully laid to one side. We sat through the proceedings impatient to hug Andy and express our pride. We drove home and celebrated with our friends and Andy's greatest admirers, Ann and Amir and Nancy and Don.

We had hoped that Andy could find a job after finishing high school; perhaps he could increase his hours at the Co-op. To our surprise, his teachers at Kenwood had suggested that he attend college. College for our developmentally disabled son—was this really possible? We had never expected him to finish high school let alone attend a college, but he had exceeded our expectations every step of the way.

As we started to explore places of higher learning, we discovered that the Chicago City Colleges were subject to a new law, Section 504 of the Rehabilitation Act of 1973, which made it illegal for institutions receiving federal funding to discriminate against people with disabilities, whether physically impaired or mentally retarded.

In addition to providing two-year programs at a variety of campuses in and around the city, the colleges provided Adult Education Classes for the Exceptional Adult, which were designed for college-age educable mentally handicapped students, sheltered workshop workers, and other disabled persons who possessed the basic social skills to attend classes on a college campus. Students received instruction in rapid reading, physical fitness, improving your math, nutrition, and the preparation of food—skills that prepared them for independent living. Unfortunately the program was given only on Saturdays when Andy worked all day at the Co-op. We were reluctant to take him away from a job, where he had been accepted and was performing well.

However, we thought he might be eligible for selected regular classes since he had been partly mainstreamed in high school. Our Sudanese friend, Amir Nour, a professor of art at Truman College, said, "Think about sending Andy to Truman. It's on the north side of the city in a relatively safe neighborhood. There's a train line running directly to it from Hyde Park, and I don't think Andy will stand out as being different because there are many foreign students there who have language and adjustment difficulties. And I promise you, I'll keep an eye on the situation."

Pete met with Mr. Paul Mall, a faculty advisor, to discuss a possible program. Mr. Mall explained, "It's our belief that young adults should have a chance to develop as well as they can, not just educationally but socially in order to enhance their quality as citizens. From Andy's previous record, it's clear that he would benefit socially, and he may be capable of learning more."

Encouraged by Mr. Mall's words, we decided that Andy would attend Truman College as a part-time student. In the fall of 1978 he registered for classes in typing, drama, and physical education. He attended college five mornings a week and continued with his work at the Co-op supermarket on Thursday and Friday afternoons and all day Saturday. On Wednesday afternoons, he went to his horseback riding class at the armory building in downtown Chicago.

Traveling to Truman College by bus and Chicago's famous 'L' train provided the biggest challenge. In the late 1800s, entrepreneurs designed an elevated railroad to bring people from the south and west sides to the center of the city. With the addition of a northwestern section in the early 1900s, the various lines were connected to encircle the center of the city, forming the structure known to this day as "the Loop."

After a few trial runs with his father, Andy had quickly mastered the ten-minute bus ride to high school. Now he faced a one-hour journey by bus and train to college. Pete went with him several times until Andy felt confident of finding the right bus (it stopped near our house) to take him to the elevated railroad station at Fifty-Fifth and Halsted. Two train lines, A and B, went into the city and to the north side. Andy had to choose the train on line A going north and stopping near Truman College. On the return journey, he had to do everything in reverse, making sure he got on the line that stopped at Fifty-Fifth Street. How many of us, in the confusion and rush of getting somewhere, have hopped on the wrong train or bus? Andy made a mistake only one time. Fortunately he realized his error when the train went whizzing by the Fifty-Fifth Street stop. He had the presence of mind to get off at the next stop and find a train going back the other way, which stopped at the right station.

Another worry was whether inner city teenagers would take advantage of a handicapped white boy traveling on his own through parts of the city avoided by many fearful Hyde Parkers. Would he be attacked or have his wallet taken? We made sure he took only a minimal amount of money with him, enough to pay for his tickets and change for a soda or two at the college. One day a boy accosted him as he descended the stairs from the platform at Fifty-Fifth Street. Andy responded, "Do you want me to scream until someone comes to help?" The boy left him alone. No doubt Andy's experience with similar situations at Ray and Kenwood schools helped him respond to this encounter.

In January 1979, Chicago suffered another of its mammoth snow-storms that hit about once a decade. The city shut down as several feet of drifting snow blanketed the urban area, causing all forms of transportation to come to a halt. Schools, colleges, and businesses were closed for several days, forcing students and workers to stay home and enjoy an unexpected holiday. City workers labored day and night to clear the streets. They had already cleared the train lines in the wealthier western and northern suburbs but apparently were giving less attention to the poorer south side where ice on the power points prevented the trains from running. As a result, Andy could not travel to college. He became bored at home and annoyed with the delay. Each evening he watched the news hoping to find out when the south-side 'L' trains would start again. Without any provocation on our part, he wrote the following letter to the mayor of Chicago:

Dear Mayor Bilandic,

If you want to keep this job of the Mayor of Chicago please work much harder, and please don't be lazy on you job.

I don't like to have some delay on the CTA trains, and please put more trians on the CTA Rial.

Please work on the snow removers to move all the snow before it melt to a flood, because it is much worst for Chicago.

Please try to work on the CTA and RTA to put more buses and trians, because people wants to get around on time to their job and college and high school and others, so we don't like to be late to where we are going to.

Please work on your plans of Chicago, because sometime we do have the worst weather in winter of December and January.

Andrew James Wyllie.

After two weeks the trains started running again, and Andy was able to return to college. In the next mayoral race, Jane Byrne capitalized on Mayor Bilandic's inability to deal promptly with the transportation problem and won the election.

Once before, during elementary school, Andy had demonstrated his independence by riding his bicycle far from home. Now he decided to show off his college status by bicycling to his former high school to visit his favorite teacher. At the school he locked his bike on the rack and had a pleasant visit with Ms. Hashimoto. On the way back, he rode along Fifty-Third Street, one of the main thoroughfares of Hyde Park. Just as he was crossing the street on his bike, having looked both ways to make sure there were no cars coming, a Bell Telephone van came around the corner. Andy did not see the van, and the driver did not see Andy. Before he knew what was happening Andy and his bike hit the side of the van, and Andy went flying over the hood and landed on the other side on the road. A police car driving in the opposite direction saw what happened, turned around quickly, and came to Andy's assistance.

The policeman picked Andy up off the street and put him down carefully on the sidewalk while he called on his car radio for an ambulance. Realizing that his young victim was mentally handicapped, the policeman was gentle and kind. Andy remembers shaking all over and feeling achy, dazed, and bruised. Fortunately he did not feel any excruciating pain and was able to walk into the ambulance with the help of the policeman. The ambulance attendants asked Andy for his name and address, which he was able to give them, as well as showing them the identity necklace that he wore, explaining that he was Down syndrome.

Meanwhile Pete received a telephone call at work saying that his son had been admitted to Billings Hospital (the main University of Chicago hospital) and asking him to come over right away to the emergency room. The caller tried to assuage Pete's alarm, saying, "It's all right, your son isn't seriously injured, but we need you here at the hospital." Pete found Andy lying on a trolley in a corridor with his eyes looking watery and scared above patches of dried blood. After a long wait, a doctor examined him but found only bruises on his backside and abrasions on his face, legs, and arms; luckily there were no broken bones. The doctor cleaned him up and released him. The Bell Telephone Company, relieved that we were not going to sue them, paid for the medical expenses as well as a new bike.

Pete was now chairman of the Department of Geophysical Sciences. Since he still had work to finish, he took Andy back to his office, giving him paper and pencil to keep him occupied. Pete's secretary, Glenda, was part Apache—a tall, stunning young woman with long, thick hair, who was often likened to the famous singer Cher. She was also a faithful Trekkie like Andy. While Pete typed and shuffled his papers, Andy wrote a letter to Glenda:

This is a Secret

You are so pretty with your hair down that way and I like it very much. So you married, I wish not, because I want you because we love Star Trek and we got things to talk about.

We are the type to get marry together because I love you so much and I want to kiss you on the lips, as soon as I am recover from this mess, then you can.

Andrew J. Wyllie

The accident may have shaken him and caused bruises and abrasions, but it had not taken away his libido or teenager's interest in beautiful women.

Unfortunately, Andy's battle scars coincided with an important interview. For some time we had been searching for long-term permanent employment and a possible residential facility for him. Through the family of Andy's elementary school friend, Lael Arnold, we had heard about the Lambs Farm, a small community for developmentally disabled adults in Libertyville, Illinois. Some of their participants lived in a dormitory on the farm, and others commuted from a variety of Chicago communities.

In May 1978, Pete met with the Lambs employment manager to discuss the possibility of Andy working two days a week at Lambs during the summer after the end of the college year. This would allow him to maintain his schedule of work at the Co-op in Hyde Park. On his application form we described his skills as follows:

Andrew Wyllie has attended swimming classes at the YMCA and spent two summers at the Y's Camp Martin Johnson, where he swam one mile in a marathon race; once a week he takes horseback riding lessons and has had piano lessons for the last four years. At home his duties are: setting the table, emptying the garbage, walking the dog, and buying the newspaper. His interests are swimming, roller skating, dancing, listening to music, and watching television. He follows baseball and football teams and makes model planes and cars.

Andy's qualifications looked good on paper, but before making a commitment, the directors of Lambs wanted to meet their new applicant. Poor Andy had to appear before his interviewers with a face marred by the black-scabbed patches of his accident. Fortunately, his appearance made no difference; the directors agreed to train him for work at the Lambs Country Inn, a restaurant open to the public. We also learned that Lambs was expecting to construct more residential housing in the near future.

The journey to Lambs was an even longer and more complicated journey than the one to Truman College, but by now Andy was a veteran commuter. He took a bus to one of the main line train stations downtown and found the correct platform and train to Lake Bluff, where a Lambs counselor met him and drove him to the Lambs Farm. The journey took nearly two hours, but it was only for the summer months. After Pete had established him in the routine, he drove down to the station a few times and watching from a distance, made sure Andy found the right bus back to Hyde Park. Andy managed it all without a hitch.

Although he was building up his self-confidence and had mastered the challenging journey to the north side of the city on his own, Andy's grades at the end of his first year in college were not good. He received a C in drama, a D in reading, and Fs for typing and English. Andy took his classes seriously and had set himself a routine at home, which included an hour or two of homework every day. We thought he was doing extremely well in typing, a task that he practiced diligently. He used all his fingers and thumbs, putting them on the correct keys; he could copy type and keep his eyes on the text—tasks that his father had never mastered. However, with two fingers of each hand, two thumbs and his eyes on the

Loving Andrew

keyboard, Pete's fingers flew across the keys, whereas Andy was as slow as a tortoise.

Failing two classes did not worry us. Clearly the college experience was stretching Andy's abilities, helping him to mature and become more independent. Moreover, it seemed that he felt accepted in a normal environment and took pride in being a college student.

Because his grades were below the minimum required to stay in the system, we had to appeal Andy's case if we wanted him to continue for another year. Andy filled out the request form required by the registrar's office, but Pete wrote the accompanying note of explanation,

Andrew Wyllie is mentally handicapped because of Down syndrome. Therefore, he cannot follow the work at the standard college pace. He does work and is proud of the fact that "I am getting there." But he cannot "get there" fast enough to get normal grades. His high school teachers in special education were anxious for him to attend Truman because he is still growing socially. Therefore, as a student he can benefit from the college program, even if academic records do not show this.

Andrew learned *how* to type last semester—not a bad achievement for a Down syndrome student! It is our hope that if he takes typing again, he will begin to catch up with the normal students, even if he cannot cope with all of the more academic aspects of typing, his skill will certainly improve. He also enjoys basic English and drama, and his determination to do well will surely lead to improvement.

The stated aims of the community college program are satisfied, because Andrew can definitely benefit from attendance. Despite the apparent contradiction between "college" and "mentally handicapped" here is a case where a mentally handicapped student can benefit immensely from a liberal interpretation of the charter for the college system.

Andy was allowed to re-register and continued with classes in English and typing. After seeing a newspaper article in November 1996, in which I had mentioned Andy's achievements, his former typing teacher, Mae Cowen, wrote the following letter to the *Chicago Tribune:*

I taught Andrew to type when he attended Truman College. At the first session I asked Andrew why he wanted to learn to type. He informed me that he was working in a supermarket, and he was told he would be promoted if he could type envelopes, labels, and short memos.

Andrew worked very hard learning to use the typewriter and turning in all assigned work. He did learn to use the machine to the best of his ability. I knew he could not become a speed typist or do difficult work, but the fact that he could place a letter properly and type with few errors was, in my mind, sufficient for a passing grade.

I became very fond of Andrew and often wondered if he had achieved his goal. I am very happy that he is at Lambs Farm where he always wanted to be. His parents have every right to be proud of this remarkable young man. He is a fine example of what a Down syndrome child with motivation can achieve. I am proud to have helped him.

At home he created weekly schedules. He organized his time on a variety of charts. One was a large, white sheet of paper pinned to his wall. On the top he had taped a heading "Weekly Schedule" printed on purple paper. Down the left side he printed the days of the week, also cut out of purple paper. All the spelling was correct, except Friday, which was misspelled as "FIRDAY." In six separate columns he listed his activities for each day: Get up Time, Garbage, Clean (he now took care of cleaning his room), Hairwash, Homework, Nap Time, Produce Work (at the Co-op), Call Perry (his friend from school). Another Weekly Schedule was carefully typed with dashes dividing sections titled Get Up, Walk Pucci, Lunch Time, Garbage Time, Clean Up Time, and Bicycle Riding. In one column was a list of the days on which he did each activity and in a second column the beginning and ending times for the activity (fig. 18.1). A handwritten chart listed his television programs (fig. 18.2). Obviously he had studied the television times and accurately copied his selected programs onto his chart.

Many people with disabilities find comfort and security in routine. During her high school years, Lindsay Yeager would lay out her clothes for the next day. She liked to have her meals on time and at the weekend was always up, showered, and dressed, never sitting around in pajamas

WEEKLY SCHEDULE

	Get Up	Walk Pucci
Sunday	9:00	9:30 & 5:30
Monday	8:30	9:00
Tuesday	8:30	9:00 & 6:00
Wednesday	8:30	9:00
Thursday	7:30	8:00
Friday	8:30	9:00
Saturday	7:30	8:00

Lunch Time

Sunday	2:30-3:30
Monday	12:00-1:00
Tuesday	12:00-1:00
Thursday	12:00-1:00
Friday	12:00-1:00

Garbage Time

Sunday	4:30-5:00
Tuesday	8:30-9:00
Thursday	8:30-9:00

Clean Up Time

Sunday	8:30-9:00
Wednesday	8:00-8:30
Friday	8:30-9:00

Bicycle Riding

Sunday	3:30-4:00
Monday	1:00-3:00
Tuesday	1:00-3:00

Figure 18.1: Andy's neatly typed list of his weekly activities (age nineteen)

Time	channel	T.V show Programs
10:00	11	Lifestyle (children)
10:30	32	Movie (comedy)
11:30	9	The Lone Ranger (Western)
3:30	9	Movie (Adventure)
5:30	9	Star Trek (Science Fiction)
7:00	7	Battlestar Galactica (Science Fiction)
12:00	9	Bozo's Circus
1:00	32	Courtship of Eddie's Father (comedy)
4:00	9	Gilligan's Island (Comedy)
7:00	7	Lucan (Adventure)
8:30	2	one day at a time (comedy)
7:00	2	Paper chase (Drama)
8:00	7	Three's company (comedy)
7:00	5	Dick clerk's live wednesday (Music)
8:00	7	charlie's Angels (crime-Drama)
7:30	7	What's Happening (comedy)
9:00	7	Family (Drama)
7:00	5	Diff'ent strokes (comedy)
7:30	9	Hogan's Heroes (comedy)
9:00	2	Flying High (comedy-Drama)
8:00	5	Godzilla Power Hour
7:00	32	Emergency one (Drama)

T.V WEEK PROGRAMS

Figure 18.2: Andy's handwritten list of his favorite television shows (age nineteen)

like other members of her family. After receiving her high school diploma at age eighteen, Lindsay attended Pasadena City College for two years. She took classes in drama, but her main interest was food services, for which she received a certificate.

In his second year of college, Andy also took physical education and a general drawing class taught by Amir Nour. In addition to his work as a sculptor, which has brought him into the forefront of African art with references in textbooks calling him the progenitor of modern African sculpture, Amir is a gifted teacher. Many art teachers leave their students to grope in the dark, fearing that too much direction will ruin their creativity, but Amir gives his students meaningful instruction and is sometimes rewarded with exciting work.

Andy's midterm grades in the spring of 1980 were A in physical education and a B for drawing. Amir told us that Andy paid close attention to his instructions and showed a drawing ability that exceeded many normal students. As a surprise Amir arranged to have one of Andy's drawings framed for Father's Day (fig. 18.3). Under Amir's tutelage, Andy had learned to organize his drawing by marking a line down the center, placing the hills and distant coast line three quarters of the way up the paper and the boat a quarter of the way from the bottom. The shape of the boat was quite clearly a rowboat with a seat inside. A variety of shading gave the drawing texture, dimension, and perspective. It was signed and dated March 1980.

While Andy was struggling with his college courses, Lisa was paging through catalogs trying to decide which colleges might meet her needs

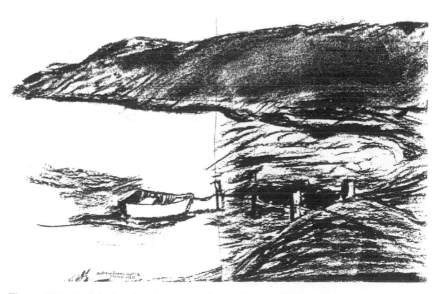

Figure 18.3: Andy's drawing for an art class at Truman College (age twenty)

and offer her a place. She had spent two months in the summer of 1979 backpacking through the mountains and wilderness areas of Colorado, Wyoming, Oregon, and Washington. Having climbed to the summit of Mt. Rainier, she now felt ready to tackle the world, pass her driving test, and challenge the limits set by parents on her ambitions. Another bird was stretching its wings and preparing to leave the nest.

John, now a freshman in high school, was concentrating on getting good grades. He still played the tuba but had given up singing with the choir after his voice changed. His spare time was taken up with soccer practices, and he was planning to try out for the swim team. During the summer he had qualified as a racing skipper on 420 two-man sailboats and attended a camp in Michigan.

Aware of his siblings' ever-growing activities and freedom, Andy continued to strive toward greater independence. Now that he was a college student, he established firmly that his basement room at home was his own apartment. He taped a succession of different notices on his door, identifying his room with an interesting variety of names, which demonstrated the broad extent of his knowledge and an ability to create his own imaginary life. The names were "Private Apartment Room," "Bachelor's Apartment Room," "Private Cottage," "Motel Apartment Room," and "Andrew's Home Sweet Home."

In addition to identifying his own space, he established rules for the rest of the family so that we would respect his need for ownership and privacy. As he changed the name of his apartment a new set of rules would appear. A notice on green paper read:

Private Apartment Room

You may come in my room to watch TV, but, soon you finish watching TV, please shot it off and soon you finish in my room, please close my door.

While I do my homework do not knock or open my door that will disturb me from doing my work.

While I am in my room, please knock first before you enter my room.

If I'm taking a nap do not disturb me.

Do not go into my Private Office.

As is evident from his television schedule, he was an ardent viewer. Lisa and John complained that he was turning into a couch potato because he spent many hours in front of the tube. However, television was his relaxation after attending college classes and working at his job. Soap operas and movies stimulated his imagination and social skills; game shows helped his vocabulary and general knowledge.

From his salary he had been able to buy a new television for the family so that he could have the old one in his room. This solved many of the fights over choice of programs. Although they would never have admitted it, Lisa and John were probably envious of their handicapped brother having enough money to buy a television set. A new typewritten notice appeared on his door:

Motel Apartment Room

New Rules

1. While I am in my Private Apartment, please knock first before you enter my apartment.

2. While I am doing my homework, please do not disturb my concentrate, live my door alone, please.

3. If you want to watch on my TV in my apartment please try get a permissin from our parents or from me.

4. As soon you finish in my apartment, please shot my light and please close my door after you.

5. Dear Parents, please live me all alone in my Private Apartment so, I can think of my business and my personnal affair and my homework, so I try by myself for a while, if I need you I will call you.

Although he was striving to be independent and set his own rules, he was also learning to abide by our rules. After being punished for taking money from his father's wallet to send to a religious organization, he was now careful to let us know if he had borrowed money. He left Pete a note on his desk saying, "I take some change from your desk for the buses for next week." It was signed, "Andy, your number one son."

In addition to honing his social skills, Andy had developed excellent grooming habits. He was particular about showering, washing his hair, and shaving. However, while in college he decided to grow a beard, perhaps to prove his manhood as well as his independence. Pete was beardless, so he was not trying to copy his father. As a teenager with fair hair, Andy did not need to shave every day, so he would not have been able to grow a proper beard. When I expressed my objections, he wrote me a note: "Mom, I like to start growing a beard in my early age, and it is my own choice. P.S. No body will stop me from growing it. No shaving." I replied on the back of his note: "You cannot live in my house with a beard." Andy replied: "Yes I can if I want to and I will."

The argument continued for several days. Now that Andy was becoming an independent young adult, it was even more challenging to find a way of deterring him from an inappropriate development. I usually tackled such situations by exploring several options. I had to find a reason that would make sense to him. In this case I tried appealing to his desire to be an acceptable adult. Although he knew he was developmentally disabled, he didn't like being labeled as such. I said to him, "Do you want to stand out as retarded?"

"No," he replied strongly.

"Wouldn't you rather be the same as everyone else?"

"Yes." He usually responded in monosyllables when we were having a serious discussion.

"Then it would be silly to draw attention to yourself by looking scruffy and unshaven. Young men and women in the working world have to look smart and clean-shaven."

"I'll think about it."

Eventually I won. It took time and patience to persuade him that at this stage of his life when he was striving to establish himself as a regular college student and an employee of a good supermarket, he would fit in better if he was clean-shaven. It was part of the socially appropriate behavior routine.

Part IV: Adult Life
Ages Twenty-One to Fifty-Two

Chapter 19:
Leaving Home

Although he had not completed his second year of college, Andy left home on March 30, 1980, to become one of the first residents of a new supportive living arrangement recently opened at the Lambs Farm in Libertyville.

For several years he had been striving to become independent. He had established his own apartment at home, but that arrangement was not good enough. It was time to sever his umbilical cord, and it was he who wanted to finalize the separation. We had been training him to think for himself, to travel around the city alone, to accept responsibility, and to work at a regular job. We had taught him to behave appropriately in public, to be polite, and to be able to communicate his needs even though his speech was not always clear. Now he wanted to prove himself. Other twenty-year-olds left home, went to college or found jobs, and lived in their own apartments. Andy wanted to do the same.

In the spring of 1980, he typed one final notice for his apartment door at home:

Private Cottage—New Rules

Dear Parents, Lisa and John, Please live me all alone. I like to be on my own in my Private Cottage forever, so I can work things out by myself.

I need some privice in my Private Cottage so please let me have it.

When I am taking a nap, please do not Disturb me. I am sleeping soundly when the sound of my clock wake me up around the time.

During one of Andy's Christmas visits to our home in California I asked him, "What did you feel when you left home?"

"You're not going to like what I have to say, Mum."

"Well, say it anyway," I urged.

"It was nice to get away from our Chicago house and be on my own. I wanted to be independent and be like Lisa and John and do things on my own. I wasn't lonely or homesick—sorry, Mum."

In spite of this show of bravado, a 1981 letter to his sister expressed different emotions: "I hope you are happy where you are now. It is quite lonely to live on our own, me and you are the ones to miss our family. I hope you can get tough to live on your own like me."

Watching children leave the nest is difficult for any parent, but letting go of a child with a developmental disability is an especially traumatic experience because we feel so responsible for their well-being. Many parents fail to take this step for a variety of reasons: lack of training workshops after high school, dearth of job opportunities, and a serious shortage of appropriate housing. In the early 1990s, there was a nationwide trend to close state institutions and hospitals and house the residents in a variety of community facilities. Not only was this highly disruptive to both patients and parents, but the new living arrangements were inadequate, poorly funded, badly managed, and lacked the skilled caretakers that had serviced the institutions. Even now the number of state-owned group homes lags far behind the number of residents ready for occupation and will soon have to double in size to keep up with demand. In spite of the array of services available for the developmentally disabled from birth to age twenty-two, there is a notable lack of opportunities upon graduation when handicapped young adults move from the sheltered environment of high school into an unknown world.

Some parents who have spent their whole lives caring for a handicapped child cannot bear to think of another person taking on a responsibility that they believe is theirs alone. They question the ability of others to provide quality care, or they think of the world as too dangerous for their naive young adult. Caring for a dependent keeps the nest from being depleted and gives a purpose to the lives of aging parents.

But what about the parents who refused to put their children into state institutions and now require help because they themselves are aging and their dependents need a place to reside? In some cases siblings may have agreed to take over, but many parents do not want to impose such a burden on their other children. Unaware that life spans have increased significantly with the help of modern medicine and better nutrition, they may hope that their son or daughter will die before they do. As a result, these mentally handicapped adults, now aging themselves and set in their ways, will have to face the disruptive experience of coping with community living in a public-run facility. If their parents had helped them as young adults to discover a life of their own in a residential community or group home, they would have benefited from job and social opportunities, and the parents, relieved of an onerous responsibility, would have rediscovered a life of their own.

Lindsay Yeager had always wanted to be independent, and in 2001, at the age of twenty-one, she moved into a two-bedroom apartment with a non-disabled resident, with HUD covering most of the rent. After Lindsay's roommate left to go back to college, her mother found her a one-bedroom apartment within walking distance of her family. Lindsay is under the umbrella of a private organization called CHOICESS (Community Housing Options: Integrated Community, Employment, and Social Services). A caseworker helps her with budgeting and handling money, grocery shopping, cleaning, laundry, and other general living needs. She attends a church where she takes a special needs Bible study class and helps with a Sunday school class for disabled children. She takes drama classes with Theradrama in Studio City and has had three auditions for television. She also does one hour a week of volunteer child care at a YMCA. Lindsay is happy to be on her own and her ability to be independent is commendable, but her situation is not ideal. In spite of her activities, Lindsay is lonely and lacks a social life because she is reluctant to take the initiative to meet friends.

Andy may not have remembered feeling homesick when he moved to the community setting of Lambs, but I was shaken to the core with feelings of emptiness and sadness. He was our first child to leave home; we had put so much effort into loving him and training him, and I worried that I had not done enough. I felt especially guilty because I had become absorbed in my own career. Since the summer of 1977, my business had taken off. I had already completed an office project and several apartment building renovations and was now involved in turning a thirteen-story building into elegant condominiums. I spent many hours at my drafting table in my home office or coordinating the construction at the job site. Work left me with little time to supervise children or participate in school and college activities.

Pete had done a great job setting up Andy's college program and helping with his traveling routines. I had managed to keep an eye on his supermarket job and riding lessons, but I was suddenly overwhelmed with all the things I had not taught him.

How would Andy cope? Who would remind him to brush his teeth? Would he now grow the beard he desperately wanted? Who would tell him when to change his clothes or get a haircut? What would he do if something needed mending? I had not shown him how to thread a needle or sew on a button, but at the last minute I put together a sewing kit for him and hoped someone would help if he could not manage himself. I imagined him lying in bed at night in his new room thinking of his familiar surroundings at home and crying himself to sleep.

I worried in vain. Like Lindsay, Andy was delighted to be free at last. He would certainly have to abide by the rules of Lambs and conform to the houseparent's organization, but he would not have his own parents breathing down his neck, telling him what he could or could not do.

As Lambs celebrated its fiftieth anniversary in 2011, the administration looked back with satisfaction on its growth from a small pet shop employing twelve retarded men and women in Chicago to a working community of more than 250 developmentally disabled adults in Libertyville, Illinois. The present seventy-two-acre complex comprises residences, country inn, country store, petting zoo, pet shop, ice cream parlor, bakery, resale shop, miniature golf course, train ride, and an antique carousel. In his 1990 book *The Lambs of Libertyville*, Tim Unsworth told the remarkable story of cofounders Bob Terese and Corinne Owen. He explained that "this world-renowned model community...one of the best in the United States" was visited by 350,000 people annually. They eat at the restaurant, buy from the shops, and attend a variety of public weekend events held during the summer.

From the beginning Bob Terese and Corinne Owen, both dedicated teachers, decided that the mentally handicapped were not just a subspecies to be supervised and kept out of the way; they were real people who deserved to be trained to do worthwhile jobs and be of service to the community.

In 1961, Bob and Corinne were fired from their jobs as teachers in the Retarded Children's Aid program at Hull House for daring to propose the establishment of a business to be run by developmentally disabled adults. After a year searching for support, they opened a small store on North State Street, the only pet shop in the vicinity of the Gold Coast's wealthy high-rises. Devoutly religious, Bob and Corinne called their new venture "The Lambs" from a passage in St. John's gospel in which Christ directs his disciples to, "Feed my lambs."

Lacking advanced degrees in special education or psychology, the co-founders had an ongoing struggle to get their ideas accepted by leaders in the profession. Nevertheless, within three years their operation was a success, and the number of mentally handicapped helpers had increased to twenty-two. Bob had found outside employment in the regular workplace for some, but the remaining employees needed more work than could be accommodated in the six hundred–square-foot space of the pet shop.

After much searching, Bob and Corinne found a fifty-acre estate that had been a working farm with a dairy barn, two houses, and a lake stocked with fish. Philanthropist W. Clement Stone solved the hunt for funding by purchasing the farm and leasing it to the Lambs for the same rent as the State Street store. At the end of three years, when Stone saw that the Lambs' leaders were making a success of their new venture, he gave them the deed to the land. Now Bob and Corinne were on the road to fulfilling the objective described in their brochure: "To provide mentally retarded adults with meaningful work experiences, social opportunities, and a wholesome living environment." The mission of Lambs is now expressed in more respectful language: "Helping people with developmental disabilities lead productive, happy lives and connecting with the human spirit in us all."

A dormitory building completed in 1974 housed thirty-four adults, and an additional thirty or more people commuted daily to work in various

Loving Andrew

businesses or in the sheltered workshop. In December 1979, Lambs had just built ten small group homes with a $2.6-million, forty-year loan from the US Department of Housing and Urban Development. They were eager to fill their new residences with people they knew, especially those who had demonstrated good work habits and qualities needed for living independently. A staff member called us to ask if Andy would like to become one of the first residents of the newly built houses. Andy's work at the Lambs restaurant in the summer of 1979 had impressed his supervisors; he was the kind of person they needed to be an anchor for future residents. It seemed a shame to cut short his college program, especially since he was doing much better in his classes. We decided to let him make the decision: "Would you like to move to Lambs and be one of the first residents in House Two? They would really like to have you."

Andy was delighted. "Yeah, at last I can live on my own. When can I go?"

Before leaving home on March 30, 1980, Andy wrote out a revised schedule for other members of the family to take over his duties. At the bottom of the list he wrote: "Be good and good luck." It was a touching farewell.

Andy decided to establish himself in his new home as "Andrew." His formal name became a symbol of his new life and independence. We all had a hard time remembering to call him Andrew. As his parents, Pete and I tried claiming the shortened name as our prerogative; after all, we had called him Andy since his birth. When we forgot, which we did more frequently as we got older and our memories shorter, he reprimanded us severely or wrote us notes with Andrew spelled out in large letters. Once or twice we were told in writing to make it our New Year's resolution to call him Andrew. During one vacation visit, Andrew wrote the following note to his father: "Dad, Please coach Mom to say 'Andrew' not Andy all the time. Thank you." Out of respect for his wishes, I shall refer to him as Andrew for the remainder of this story.

The new houses, originally known as SLAs (supportive living arrangements), are now called campus group homes. The functional, wood-framed residences sit on the shores of the lake. Each house accommodates twelve adults, six men on the ground floor and six women upstairs. Each resident has a private bedroom and shares a bathroom with one or two neighbors. A dining room, kitchen, and airy, high-ceilinged lounge provide general living space. Each room is carpeted and furnished with bed, dresser, and armchair. We purchased this furniture and added a desk, bookcase, and accessories from home for Andrew. As with his apartment at home, he made numerous floor plans to change the furniture arrangement several times a year, usually just before we would visit. He took pride in his room and always kept it neat and clean.

Most of the residents have individualized their rooms with a variety of decorations. Andrew squeezed in a stereo and television set, and his walls were covered with *Star Trek* posters and framed photographs of movie stars, sports heroes, and friends. Another member of House Two hung model planes from his ceiling, making it look like a cave full of bats. Although residents mingle freely with other houses, each house has developed its own identity and organizes outings to restaurants or movies. Each member is responsible for maintaining his or her room and bathroom, and all share in the running of the house, with rotating shopping, cooking, and cleanup duties.

When Andrew first moved to Lambs, house parents lived in the upstairs apartment and supervised the operation of the house. After the first two years, House Two was assigned a higher level of independence; in the place of house parents, a daily aide coordinated doctors' appointments, organized the shopping, and supervised preparations of the evening meal. Andrew was one of the few residents who was allowed to cook unsupervised. His favorite recipes were meatloaf and stir-fry.

By the early 1970s, Lambs had become a more complex operation. As gifted teachers, Bob and Corinne had focused on their mission to care for and educate the developmentally disabled, but they had never been comfortable with fundraising and handling the business side. It also became important for Lambs to acquire some state funding and seek accreditation. In the mid-1970s, the governing board decided that Bob and Corinne should hand over the administrative reins of Lambs to a professionally trained director.

During Andrew's residency at Lambs, there were several executive directors, some more successful than others. With many added responsibilities, the leadership title has now been elevated to president and chief executive officer. Recalling the important role played by Corinne Owen, the current leader is a woman. After spending nine years on the board of directors, Dianne Yaconetti was elected president and CEO in 2001. She brings strong credentials, several awards, and many years of corporate experience to the job and without children of her own, relates to the participants as if they were part of her family. They all feel free to share their triumphs, sorrows, and frustrations with Dianne.

Over the years Lambs has developed a strong framework of support personnel. All the professional staff members have degrees in either education or social work. New members attend an orientation program, which includes an explanation of the Lambs philosophy and instruction in different ways of approaching participants, stressing the importance of individualization. Andrew had a social services coordinator or case manager, who kept an eye on all aspects of his life: work, medical needs, relationships with peers and staff, and his love life, which turned out to be the most important. A community resource coordinator oversaw his work schedules and performance. A job captain stayed in touch with his supervisor and periodically visited the supermarket where he worked. A recreation and leisure counselor helped Andrew with his participation in various sports and exercise programs. House parents and daily aides under the supervision of the supportive living coordinator kept tabs on Andrew's residential life and needs.

Communication between the departments is excellent. Each participant, with parents, if possible, meets once a year with his or her interdisciplinary team for an individual program plan (IPP) review. In addition to reviewing progress, participants are encouraged to develop new goals. At one time Andrew's goals were learning to barbecue and using a lawn mower.

Until his death in 1999, Bob Terese participated as much as he could in the operation of Lambs and kept his former partner, Corinne, abreast of developments. During a visit in 1995, I had lunch with Bob in the Country Inn. We were waited on by a Lambs resident who attended to Bob's needs with loving attention and made sure his glass of iced tea was constantly refilled.

I asked him, "As a cofounder, what do you feel about your work setting up the Lambs program?"

"It's been very satisfying, a pleasure," responded Bob enthusiastically. "I can't think of anything I could have done that would have given me greater pleasure. Lambs is not just for the benefit of the retarded but for everyone who works here and visits. This in itself has created another level of achievement."

"What is the reason for the success of Lambs?"

Without a hint of hesitation, Bob replied, "God. Every step along the way, the Lord has answered our prayers. When we needed money to buy the farm, a donor turned up; and many other incidents have just happened coincidentally to our benefit. I feel strongly that God has been involved in the progress and success of Lambs."

"Lambs has grown steadily. Do you have any concern that it is becoming too large or too commercial?" I asked.

"Thank God we are as commercial as we are, as we can't depend on government support. It is a great place for middle-class families, who can't afford Great America or a Disneyland, to enjoy an outing without spending a fortune."

From its inception, much of the Lambs's income has been derived from contributions, both corporate and private. Bob told me about one gift: "I had a telephone call telling me that the Lambs was to receive half a million dollars. I had never heard of the donor, a lady. Evidently she had visited Lambs with a seniors group, liked what she saw, had the money, and decided to give it to Lambs. Many of our donors are from middle-class, hardworking suburbs. We are in the same category as the Salvation Army: stable and steady."

In addition to the Lambs's excellent fundraising department, Lambs parents, from the early days of the pet shop, have always been a hardworking, dedicated group who give many hours managing events at the farm or organizing fundraising functions. Parents also represent each house and help with seasonal functions and special events.

When Andrew first moved to Lambs, he kept to himself and resisted joining sports activities or recreational clubs. If we encouraged him to participate, he told us, "Don't worry, I will. Just give me time; I want to get settled first." I think he wanted to relish his freedom and do exactly what he felt like doing without being pushed into anything. Inevitably it was an adjustment, a new home, new job, new routines, new rules, new surroundings, and many new faces.

An article in the 1980 Lambs Annual Report described the new houses and some of the residents. A photograph of Andrew showed him at work stocking shelves:

> Soft-spoken and introspective, Andrew says he enjoys meeting people at his job in a nearby grocery store. "I want to learn about others. I want them to learn about me." He speaks openly about his handicap, Down syndrome, and will tell you matter-of-factly: "I'm Down's. I want to set an example for my kind of people."

For the first six months of 1980, Andrew worked in the Lambs restaurant as a trainee. The Country Inn, a full-service restaurant open to the public, serves as the main training place for many of the residents. Opportunities to perform a variety of tasks help the supervisors observe and evaluate a resident's ability to do the job and relate to the public.

Bob and Corinne believed strongly that pupils had their individual levels of achievement. If mentally handicapped people were working below their level, they would become bored and vegetate; if they were stretched too high, they would become frustrated and afraid of failure and would regress. Participants needed to gain enjoyment and satisfaction from a job, and this could only happen if the job was right for them.

In Andrew's case, having completed a six-month probationary period with flying colors, he had proved himself ready to work outside the Lambs campus. In the fall of 1980, his vocational counselor, citing his previous experience at the Hyde Park Co-op, was able to find him a job in a nearby community supermarket.

Under the umbrella of Lambs, Andrew now had a home, a job, and an active social life. We felt satisfied and relieved. Moreover, Libertyville was only an hour's drive from Hyde Park. We visited Andrew about once a month, and if any problems arose, we could meet with his counselors or house parents at any time.

Unfortunately, this comfortable arrangement came to an end in 1983 when Pete accepted the chairmanship of the Division of Geological and Planetary Sciences at the California Institute of Technology. It was an invitation he could not refuse, a position at one of the most prestigious scientific institutes in the world, a warm climate, and when the earth shakes, a chance to experience geology in action.

It was true that our parental responsibilities were decreasing: Lisa was in her second year of college in Massachusetts, and John, who had just graduated from high school, was eager to attend a university in California. Nevertheless we worried about Andrew and thought that he should move with us. We looked for a suitable residential community for the developmentally disabled in Southern California but found none that came up to the standard of Lambs. We expressed our concern to Andrew, thinking that he would feel lost without us nearby.

His response was strong and clear: "Mum and Dad, your kids are grown up now. You must lead your life, and I will lead mine. And mine is here at Lambs."

Chapter 20:
Lambs Farm: Work and Play

Except for a train line going to Chicago, the rural area around Lambs lacks public transportation. As a result, residents who have jobs away from the farm have to be transported, so the counselors look for positions as near as possible.

Andrew's first job was at an A & P supermarket in Libertyville, where he worked part-time at a variety of tasks: stocking shelves, inventorying magazines, and bagging. After a year the store closed, and Andrew was relocated to an A & P in Lake Forest, where he stocked frozen foods. Unfortunately, the A & P organization went out of business, and Andrew was out of a job. After a short interval, Lambs found a position for him at the Eagle Supermarket in Libertyville, where he handled the bottle returns and worked as a bagger.

For his first job in Hyde Park, Andrew was kept out of sight of the public; now, in Libertyville, he had graduated to a position at the front of the store relating directly with the customers. However, his new jobs were not without problems. Checkers complained that he bagged too slowly. He tried to speed up, but if a checker pushed him too hard, he would get confused and annoyed. Sometimes a supervisor would give him several tasks to do, reciting all the instructions at one time. Like many of us, he could absorb only one direction at a time unless he was given a list of the tasks in writing, but what store manager would have time to write a list? I encounter the same problem at home when I ask my husband to do some chores; I have to write them down. Pete has a PhD and is a renowned scientist, but owing to a lack of interest or just poor memory he reacts the same as his son with Down syndrome, who says firmly, "Mum, one thing at a time, please."

In 1983 Sunset Foods, a supermarket specializing in superior service for the communities of Lake Forest and Lake Bluff, wanted to support the Lambs program by employing one of their residents. They spotted Andrew at the Eagle and in cooperation with the Lambs Vocational Department, asked him if he would consider accepting a job with them. How could he refuse? The move provided him with a forty-hour-a-week position as a bagger and a pay raise.

When Andrew first started working at Sunset Foods, he had to learn to stand near the checkout counters looking eager to bag as soon as customers had paid for their groceries. During slow times he would get bored and was sometimes reprimanded for slouching, fiddling with his hair, sucking his thumb, or picking his nose—behavior inappropriate in any job and especially in a high-class store.

To counteract the tedium, Andrew's counselor suggested that the store manager move him around to different assignments. During rotations he worked in the grocery and soft drink sections and stocked shelves. In the soft drink department, he was given a lapel badge reading "pop manager." The title was probably intended to boost his morale, but instead it overextended his self-confidence: taking the nomenclature at face value, he made some inappropriate decisions, which included refusing to fill a large order because it would have depleted his supply.

If Andrew had been employed outside the umbrella of Lambs, he might have been fired for his transgressions. Fortunately, his job was monitored, and the management consulted with the Lambs Vocational Department when a problem arose. If the incident was serious, the counselors telephoned us so that we could discuss the situation with Andrew. Although thirty-one-year old Lindsay Yeager is exceptionally high functioning, she has had difficulty finding and holding a job. An organization called Foothill Vocational Opportunities has helped her with a résumé, job opportunities, and applications. But it is a far stretch from the services provided by Lambs, which provides a variety of job opportunities on campus if a resident does not qualify for a position in the community.

Bob and Corinne reminded everyone that "learning to relate to the retarded is a process." Without any training or previous experience working with a handicapped person, it was understandable that the store person-nel did not know how to get the best out of someone like Andrew. More-over, he did not like to be yelled at. If he sensed rejection, he would act negatively; he needed praise and encouragement to keep doing a good job.

During a visit to Chicago in 1995, I discussed his progress with Steve Davis, the assistant store manager, and Pete Cummins, the front end manager in charge of the cashiers and baggers. Both of these young men were part of the Sunset family and had worked their way up to their pres-ent management positions after starting at the store about the same time as Andrew.

It was clear from their reports that during his thirteen years at Sunset Foods, Andrew had grown into a mature and reliable employee. Steve, who had worked closely with Andrew in the stock department, told me, "I don't see Andrew as having Down syndrome. Andrew is Andrew, just another one of the people who work here. He's a conscientious person. He cares about everything and he wants to be everybody's friend, but sometimes he has his moods when he's obnoxious."

"In what ways is he obnoxious?" I asked.

"If he doesn't want to listen, he won't listen. The only one he'll listen to is Pete because Pete's his supervisor right now. Andrew is like my six-year-old kid; if he doesn't want to do something he won't do it, and that's it."

Sometimes Andrew upset a supervisor by refusing to do something or by doing a job that was not part of his routine and then answering back when censured.

Pete Cummins explained it another way: "I think Andrew considers himself to be one of the top dogs because he has been here a long time. He thinks that he knows more than the supervisors who haven't been here so long and he shouldn't have to do what they tell him."

"Does it help if things are explained to him?"

"Right," said Pete. "You can see on his face that he's wondering why you are asking him to do this, especially if it's a little bit out of the norm. If you don't explain and just tell him to go do it, you're going to hurt his feelings."

"Like many people with Down syndrome, Andrew has difficulty analyzing a task and putting together a plan," I said. "Also, the developmentally disabled often lack mental flexibility and are inclined to connect with one person. You have worked with him all the time he has been at Sunset, and he has developed confidence in you and a strong attachment."

"It's no big deal to me. Certainly when I'm around he never has a problem. When I tell him to do something, he asks no questions; he just does it. It's when I'm away that he winds up with a problem with one of the other supervisors. Maybe they're just short with him, but it's nothing serious."

Pete, who has a soothing manner, exhibited remarkable patience and understanding with Andrew. If it was a busy day and Andrew's bagging was holding up a customer, Pete would get someone to help him out. "Sometimes he gets upset because he likes to do it all by himself, but I'll explain, 'Andrew, today we're really busy and we need to get these orders out quicker' and he'll say, 'OK, OK,' and everything is fine."

"Do you have any problems understanding what he says?"

"Only when he's excited—then he can't get the words out and he starts to stutter," replied Steve. "I'll tell him, 'Just go slow, I'm just asking you a question,' and he takes a deep breath and says it."

Pete recounted, "I think some people might have a bit of a hard time understanding him, but he gets his point across. It's nothing that we can't overcome. We have a language barrier with all the Mexican employees, and it's easier to tell Andrew what we need done than with some of the baggers who don't understand English well."

In a few areas, Andrew's lack of physical strength and coordination interfered with his job performance. "Andrew's reaction time is slow," reported Steve. "When we have a chain of people unloading bags of charcoal off a truck, Andrew will slow down the chain. He would catch the bag, but he really had to think before he turned and handed it to the next person."

Pete said that Andrew cannot lift heavy things, "He wouldn't be able to carry six gallons of bleach in a case." Like many people with Down syndrome, Andrew was born with an umbilical hernia, which was not serious enough to require surgery. Eventually the hernia healed itself, but it left Andy with weak muscles in the stomach area, which probably affected his lifting ability.

"But then we would find other things for him to do, like wheeling things out to the floor or stocking the shelves," continued Pete.

"And he always remembers where everything goes," added Steve.

On one occasion, Andrew was responsible for a customer taking the wrong groceries home. When customers drove their cars to the door, the bagger loaded the groceries according to a number they were given. Andrew mentally transposed the numbers and gave a customer with number sixty-nine the groceries labeled ninety-six. Unfortunately the error was not discovered until the customers unpacked their groceries at home. After this Andrew continued to bag but was not allowed to handle the numbers.

By 1997 Andrew had completed fourteen years at Sunset Foods. The earlier problems had been resolved, and except for occasional lapses, Andrew maintained a good relationship with his bosses and became part of a happy family, referring to his manager and coworkers as his good friends. Andrew's vocational counselor said, "Andrew does a great job in his position. He certainly has the grooming and the necessary social skills to deal with the public. He is aware that he needs to accept directives from other supervisors, and he assures us that he is working on it."

Andrew chatted with the other employees and joined in the teasing and joking. He enjoyed attending the company's social functions and participated in the occasional football pool, once winning the pot on his first try.

I asked Steve, "Did you think that his win wasn't fair?"

"Oh no, I thought it was great. I'm sure he could use the money just like anybody else."

This participation heightened Andrew's interest in professional football and provided good mental exercise. As well as following games on television, he read the sports section of the newspaper to track the teams he listed as possible winners.

Steve told me that soon after Andrew joined Sunset, a number of customers commented how nice it was that the store had employed him. Soon many of them knew him well and stopped to chat. Andrew especially enjoyed talking to the babies.

Pete spoke enthusiastically about Andrew: "One of the things we like about Andrew is his attitude. He looks forward to coming to work, and he likes to do everything real well. If you try to rush him he gets upset because he knows that if he tries to go faster, he might botch the job up. A lot of the cashiers would rather have him bag for them than anybody else. There are other guys who are faster, but Andrew makes sure that all the meat gets wrapped in plastic and all the cold things are bagged together. Customers often stop the cashier and say, 'Hey, can I get Andrew to bag for me?' because he does a really good job of packing."

I asked both managers, "Do you feel you have learned something from your experience of working with a person who is developmentally disabled?"

"Oh definitely," replied Pete. "Andrew was the first person with Down syndrome that I've ever worked with or had this close of contact with. I thought he might need more special attention. It's surprised me how well he could adapt to all the different tasks and jobs that needed to be done. He's a great employee."

"And of course he was always here on time," I commented.

"Oh, he's not just here on time," replied Pete emphatically. "His punctuality—it's outstanding. I use him as an example many times. When other employees are tardy, I print out from the computer a report of Andrew's weekly punches on the time clock and show it to them and say, 'Andrew is supposed to be handicapped. What's your problem?' His record is perfect."

For Steve, Andrew became a friend. "He came to my wedding. He was dancing and having a good time. Sometimes I find him annoying but he's a good guy; he's Andrew."

As well as being a high-class, specialty supermarket, Sunset Foods established a family of employees. Andrew was fortunate to be a member of this special family. We reminded him often to work hard and do what his supervisors told him. Andrew worked eight hours a day, five days a week; Sunday and Tuesday were his days off. Although this left him little time, he managed to take an active role in Lambs's recreational and social programs.

When he first moved to Lambs, he took several months to adjust before signing up for any activities, but before long he was bowling, playing tennis, attending exercise classes twice a week, and participating in plays and musicals.

From 1979 to 1998, Julia Robberson, known affectionately as JR, ran the recreational program. A dynamic woman with a strong, deep voice, JR had degrees in physical education and physiology, special education, and counseling and was a college professor for several years. In 1991 she was elected a coach for the International Special Olympics.

She loved working with the developmentally disabled and was especially thrilled when Lambs was able to complete its Founders Building in 1991. As well as housing the administrative offices of Lambs, the new building has a large gymnasium with weight and training rooms around the perimeter. This enabled JR to organize many activities for the participants on the campus instead of renting facilities in the nearby communities.

"In preventive health we have really gone into the fitness aspect," explained J.R. "Now we have aerobics, weight training, and circuit training. As our participants get older, they need this more. We will continue this in the geriatrics program."

Andrew was a member of the Lambs Bowling League and won several ribbons in Special Olympic bowling events. The Lambs team also competed against other developmentally disabled teams in different parts of Illinois. When the bowling league met on one of Andrew's workdays, Andrew's social worker helped him join a regular bowling league, which met on a Friday evening at lanes located a short distance from Lambs. In good weather Andrew was able to walk there on his own, and in the winter months, someone from the league picked him up and a counselor brought him home. Andrew told us he scored over 100, but most of the other members scored higher. It gave him another opportunity to make new friends and participate in regular life outside of Lambs. He was especially proud to be "out in the community."

Andrew also took up tennis. As a child he had lessons in Florida, and encouraged by JR, he decided to give it a try. A local tennis professional, Celeste Pregracke, was a state tennis director for Special Olympics and gave classes once a week for a group from Lambs. She had that special charisma and patience that can produce exciting results from a group of young adults with varying handicaps and abilities. On several occasions members of the Lambs tennis team competed at the International Special Olympics.

Because of the intricacies of the game, both mental and physical, tennis is not a sport that is easily mastered, and certainly not by someone who is developmentally disabled. But the effort to coordinate eyes, hands, arms, and feet, as well as the need for clear thinking, makes it a wonderful exercise for the handicapped. Celeste believed that these special athletes had the ability to play, and she instilled that belief into her pupils.

JR described Andrew's performance: "His motor development is good, and he has very fine coordination. Tennis takes good timing, and Andrew's timing needs work; you have to be able to judge where the ball is going and to move quickly. He thinks things out; he's an analyzer. In tennis that doesn't always get the ball, but he's getting better and faster all the time." JR believed in the importance of mental stimulation: "If we are mentally stimulated, then we are growing and developing. Once our participants become stagnant and sit in a chair doing nothing, then we are in big trouble. We give them activities to think, to use the whole body to organize and to manage."

Once again our preconceived notions about the limitations of Down syndrome were being cast aside. During one of Andrew's visits to California, I practiced with him on a friend's private court and was amazed at his ability to move, hit the ball, serve correctly, and keep score. Although he would never reach the World Special Games, he did win a first place in singles at the regional level and a bronze medal for third place at the state level—an amazing achievement for a thirty-eight-year-old with Down syndrome.

Andrew worked hard and played hard, but he still liked to watch television and enjoy quiet times in his room when he could play one of his videos or watch a favorite program. Unfortunately, Lambs residents were not spared junk mail. In 1988 Andrew received a "check" for $50 for a twenty-inch television set. For some time he had been dreaming of succeeding in one of the heavily advertised sweepstakes; he kept thinking he had heard his name being announced on television. Now it had actually happened; he was a winner. Without telling any of his counselors, he filled in the necessary information and sent in his $50 purchase certificate.

A short time later, the company sent him a bill for $279 to cover the purchase of the television set. He was given permission by his house parent to pay some bills and used the opportunity to write a check for $279 and mail it to the company. A few weeks later, Lambs received a package addressed to Andrew Wyllie with an additional $23 due on delivery for shipping and handling.

The Lambs staff had discovered Andrew's venture into mail-order purchasing. His social worker called us, and poor Andrew had to face a barrage of questions and reprimands from concerned parents and counselors. In making the purchase, Andrew had demonstrated his independence and purchasing capability, but the incident had also revealed the vulnerability of a gullible handicapped adult. Obviously Andrew's freedom to write checks had to be questioned, but he also had to learn to recognize mail order scams. With the help of his social worker, Andrew learned to discard his junk mail and resist the temptation of enticing propositions. If he did want to mail in a certificate or respond to a questionnaire, he discussed it first with his counselor. Rules for check writing and large purchases were tightened: any purchase over $50 had to be approved by both his house parent and a senior supervisor.

Andrew's love for television had other repercussions. Reverend and Mrs. Arnold, Lael's parents, came to regard Andrew as their television repairman. Before moving to their present apartment in a high-rise retirement building in Hyde Park, they lived in a house that bordered the bank of the Illinois Central train line. Although they had a good-quality console television, they always had a snowy picture. They presumed that the railroad bank behind their house was the culprit, so when they moved to an eleventh-floor apartment, they expected to get a clear picture. However, it was still fuzzy.

When Andrew and Lael were visiting one weekend, Andrew said, "I know what the problem is, and I can fix it." Following Andrew's instructions, the Arnolds purchased cable and special connectors, which Andrew proceeded to screw into the back of the television set and connect to a television outlet in the wall, and *abracadabra*—the picture was perfect. Our simple-minded son had realized that a connection to the building's central antenna would solve the Arnolds' problem.

Chapter 21:
Andrew: a Life of His Own

In Chicago, Andrew lacked a social life of his own. He made only a few friends at school, and we were afraid to encourage further activities with the two or three schoolmates who visited our house because they lived in the ghettos.

Andrew had desperately wanted to attend his high school prom, but there was no one for him to take. We asked him, "Would you like to take your sister?"

He responded, "My sister as a date—no way."

I felt he should go to the prom; we could have asked his teacher if there was a girl in his class he could take, but Pete was against the idea. In the end we let it go, thinking that he would feel out of place at the kind of elaborate event that proms had become.

As a family we went to movies or made special outings to restaurants, a show, or a museum. Andrew enjoyed his horseback riding and swimming classes at the YMCA. He belonged to the Flamingo Pool Club, a summer swimming pool where Lisa and John had jobs as lifeguards; he occasionally participated in parties organized by a neighborhood social club; but he had no friend with whom he could go to the movies, for a bicycle ride, or to an ice cream parlor.

We never expected Lisa or John (and they never offered) to take their older brother along on outings with their friends. Andrew needed his own peers, people who had the same limitations and the same interests, men and women he could regard as equals and who would accept him without questions. A community for the developmentally disabled such as Lambs, which was not shut away in isolation, gave him social contacts, organized activities, recreational sports, and the opportunity to visit shopping malls, movie theaters, and places of interest.

During his adolescence, Andrew developed in the same way as any teenager. He had the same dreams and the same crushes on girls and women. His sexual development was no different from that of his brother, although he may not have known how to manage his changing body as well. He was quick to respond to a woman, but he was selective; invariably he liked pretty women, usually with blonde, long hair, especially if he had a chance to perform his hairdressing techniques on them. Like anyone else, he loved receiving attention, so any woman visiting our house who bothered to talk to him and take an interest in him became an object of his passion. This was often expressed in the form of love notes and pleas to visit his room at bedtime to kiss him goodnight. Depending on the visitor, these demonstrations were usually innocent and inoffensive, but occasionally we had to curtail his note writing.

Andrew first met Lael Arnold, who had Down syndrome, in elementary school in 1966 but lost touch with her when he joined the educable classes in Ray School in 1968. He met her again when he started going to the Lambs Farm for summer work in 1979. Occasionally they travelled together on the train, and she soon became a close friend. Lael, whose round face was framed by softly curled red hair, was short and cuddly and like many people with Down syndrome, struggled to control her weight. Her family lived in Hyde Park, and she and Andrew walked to each other's houses.

One day in 1982, after finding them together in Andrew's room with the door closed, I realized that they were becoming more than just good friends. Later I had a talk with them about feelings, relationships, the facts of life, and the problems of intimacy. None of us found the discussion easy, but in retrospect, I think we were glad to have talked openly about sex.

Concerned about Andrew's responsibilities if he became sexually involved with a woman, I researched the question of sterilization. Unlike the first half of the twentieth century, the law now protected the developmentally disabled from forced sterilization, and unless the parents were legal guardians, they had no authority to request it. I asked several medical specialists at the University of Chicago Billings Hospital whether a male with Down syndrome could sire a child and whether a vasectomy would be advisable.

In consultation with an urologist specializing in birth control, I learned that if there was a total absence of spermatozoa in one test, it could change in the next test. He told me it would be necessary to take a sperm count every three months for about a year. After observing the pattern, there still would be no certain answer. Therefore, any attempt to verify whether Andrew's sperm count was too low for impregnation would not reassure us, even though it is generally believed that Down syndrome men have a lower fertility rate than the general population. According to the National Down Syndrome Society (www.ndss.org. 2011), information on the fertility of men with Down syndrome is limited, with only two documented cases of fatherhood. Records show that women with Down syndrome have given birth, but 35 to 50 percent of their offspring are likely to have Down syndrome or another type of disability. The question remains whether a Down syndrome couple can reproduce.

Even though Andrew was capable of understanding the need for sterilization and making the decision for himself, the hospital's legal counsel advised us that we must have a court order giving a doctor permission to perform the surgery. I did not want to discuss the problem with Andrew until I had worked through some of the medical and legal tangles. Faced with all these barriers, I never introduced the subject, but I did report my findings to Mrs. Arnold.

Once Mrs. Arnold realized that Lael might become sexually active, she arranged to have a tubal ligation performed at Michael Reese Hospital. Unfortunately the administration, anticipating a possible lawsuit, put a stop to the surgery because Lael had not signed the permission form herself. Concerned about an accidental pregnancy, the Arnolds then asked their doctor to prescribe a contraceptive pill for Lael. However, Lael had a heart condition, so this was not been the best treatment for her.

In 1994, fifteen years after the Arnolds first requested a sterilization procedure, Lael telephoned me and said, "Mrs. Wyllie I want to tell you I'm going to have my tubes tied. I've made the decision myself." I was touched that she wanted to share this information with me. Now aged thirty-eight and with sufficient understanding of her health needs, Lael was able to make the decision for herself. This time Mrs. Arnold found the doctors and the administration willing to do the procedure.

After the surgery, Lael called me again: "Mrs. Wyllie, I had my surgery and I'm doing fine. I wanted you to know." I sent her a get-well card and a note of encouragement.

Lael became a full-time resident at Lambs soon after Andrew moved there. Their friendship grew like a tender sapling. In the early years, Andrew was more assertive and at times bossy; Lael tended to be possessive and jealous if Andrew paid attention to other women. One time she started crying because he had been dancing with someone else. The other woman told Andrew, "You need to hit her and knock some sense into her." Andrew, without thinking whether his actions were right or wrong, slapped Lael. This caused a major upset. When Lael's brother heard about the incident, he said, "I'm ready to take on anyone who treats my sister so badly." Fortunately, with its built-in support system, Lambs was able to help both young people learn how to cope with their feelings.

Except for minor differences, the love of this young couple remained strong and faithful. Their social worker told me, "I see a real caring, supportive relationship."

During a visit in 1997, I took them out to the Lambs Country Inn for dinner.

Andrew told me, "I sometimes bring Lael to this restaurant."

"Yes, for my birthday."

"And we order a special drink."

"A giddy cocktail," said Lael.

"What's in a giddy cocktail?" I asked.

"Well…" Lael thought for a minute. "A cherry."

"And something fizzy, like Seven Up or some fruit juice."

"No alcohol?" I queried.

"No, no alcohol, it's like a kid's cocktail," explained Andrew.

Listening to this charming exchange, I conjured up an image of Andrew and Lael enjoying a romantic evening together, perusing the menu in their studied fashion, choosing their special drink, and with a minimum of conversation, enjoying each other's company as they plodded through the serious business of eating.

On Sunday morning as I drove them to church, Andrew and Lael recalled their friendship in elementary school.

"Mrs. Wyllie, the Murray school isn't there anymore. The buildings have gone," explained Lael. "And they cut down our tree in the playground."

"It was an oak tree," said Andrew. "We used to sit under it during recess. I drew a heart on it like this"—he made a heart shape in the air—"and put an arrow through it and wrote 'Andy loves Lael.'"

Their reminiscences made me realize what an important role Lael played in Andrew's life. She was a link to his past, his childhood, and his family.

In spite of realizing that marriage was a distant and unrealistic dream, Andrew and Lael became engaged. They exchanged engagement rings; Lael lost hers several times, but Andrew happily bought her a new one, managing to keep a limit on the cost.

In 1981 Andrew wrote a letter to his sister at her college:

It is quite hard to live on your own like me at the Lambs, but I got someone at Lambs and that is Miss Lael Arnold.

Lisa, I just bump a question to Lael and she say yes to marry me in the future.

I'm in love with Lael Arnold and she is in love with me.

In another letter he wrote:

When I am with Lael I feel weak and I fall in love for marriage.

When I am in my apartment by myself playing my stereo or watching TV I feel much stronger and I'm not in love for marriage at all.

It is great for me to be on my own, because I don't feel I miss my family. I don't show my feelings towards it because I'm having fun out here at Lambs Farm to join the activity like you say to be out door more. I was taking softball and now I move up to soccer then basketball and more to come if it won't affect my job at A & P.

In light of Andrew's and Lael's feelings toward each other and with the Arnolds' encouragement, I raised the question of married housing at a parents' meeting in 1982, a year before we moved to California. A small group supported the idea, but many families felt that it should not even be discussed. Some parents believed that their sons or daughters were incapable of a physical relationship because they did not have sexual urges.

Four couples supported married housing. We formed a committee, and I composed a letter that was sent to the program services committee of the board of directors. This is an excerpt:

> Some of these parents have sons and daughters who have expressed a desire to get married. The parents involved support the idea of marriage. We feel that our young people are capable of a permanent relationship and deserve the chance to lead a completely normal and fulfilled life. However, we would like them to remain at Lambs. They will always need the protection and guidance, jobs, and social life that Lambs provides.

We acknowledged the many problems that would have to be overcome. Marriage embraced by Lambs would require different residences than the SLAs; perhaps housing could be built or acquired in a nearby community. Although residents pay a percentage of their earnings for rent and food, parents are responsible for monthly contributions, which make up the cost of living at Lambs. If a couple married, the respective parents would have to agree to remain responsible for their dependent's financial obligation. What would happen if one family lost the means to support their son or daughter at Lambs?

What would happen if a couple had a baby? The administration could not be responsible for children; they have enough to do caring for their own Lambs. If normal couples find parenting an onerous responsibility, how could a developmentally disabled person, however advanced, become a parent?

According to an article in a 1995 British edition of the magazine *Marie Claire*, the Queen Fabiola Centre in Belgium allowed their residents to live as couples in a sexual relationship. However, a legal marriage was discouraged because it implied a right to procreate. Instead, couples participated in a ceremony to make their union official. All couples had a counselor to help them with the ups and downs of their relationship. Any woman joining the center had to consent to the use of a slow-release injectable contraceptive called Depo-Provera, because the administrators felt that a developmentally disabled couple could not take on the responsibility of a child.

Naturally, such arrangements spawned a heated debate. Some experts felt that the contraceptive requirement was an infringement of human rights. In spite of questioning their abilities as parents, some believed in the right of the mentally disabled to bear children; others felt that there was no need for sex, and it was wrong to introduce the idea. But many said, "Of course they should be allowed to have sexual relationships."

Like the participants in Belgium's Queen Fabiola Centre, Andrew needed special guidance in sexual matters, just as he needed extra help in learning to read or do arithmetic. One evening during a Christmas vacation, we were browsing in a bookstore while waiting to pick up a pizza for supper. I was perusing the magazines, and Andrew wandered off in the direction of the children's books, presumably to look at videos. When I walked down the aisles, I found him studying the titles along a row of adult books instead of the children's entertainment.

"What are you looking for?" I asked.

He pulled from his pocket a slip of paper on which he had written the title *How to Be the Perfect Lover.*

"How do you know about this book?"

"I found it in my brother's bedroom, but I don't want to take his copy, so I would like to buy my own."

I explained that the book was probably out of print, but if he would show it to me, I could help him find something similar.

"Why do you want a book on lovemaking, Andrew?"

"I want to know how to please my woman."

A few days later, we found a small booklet on love and sex. I told Andrew that he should regard such matters as personal and keep the book in a drawer in his room. Although I was not sure how much of the book he would actually read and understand, I was touched by his willingness to share this aspect of his life with his mother and that he could accept my guidance in finding appropriate literature.

Speaking about his parents to a counselor, Andrew said, "Dad's my business manager, and Mum—she's just precious." He expected his father to handle his vacation plans and book his plane tickets, but he preferred to have his mother help him select clothes and guide him in personal matters.

Many parents avoid the subject of sex with their normal children and probably never think to broach it with their special needs children. However, as adults with developmental disabilities become more integrated into normal life and a greater number develop relationships or get married, the questions of sex, birth control, and sexually transmitted diseases need to be addressed. Although counselors in residential communities may offer general information on sexual subjects, not all handicapped adults live in such settings. Parents need to realize that their disabled children are capable of developing sexual relationships and to consider whether they should be given the opportunity and knowledge to enjoy lovemaking safely and to the best of their ability.

When I interviewed Lindsay Yeager at age seventeen in 1997, I asked her about her hopes and ambitions for the future. She told me, "I want to have two cats, a dog, and a husband (probably in that order). I would like to live independently and get married to a man who will understand and help me, especially with money." She thought that children would probably be too great a responsibility because she had been a lot of work for her mother. She said, "Maybe I should have that operation."

In response to our request regarding married housing, the president of the Lambs Board telephoned me and was not encouraging; there were too many problems to overcome, and the cost would be too great. Marriage for developmentally disabled adults would open up a Pandora's box of problems. In 1982 other priorities were taking precedence: a geriatric facility, one of the first in the country, had just been completed.

During my visit in 1995, Bob Terese told me that he favored the idea of married housing. "I would like to see married housing as part of Lambs," said Bob. "I am quite comfortable with the concept. I am good at seeing the big pictures; others are better at implementing them." But it was unlikely to happen in his time. However, he told me with great pride in his voice, "Lambs has just purchased the last six acres of the farm, which should take care of our growth for the next twenty-five years. Our immediate priority is a nursing center to add to the facilities of the geriatric unit. It will give the parents a good conscience to know their child will be cared for." Although many participants are aging and some have had to move away to nursing homes, the present directors feel that a nursing center on the campus is beyond the scope of their mission.

However, Lambs is constantly studying ways of helping their participants lead as normal a life as possible, but always keeping in mind that they need support services and peers with whom they can socialize. The 2010 annual report listed nine group homes housing twelve residents in each; the W. Clement and Jessie V. Stone apartment building for sixteen residents on the campus; six homes in neighboring communities for residents who are capable of more independent living; and sixteen beds in the Green-Field Residence for retirement-age participants.

I still hope that in the future a way will be found to overcome the hurdles of establishing a few apartments suitable for married couples to enjoy a fully rounded life yet at the same have the security of the Lambs organization behind them. Many of the Lambs residents feel they have enough to cope with just dealing with their everyday needs; they are not interested in considering marriage. Fortunately, Andrew and Lael seemed content in their relationship and managed to accept the fact that the Lambs living arrangements and rules (residents were not allowed to visit in each other's rooms) stymied opportunities for intimacy. Because of space limitations in the Arnolds' apartment, Andrew and Lael were allowed to share a bed when they went to visit Lael's mother. However, Andrew told us that Lael insisted on "no hanky panky."

When Lael's father died, Andrew, wanting to support his sweetheart, asked if he could attend the memorial service. After several family members had memorialized their father, Andrew went up to the lectern and spoke.

"I am Andrew Wyllie and am representing the Wyllie family. We have been neighbors for eighteen years when we were living in Chicago. I was very fond of Harvey Arnold, and I know his daughter for thirty years."

"And that's when I got embarrassed," said Lael. "And Andrew did cry."

"Yes, I was very touched when I heard the news," added Andrew. "I do care for him."

"I called Andrew at his work and tell him," explained Lael. "Both my sisters like Andrew and say I have good taste and I should keep him."

I was impressed that Andrew had the courage and presence to speak at the service. His actions stemmed from a desire to express his condolences and were a mark of his self-assurance.

— ★ —

Every Sunday Andrew, Lael, and another resident of House Two, Marc Henry, attended St. Lawrence Episcopal Church in Libertyville.

Soon after his move to Lambs, when his housemates began to join churches, Andrew had phoned us to ask, "Mum and Dad, what is our church?"

"It's the Episcopal church, Andrew."

"Can I join and be confirmed?" he asked.

"Of course, we would be delighted for you to join the church. You were baptized in the church where Dad and I were married in Yorkshire, England. It was an Episcopal church called All Saints."

"Oh, good," he said.

Andrew's interest in religion, which had begun when televangelists captured his attention, would now find an appropriate outlet. Warmhearted Mrs. Lloyd, a member of the Libertyville church, took Andrew, Lael, and Marc Henry under her wing. She picked them up for church every Sunday and brought them into the fold of the community by involving them in service activities. They participated as babysitters and acolytes; they worked as ushers, taking the collection and helping to count the money. The church congregation opened their arms to these developmentally disabled men and women and accepted them as their own in the true spirit of Christianity.

During one of my visits to Libertyville, I stood in for Mrs. Lloyd, who was away on a trip, and took Andrew and his friends to church. Andrew was eager to introduce me to the minister, Father Jedediah Holdorph, who told me, "Andrew is very reliable and deliberate in his role as an acolyte."

After church I took the three Lambs residents to lunch at their favorite Burger King. While we were there, one of the church wardens, John Mullen, came in with his wife, Nancy. As we chatted with them, Andrew said to John, "You know, Jim Brown, who was the chief acolyte today, had the wrong color rope on, and it was too short."

Andrew was referring to the rope or cincture that the acolytes wear around their white robes.

Nancy Mullen explained, "When we bought the ropes for the acolytes, we thought they would be for young people. We didn't expect that they would have to go around the girth of a middle-aged man. But we will take your suggestion for a longer rope under advisement and remember to use the right color."

I was impressed with John and Nancy's warmth and naturalness as they conversed with Andrew. In their eyes, the Lambs residents were just the same as any of the other members of the church. They took Andrew's comment seriously and appreciated his attention to detail.

I asked John, "Have you made any special adjustments for Andrew and the others?"

"Oh no," he responded. "They do just fine. Andrew is a team leader and has to be responsible for his team of acolytes when they are on duty."

Our first opportunity to observe Andrew's role in St. Lawrence Church was an especially moving occasion. As the organ played the processional hymn, our mature son, dressed in a white acolyte's gown, lifted the golden cross high above his head to lead the ministers and red-robed choir down the aisle. A lump in my throat inhibited my singing, and tears rolled down my cheeks. As he reached the chancel, Andrew placed the cross carefully in its holder and stood at the side of the altar to assist the minister during the communion service. He faltered only once when he forgot to move the prayer book.

As a teenager looking for comfort and companionship, Andrew searched for God and heard the messages of Rex Humbard and Robert Schuller. Now as an independent adult, his quest had been fulfilled through his role as an active member in an Episcopal community of caring Christians. From time to time Andrew reminded us, "God loves you, so keep him in your heart and in your life."

Chapter 22:
Delusions and Hallucinations

In April of 1997, Andrew celebrated his thirty-eighth birthday. His life appeared to be on an even keel. Lambs Farms, where he had lived for seventeen years, was his home and provided him all the mental and physical support that he might need. He had a full-time job at a specialty supermarket; he had a loving relationship with his longtime girlfriend, Lael Arnold; he served as an acolyte in a nearby Episcopal church; he participated in a variety of sports activities and competed in Special Olympics events; and Lambs provided a social life as well as freedom to go shopping or to movies in the community.

Andrew always spent his vacations with us in California, two weeks in the summer and two weeks at Christmas. During his vacation in June, he expressed concern about losing his job. He was especially fixated on having trousers of the right color, believing that someone was insisting that his trousers were dark blue and not really black. After he returned to Lambs, he seemed bothered by something in his house, but he would not tell us anything during our Sunday telephone calls because "the walls here have ears." Then in July, Andrew's life began to unravel.

Since his teenage years, Andrew had been fascinated by hairdressing and loved to have his hair styled in the latest fashion. He used the Lambs bus service, known as the Rainbow Run, to go to a hair salon at one of the local shopping malls. Evidently the same hairdresser always cut his hair, and Andrew probably flirted with her in his own innocent way. This time he asked her to marry him and presented her with a ring. The owner of the salon, realizing that this was out of the ordinary, reported the incident to a Lambs counselor. Because Andrew's behavior had been unusual in other ways, Lambs staff arranged for him to see a psychologist. Andrew told the psychologist that he believed the hairdresser was the daughter of his boss at Sunset Foods and that he needed to marry her to keep his job, and that the police had come to the supermarket and taken him away in handcuffs.

The counselors also reported that Andrew had been acting strangely and irresponsibly with Lael. He took her to a fair and left her there and did not turn up for a date to visit her mother's home in Hyde Park. He said that he loved her dearly but wanted time alone.

Things came to a head when Andrew started to pack up his room, put all his belongings into plastic bags, and threw them in the trash. He believed he was going to get married and leave Lambs. A general practitioner, after being told by Andrew that the clouds were talking to him, suggested that Lambs have him admitted to the psychiatric ward of a local hospital. He spent the weekend seeing specialists, having a battery of blood and other tests, and no doubt feeling scared and wondering what was going on. We were all scared. We talked to Andrew on the telephone, and I asked his sister, Lisa, to call because often he felt able to tell her things that he did not want to discuss with his parents. Here are snippets of their conversation:

"Are you OK? You can't be that good if you are in the hospital," said Lisa.

"Yeah, well, um, I did some crazy things."

"Like what kind of crazy things?" asked Lisa.

"Like I packed up my room, and I did a bad mistake. I asked a lady to marry me."

Andrew explained that the lady to whom he had proposed wasn't Lael. He told his sister that he was having trouble at work and something big was coming up in September when he would have been there fourteen years. Lisa asked him about this big thing.

He replied, "They are talking about making me store manager."

Lisa explained that this was very unlikely because he was Down syndrome and that sometimes our minds play tricks with us; maybe he was imagining this. Andrew agreed: "Sometimes my mind does play tricks."

Lisa asked if he was actually hearing people talking about him at work or if voices were coming from somewhere else, or if perhaps it was just in his mind. He said it sounded like people were talking about him.

He seemed to have adjusted to the hospital routine. He liked the food and was attending group sessions, talking about his problems, and getting to know the other patients. For a person with a learning disability, he demonstrated surprising clarity when talking about his delusions and mixed-up thought processes. Although much of his thinking was abnormal, all of his imaginings were founded on the real world in which he lived. The basis of his worries seemed to be his job security.

The battery of tests at the hospital produced one important abnormality: Andrew's thyroid count was twenty-two, well above the normal six. He was severely hypothyroid. Could this account for the delusional symptoms? We discovered that an untreated underactive thyroid could lead to dementia, delirium, and occasionally hallucinations or "myxedema madness." We clung to this information with the hope that once medication had brought Andrew's thyroid into balance, his mental health would right itself. The psychiatrist treating Andrew also put off prescribing any medication for his psychosis until Andrew's thyroid was corrected.

Keeping in mind Andrew's worries about his job, we wondered if something had happened at the supermarket to trigger his breakdown. It was possible that fellow employees had teased him about the color of his trousers and had suggested that he become the store manager when they heard him boasting about his upcoming fourteen-year anniversary.

During one of his regular visits to the Adult Down Syndrome Center run by the Advocate Medical Group and headed by Brian Chicoine, MD, and Dennis McGuire, PhD, in Park Ridge, Illinois, Dr. McGuire concluded that Andrew was suffering from either delusional, obsessive-compulsive, or bipolar disorder. His report discussed possible causes for Andrew's behavior: "We have seen many individuals at our center who begin to compare themselves to their brothers and sisters and others in the community." Andrew's younger brother and sister were both married, and his sister already had three children. Andrew and Lael loved each other and wanted to marry, but as long as they lived at Lambs, marriage was out of the question. Some of Andrew's fellow workers, who had joined the Sunset family at the same time as he had, were now managers wearing distinctive blue jackets, while Andrew was still a lowly bagger.

Throughout his childhood, we had encouraged him to do everything his siblings did and to lead as normal a life as possible. He had attended a city college, worked in regular employment, and learned to socialize with our close friends. So perhaps it was not surprising that his present frustrations stemmed from a concern over job security and a fixation on getting married. His dream was to leave Lambs, get a job, and find a woman to marry. It was also possible that Andrew's problems were rooted in his frustration with being handicapped. He had stated clearly, "I'm not Down's; I'm standard."

Other high-functioning people with Down syndrome have similar challenges. For instance Lindsay Yeager, who is not suffering from any delusional disorder, maintains that she is "really more into normal people." Having had her mosaic phenomenon explained to her, she claims that she only has a little bit of Down syndrome and that her problems are due to a learning disability. As a teenager she spoke of her aspirations to find a husband and perhaps have "that operation." Now her ambition is to have a baby, probably because her siblings are married and her sister has a new baby.

What about other causes for Andrew's delusions? We realized that there could be a breakdown in the neurotransmitters of Andrew's brain and that this might be the onset of some form of mental illness. A few days after he returned to Lambs, Andrew attempted to telephone his sister from another house because the phone in his house did not work. When the house manager came to get him, he ran away. At his appointment with the psychiatrist a few days later, Andrew said he ran because he thought the house manager was the police. Concerned about these persistent delusions, the psychiatrist prescribed Zyprexa. This was the beginning of a long regimen of different antipsychotic drugs before the most suitable medication and dosage were found.

There is a greater prevalence of mental illness in people with intellectual disabilities than in the regular population, so perhaps it was not surprising that Andrew's psychiatrist decided to add an anti-depressant, Zoloft, to Andrew's new arsenal of medications. However, the combination of Zyprexa and Zoloft was disastrous. Andrew developed a voracious appetite, put on a lot of weight, and became like a zombie. He joined us on a visit to his sister's home in Pennsylvania over the Christmas holidays. He did well shopping for gifts and adding up the costs to stay within his budget; he enjoyed watching television with his three nephews and learning from them how to play Nintendo games, but he was having difficulties in other areas. He fell asleep frequently and took long naps in the afternoons; he had a hard time finding words and expressing his thoughts; he had less flexibility with small motor movements; he became obstinate and belligerent when we ate in restaurants and he could not have everything he wanted. We concluded that most of his problems were side effects of the medications.

From mid-1997 through late-1999, we all felt we were riding a roller coaster with many ups and downs as well as unexpected twists and turns. There were changes in medications, changes in psychiatrists, changes in social workers (six in two years), and changes in task assignments at work—all contributing to Andrew's confusion and instability. Concerned about the first psychiatrist's medication recommendations, I urged the Lambs staff to find another specialist, who agreed that Andrew's hypothyroidism was probably the cause of his mental breakdown. He discontinued the anti-depressant Zoloft and added Ritalin and Wellbutrin as stimulants, hoping to counteract the zombie-like effect of the Zyprexa.

Andrew had taken a long medical leave from Sunset Foods and worked at the bakery on the Lambs Farm grounds, but it was psychologically important for him to return to Sunset, because it was the fear of losing his job there that had triggered his mental breakdown. However, doing well at Sunset was a challenge. When he returned in the summer of 1998, Andrew had slowed down and was not able to keep up the pace needed for bagging, so he was given other tasks, like fronting shelves or helping with unloading supplies. He had difficulty staying awake and on task, and at times he seemed to space out. When he told one of the managers that he was quitting, the manager took him at his word until Andrew explained to his job coach that he did not mean that he was resigning, just that he was "quitting acting funny," so his job was saved.

In his house at Lambs, Andrew became lazy about picking up and cleaning his room (usually he kept his room immaculate), and he behaved badly toward Lael. She did not understand what was happening to her dearest Andrew, and when he was unkind to her, it was especially upsetting. She phoned me once or twice, and I tried to explain that Andrew was not well and did not always know what he was doing.

When Andrew came to visit us in the summer of 1999, he seemed much brighter and more talkative, but we were concerned about his weight gain of thirty pounds. In October, a new psychiatrist, Dr. Rosanova, who specialized in adults with developmental disabilities and visited Lambs Farm on a regular basis, took over Andrew's case. She gradually weaned him off the Ritalin and Wellbutrin, and began to lower the Zyprexa dose. She also agreed that Andrew's mood disorder was probably associated with his hypothyroidism, and she explained that it was typical for patients taking Zyprexa to gain weight.

After his Christmas vacation with us, I wrote the following note to the director of residential services:

> We are delighted to say that we found Andrew wonderfully improved. He was cheerful, responsive, and much more alive. He answered questions promptly most of the time, he no longer had to struggle to find the right word, he didn't need to take long afternoon naps, and he wasn't always glued to the television, except for his regular programs. We could reason with him over whether he should do something or not, and the grumpiness and aggression evident during the last two years had gone. On one of our outings I offered to buy him some popcorn. He said he would prefer a hot dog, but when I reminded him that we were going out to dinner and a hot dog might spoil his appetite, he agreed and didn't make a fuss. We could carry on a conversation with him—something that had been a real struggle during his illness. He wrote very nice thank you letters to his godmother and others with far fewer grammatical and spelling mistakes than a year ago.
>
> We are sure this vast improvement is the result of discontinuing the anti-psychotic medications. It is as though he has woken up from a long sleep or zombie-like trance. He is mentally alive again and well on his way back to being the old, cheerful, and responsive Andrew.

Soon after the New Year, the psychiatrist discontinued the Zyprexa. Andrew was now free of antipsychotic medications. He was cured. We rejoiced and relaxed.

Chapter 23:
The Demons Return

Every Sunday we chatted with Andrew on the phone. In March 2000, we detected symptoms of psychosis returning. Andrew sounded hyperactive, agitated, and focused on Valerie, his former housemother, who seemed to be identified now as a persecutor. Andrew claimed that she was coming between him and Lael. During one of our conversations, he had been bright and clear, remembering his bowling scores for several weeks, but claiming that Valerie was now "calling the shots." With the increase in paranoia, Lambs counselors consulted with Andrew's psychiatrist, who prescribed 25 mg of Seroquel twice a day, but Andrew refused to take it because he thought that Valerie was prescribing it.

On April 1, three months after being taken off his previous medication (Zyprexa), Andrew was back in the psychiatric ward of the local hospital. He had been wandering around the grounds dressed in his best suit because he believed that the police wanted him to go to the courthouse and marry Valerie. Andrew thought she was in love with him; marrying her would solve all his problems. Earlier, staff had found him outside in the rain without a coat and persuaded him to go to bed. He had complied, returned to his room, locked the door, cleared off his desk, taken the screen off his window, and climbed out. Mike Impastato, Andrew's houseparent since 1999, just happened to be coming out of a nearby house. Worried that Andrew might wander off grounds, Mike got permission to have him hospitalized.

We spoke to the nurse in charge of the psychiatric ward, who told us Andrew was being cooperative and eating well but was continuing to refuse to take the Seroquel, claiming that it was the wrong color and made him sleepy. In desperation and to help Andrew cooperate, the hospital psychiatrist prescribed Haldol, an older antipsychotic with potentially severe side effects. Finally Mike, who was both firm and kind and had a special gift for reasoning with Andrew, managed to persuade Andrew to let the doctor put him back on Zyprexa.

I decided we should go to Chicago. In particular I wanted to arrange a meeting with both psychiatrists to get their opinion as to the nature of Andrew's illness and what was causing it. With difficulty, a meeting was scheduled at the hospital, and Andrew joined us. He was quite clear about Valerie interfering with his life and that he believed his psychiatrist had prescribed a green pill even though the doctor had told him that it was peach-colored. In spite of the doctor explaining that it was she who had phoned, Andrew said, "But I also heard Valerie's voice saying, 'This is Valerie.'" The doctors agreed that Andrew's relapse, after he had been medication-free for nearly three months, indicated that the problem was not based on his thyroid but was probably bipolar disorder. We finally had to stop clinging to our hope that he had myxedema madness and that balancing his thyroid would cure him. Our worst fears were realized: he had a permanent mental illness.

Bipolar disorder is the modern name for manic depression, a mental illness with alternating episodes of severe depression and hyperactivity. Symptoms include rapid speech, disconnected thoughts, grandiose ideas, hallucinations, and extreme irritability. It tends to run in families, or a person can be at risk for the disorder if there is a family member who has suffered a major depression. Our family history fitted this profile: I had an aunt with severe depression and a brother with manic depression. Some experts believe that bipolar disorder is only one link on a chain of psychiatric disorders ranging from schizophrenia to major depression, differing in expression and severity but sharing a common biologic cause. However, recent studies indicate that the two conditions are distinct and caused by different mechanisms. These illnesses usually become evident in late teens or young adults, although both can appear in people over forty.

Andrew was thirty-eight when his mental problems materialized. His symptoms appeared to fit the description: he had disconnected thoughts, as demonstrated by his statement that his psychologist ran the riding stable; his ambition to be a store manager was grandiose for his limited abilities; and he was suffering from a variety of hallucinations, which we came to regard as his demons. Andrew seemed to both hate and love Valerie, who was in charge of his house, when he had his first episode of delusional disorder. He was certainly fixated on her and blamed her for many things. He believed that she followed him everywhere: she watched him at work, at tennis, in his room, and even knocked on his door at 2:00 a.m. (Andrew claimed that he knew her knock.) He imagined that she was looking through the window at church and he could hear her voice in the background or on the phone. When he returned to Lambs, he asked a staff member to call security because he knew that Valerie "would never give up until we are married."

After a week in the hospital, Andrew returned to Lambs with a prescription for Zyprexa, and the hope that once he was stabilized, he would agree to take the Seroquel again. This was a newer drug with fewer side effects and potentially less weight gain.

It took another two years to find an appropriate combination of medications and the best dosage to keep Andrew's demons at bay. The rest of 2000 was a challenging time. Lambs staff drew up a behavioral contract to persuade Andrew that he needed to put in time at the job shop before he could earn points to return to Sunset Foods. Several times he had tried to get on the bus to Sunset and even started to leave the Lambs grounds with the idea of walking to the supermarket. In spite of the contract, his attendance at the job shop continued to be intermittent, but when he was there he stayed on task and performed well. The contract included rules of behavior for when he earned days back at Sunset: he was to remain at his workstation and not disturb his coworkers or customers.

In June of 2000, Dr. Rosanova decided to discontinue the Zyprexa and try Risperdal (Risperidone). Within a few days, Andrew developed a rash and the Risperdal had to be stopped. The doctor replaced it with Seroquel. Although Andrew was concerned about getting sleepy, he agreed to the change and even accepted the pill's color. As it turned out, the Risperdal had not caused the rash. Andrew had a case of shingles, from which he soon recovered.

Unfortunately, none of the medications that had been tried seemed to help resolve Andrew's delusions or calm down the voices. He broke up with Lael and became fixated on someone called Evelyn. Apparently he had met Evelyn at church, but in his mind she had rescued the engagement ring he had given his hairdresser in 1997, she was an instructor at the riding stables, and according to his supposed search in a telephone book, she was single and living with her father. He told us that he was ready to leave Lambs, get a job on his own, and marry Evelyn.

By the end of July, there were signs of improvement: Andrew had gone over to Lael's house and made up with her; he had been thrilled to have saved a resident's life when she fainted in Wal-Mart (she was diabetic); and he was attending the job shop more consistently as well as going back to Sunset two days a week. Every thread of progress cheered us. But there was still a long way to go. In August, Andrew flew to California for his two-week vacation. He must have expected to leave his demons behind in Chicago, but that did not happen. According to postcards that he wrote to Lael and Mike, "they" had followed him:

> When I left the airport, they went in the other plane with my air ticket, both of them follow me to California. They are here to try and take me back to Chicago. My parents won't let them. I'm trying to relax and do things. One of them put a red label on my bottle of meds. I don't think that's very nice to use my airline ticket.

Wherever we went, "they" plagued him. We spent a few days in Santa Barbara, where he insisted that we keep the television volume low in the motel so that "they" would not know what he was watching. In restaurants, Andrew would want to sit inside with his back to the windows so "they" could not see him. One time he put his face in his hands and said, "I don't want to scream in here, but those two are talking to me." While walking along the beachfront, he did not want to talk because "they" would hear him. During a movie, he changed places with his father and said on the way out, "Valerie was in there. She whispered in my ear." He told his sister on the phone, "I'm just waiting for those two to get out of my life." It was really hard to know how to react to those persistent voices. We did our best to comfort Andrew and assure him that the voices were not real; they were just figments of his imagination. But our assurances fell on deaf ears. For Andrew, and anyone suffering from hallucinations, the voices and imagined scenes were absolutely real.

Martha Eaton, a psychologist and one of our closest friends, lived in Santa Barbara. She had known Andrew since he was a baby. After talking to him, she concluded that he was highly psychotic and that his symptoms fit the diagnosis of paranoid schizophrenia rather than bipolar disorder. She suggested that he see a psychologist on a regular basis. It was important for him to talk about the voices and delusions and work through them as much as possible so that he could be helped to understand that they were not real.

After Andrew returned to Chicago, we wrote to Lambs staff expressing concern over his approximately forty-four-pound weight gain and questioning the current diagnosis of bipolar disorder. Although Andrew's mood certainly cycled and at times he seemed more energetic or hyper than at others, we had seen no signs of extreme depression. As voices and delusions appeared to be dominant, could he be suffering from paranoid schizophrenia, and were there other medications that might do a better job?

According to a report from the Mayo Clinic (www.mayoclinic.com/health/paranoid-schizophrenia, 2010), "paranoid schizophrenia is one of several types of schizophrenia, a chronic mental illness in which reality is interpreted abnormally (psychosis). The classic features of paranoid schizophrenia are having beliefs that have no basis in reality (delusions) and hearing things that aren't real (auditory hallucinations)." In an interview for the *Los Angeles Times* (January 29, 2011) Elyn Saks, author of *The Center Cannot Hold: My Journey through Madness,* described schizophrenia as "a waking nightmare." Normal people wake up from their nightmares and all the scary things dissipate. "No such luck with a schizophrenic episode—you can't just open your eyes and make it go away."

Some people with Down syndrome, as they age, are predisposed to develop mental health issues, such as dementia, Alzheimer's disease, and depressive and obsessive-compulsive disorders, but it is rare to find cases of schizophrenia. One of the reasons may be the difficulty in diagnosing abnormalities of thought and of psychotic experiences in people with an underlying mental impairment. Andrew's case may be unusual, but his ability to describe his delusions and auditory hallucinations—the voices that seemed to be controlling his life—was crystal clear and provided a window into a little-known world.

We had another chance to observe Andrew closely during his Christmas vacation in 2000. The voices were still prevalent with the list of tormentors increased by two Lambs residents who were trying to take over his room and steal his checkbook. He also talked about "them" sending him dreams via a "Dream Machine." However, it appeared that the voices had become more of an annoyance rather than invoking the fear that had been evident during our summer stay in Santa Barbara.

Although the Seroquel dose had been increased, it did not seem to combat the voices, and Andrew was still gaining weight. In April of 2001, a year after his second hospitalization, Dr. Rosanova decided to try Risperdal again, keeping the dose as low as possible because it can cause tardive dyskinesia.

Andrew was now back at Sunset Foods part time. He did have another stay in the hospital, but this time it was not his mind that was sick; it was because of a blood clot in his leg, which had started as calf pain while he was visiting us in Pasadena. We thought it was a pulled muscle and he flew back as usual, but it turned out to be the more serious flyer's curse—deep vein thrombosis (DVT). He was prescribed a blood thinner and advised to wear support hose, at least for work and flying. It took some time and frequent urging by his doctor and the Lambs nurses before he adjusted to wearing the restrictive and hard-to-put-on support stockings.

By the end of 2001, he showed marked improvement. When we asked him about his voices during his Christmas visit with us, he said he occasionally heard a tape recorder, but he seemed free of fears and anxiety. He was able to carry on a conversation and even volunteered information about a proposed new apartment building at Lambs. Although his weight was much the same, he appeared trimmer as a result of steady attendance at workouts in the Lambs gymnasium and participation in Special Olympics sports events. Finally, he was less focused on himself and able to show consideration for others. An example of this was his comment when I expressed sadness at selling my seventeen-year-old red sports car: "Mum, it'll be all right. You'll get over your old car and will soon fall in love with your new car."

In January 2002, the behavioral staff reported that Andrew's psychotic symptoms were down to two or three a month. Risperdal had certainly proved to be the magic potion for getting his voices under control. In order to keep stress to a minimum at the supermarket, he was now a steady part-time utility clerk, unloading carts and facing shelves. It appeared that Andrew's life, although radically changed, was back to a balanced state.

In November, tragedy struck. Andrew's beloved Lael died unexpectedly at the age of forty-seven. In March 1960, just before her fifth birthday, she had open-heart surgery to place a patch over a hole between the chambers of her heart. At the time she was only the third person to survive such a procedure. Now the patch was collapsing, and sadly it was decided that another repair was out of the question. Andrew visited her in the hospital before she slipped away. Lael was one of the sweetest, most generous, and most gentle of people. Andrew and Lael had known each other since elementary school. After they both moved to Lambs, they became steady sweethearts and agreed to marry if that ever became possible. In spite of Andrew's occasional delusional cravings for other women and his passing rejection of Lael, they remained faithful to each other. They exchanged rings, replacing those that got lost. Lael was an important anchor in Andrew's life, representing the security of his childhood years. He bore up well and was encouraged by Lambs to attend grief counseling. In December 2002, he wrote a letter to his godmother in England, demonstrating his ability to express his feelings and talk about the tragedy.

Dear Mary,

Thank you for your sympathy. It is rough over the holidays without Lael. I hope your husband get better I know it is rough for you, I went through it too when I heard about Lael dying from stroke, and also she had open heart surgery when she was five years old.

From your godson, Andrew James Wyllie.

P.S. I got a new girlfriend name is Sue.

He hid photographs and other reminders in an effort to put his relationship with Lael behind him. From time to time he made an effort to find other girlfriends, but no one ever replaced his "sweetie pie."

Whichever medication program is effective, the antipsychotic drugs and dosages have to be constantly adjusted. After a while, Dr. Rosanova added Abilify with the hope that Risperdal could be discontinued to avoid its side effects. Unfortunately, the voices became more insistent, with Andrew telling everyone that Lael was still alive. Dr. Rosanova suggested that he be hospitalized again, but to the credit of the Lambs counselors, they decided that hospitalization was unnecessary. They could keep a close eye on him at Lambs. We were especially relieved because Andrew had told us firmly, "I never want to be put away again." After some adjustments of quantity and timing, a combination of Risperdal and Abilify was established.

Side effects of antipsychotic medications are a constant concern, and all of Andrew's team, his doctors, and we, his parents, were always watching and worrying. Occasionally, he complained of feeling dizzy. During his Christmas visit in 2003, we witnessed Andrew having a seizure. Just after getting up from the couch, he fell over and started shaking. The episode was over in a few seconds, but another similar incident spurred us to alert the Lambs staff. A neurologist ordered tests, but there appeared to be no indication of anything wrong. When Andrew passed out at work, the doctor took the symptoms more seriously. He recommended a reduction in Risperdal and started Andrew on Depakote, an antiseizure medication. The addition to Andrew's ever-growing cocktail of medications seemed to control the seizures but made Andrew dopey, hungry, out of sorts, and slow. After the dosage was increased, Parkinsonian-type symptoms (slow gait and rocking from one foot to another) also manifested themselves. A year later, another neurologist weaned Andrew off the debilitating Depakote. He did recommend changing his antipsychotic medication to Seroquel because Abilify and Risperdal can cause dizziness and seizures, but a previous trial had shown that Seroquel was no good at quelling Andrew's voices.

As with most sufferers of paranoid schizophrenia, Andrew's voices continued to hover in the background, but at least they were no longer affecting the quality of his life. One important improvement was a significant weight loss helped by a rigorous nutrition and exercise program. Throughout this rough period, Andrew had kept up his sports activities, winning medals in state and regional Special Olympics events. On one extremely cold April weekend in 2005, we watched him win a gold medal in standing long jump and a silver medal for striding into second place in a 220-yard race.

Responding to the routines that we had established in his childhood, Andrew always did better when his schedule was regular and his surroundings were constant. Since the onset of his mental illness, he had a harder time dealing with change. In 2004, the group homes at Lambs were renovated and upgraded. The construction work required moving the occupants temporarily to other houses. This was probably disruptive to all the participants, but Andrew found it especially disturbing, forcing him to take yet another leave from Sunset Foods. After the work was complete, he and most of his original housemates were moved into a newly renovated House One, where Andrew was given a room in the same location as his former house. To help with the transition, we gave his room a new look with new furniture.

In spite of his many ups and downs, Andrew continued to be a much-loved member of his house community. Mike Impastato, who had also moved as house parent to the new residence, recalled a snow day when the satellite dish went out, leaving the residents without television. He said:

> I told everyone we would have to wait for the snow to melt, but Andrew didn't accept this. He decided that the best course of action was for me to climb on the roof and clean off the snow.... He assured me, of course that I wouldn't fall. In fact, he promised me that I would not fall. I have to admit, I actually thought about doing it for a while, but in the end, we all decided to play it safe and wait until the snow melted.

Mike also told us about an incident that Liz Alvary, one of Andrew's closest friends, remembered. It took place at Target, where House One did a weekly shop. Andrew, in particular, liked to stop at Target's snack bar for a pizza. Mike wrote:

> Andrew was done with his pizza, and he told us he was just going to wash his hands and then join us in the van. Well, we waited in the van for a while, but Andrew did not come out. I went inside, and Andrew was just finishing up his second serving of pizza. I said, "Andrew, you told me you were going to wash your hands and come right out." Andrew replied, "I know. I did say that, but after I washed my hands I decided I wanted to have two more pieces of pizza just to make sure I would not be hungry later on." When we got back to the van, everyone was laughing when I told them what took Andrew so long to come out. That was just Andrew. When he wanted to do something, he would do it.

In the summer of 2005, Pete and I celebrated fifty years of marriage by taking our family of thirteen to a Club Med in Mexico. Although he enjoyed some aspects of the vacation, Andrew was uncomfortable physically and mentally and apologized to us for bringing his troubles with him. During a recent visit at Christmas, John and his family flew in from Utah for a few days. They occupied two bedrooms upstairs, and Andrew slept in my first-floor studio, where he had a comfortable bed and a private bathroom. In the past this arrangement had not been a problem, but this time Andrew was so disturbed that he repacked his suitcase with the idea of returning to Chicago. On his next visit to Pasadena, he reminded me that he would never sleep in my studio again. His brother could sleep downstairs.

Every September Andrew looked forward to marking another anniversary of his employment at Sunset Foods. In spite of his illness and medical leaves, Sunset had kept his job open and accommodated his limitations by reducing his hours and adjusting his responsibilities. There were periods when Andrew did better or worse depending on his immediate supervisors, but with the help of the Lambs's job coach, he had worked at improving his performance and accepted his new role as "cart manager," greeting customers and handing out carts as they entered the store. In September 2008, Andrew proudly earned his twenty-five-year pin. Unfortunately, this seemed to mark the limit of Sunset's patience with Andrew's increasingly poor performance. The management reported that he seemed to be spacing out and sleeping on the job. They cut his five half-days to one half-day. Andrew was devastated. Every time he went to the store, he looked at the next week's schedule, hoping and expecting to see his name listed for more hours. Finally, in anger and desperation, he decided to quit, although he didn't seem to realize that quitting was permanent.

For four months, Andrew mourned his lost job. He was so proud of having worked in regular employment since he was seventeen, and it was a terrible wrench to give it up. Finally, he accepted a position at the Lambs Vocational Work Center. Pay was minimal and depended on the number of contracts and amount of piecework acquired by the center. In spite of not being able to remember what projects he worked on, Andrew was happy, proud of his employment, and fond of the supervising staff.

In their 2006 book *Mental Wellness in Adults with Down Syndrome*, Dennis McGuire and Brian Chicoine wrote: "People with Down syndrome seem to age more rapidly," and once they reach thirty-five or forty, it is not unusual to consider adding five, ten, fifteen, or even twenty years to their chronological age. The authors also explained that in middle age some people with Down syndrome "begin to have health problems associated with being older, and they tend to 'slow down' sooner than others." Taking into account the variety of problems occurring in Andrew's brain, it was not surprising that he was now showing signs of Alzheimer's disease, a condition in which nerves in certain brain areas degenerate and progressive dementia results.

Some days Andrew's short-term memory worked well, but other days it was extremely fragile. He frequently repeated himself and at times appeared more confused than could be accounted for by his paranoid schizophrenia. He moved more slowly, and his coordination had diminished. His muscles seemed weaker, and he had difficulty getting up from a couch or out of a car. Other skills, such as writing, also deteriorated.

He used to be hooked on television soap operas, but now only wanted to watch the Weather Channel. He also lost interest in activities and sports. Even bowling, one of his favorite weekly pastimes, was forsaken. A bowling outing had always been part of his vacation schedule. One time, unknown to the counselor who had accompanied him to the airport, he had even brought his own bowling ball in his carry-on bag.

However, until recently those habits and memories that were well ingrained in his system continued to function at full capacity. He was still capable of looking after his everyday needs, performing adequately at the work center, and keeping up his duties as an acolyte at St. Lawrence Church. The volunteer church member in charge of the acolytes, recognizing Andrew's physical and mental decline, had replaced the heavy brass cross with a lighter wooden one so that Andrew could retain his position as one of the lead acolytes in the church procession.

As we settled into our retirement years, it was especially hard to witness Andrew's decline. His vivid descriptions of the voices provided an insight into the mystical world of schizophrenia where real people and events seem to have been thrown into a mixer and evolve as some bizarre mirage. How did Andrew know to use the phrase, "Don't put me away"? Perhaps he heard it from Lambs residents or in the hospital's psychiatric ward. For us it conjured up visions of lunatic asylums and lobotomies given as treatment for my aunt's deep depression two generations earlier. Fortunately, today a victim of schizophrenia like Andrew can be helped with drugs, psychotherapy, and the watchful eyes of dedicated counselors. While we monitored his struggles with mental illness and Alzheimer's, we also gave thanks for the many years that he led a successful and fulfilling life. He achieved so much more than what we were led to expect when he was born. Even during his troubles, he continued to work, be active in sports, and participate in his house activities.

Only since turning fifty did he appear to be descending the staircase of life. In his retirement years, Andrew found comfort in the stability and familiar patterns of his life at Lambs, which had been his home for the last thirty years. As recently as the summer of 2010, he told his father before boarding his plane back to Chicago, "I'm happy to go home to Lambs," a sentiment that brought great comfort to his parents and reminded us of the statement he made in 1983 when we moved to Pasadena and tried to find a residential community in California: "Mum, Dad, you lead your life and I will lead mine, and mine is here at Lambs."

Chapter 24:
A Steep Decline

As usual, Andrew spent his 2010 Christmas vacation with us in California. The journey from Chicago had a rough start. The day before
his flight, Andrew could not find his wallet, which contained his ID card,
now essential for boarding a plane. The Lambs staff helped him look
everywhere, but the card was not found. We managed to get him on a
later flight the next day to give Mike, his faithful airport chauffeur, more
time to take Andrew to a DMV center to get a new identification card.
This task was made harder because the DMV centers now require an
original birth certificate, and the original of Andrew's certificate was in
California. After several phone calls, fax exchanges, and failure to reach
a DMV supervisor, Mike decided to take Andrew to the nearest center
with the hope of talking his way through to a supervisor and persuading
her to make an exception. Fortunately, he was successful, and Andrew,
now thoroughly stressed and exhausted, caught his 6:00 p.m. flight.

Wisely, Mike had ordered a wheelchair for both airports. When Pete met
Andrew at the gate, he was in a state of mental and physical exhaustion, asleep
in the wheelchair, and barely able to stand unsupported, let alone walk. The
stewardess explained that Andrew had become agitated on the flight, probably
because he had a window seat instead of his usual aisle seat. Pete collected
his bag, drove home, and helped Andrew into bed. It was now about 2:30 a.m.
Chicago time.

After a few days, Andrew recovered from his difficult journey, but we
were soon aware of how steeply he had declined since his visit in August
and how much more we had to do for him. In general, he was more

confused, forgetful, disoriented, no longer interested in television, and disinclined to do much. His small motor skills had deteriorated, and he was unable to sign his name. When I encouraged him to try, he replied pathetically, "I can't." As always, he enjoyed his food, brief outings to the store, a couple of movies, and church on Christmas Eve. He was excited to go back to Lambs and did well on the return flight.

A few days after his return to Lambs, Mike discovered that Andrew had a urinary tract infection, which in hindsight he probably had during his vacation. Suddenly, he required more attention and help. Most worrisome was an incident in which Andrew changed into his smart clothes, put on his hat and coat, and left the house at 10:00 p.m. on Tuesday thinking that a car warming up outside was his ride to church. He had even taken the sign-out book for the driver to sign. Dianne Yaconetti, the CEO of Lambs, phoned us with the news that "the time has come," meaning that Lambs could no longer meet Andrew's needs and it was time to find a nursing home for him.

We found ourselves in a tailspin of shock and despair, feeling that a move away from Lambs, his home of thirty-one years, would only add to Andrew's decline. Not only would he lose all his friends and the comfort and support of his counselors, but he would also lose contact with his church, which had served as his religious family ever since he had moved to Libertyville. We wrote an appeal to Dianne, giving our reasons for wanting Andrew to stay put for now, and also suggesting that once his urinary tract infection was under control, he might need less attention. Dianne agreed to move Andrew to a house where there would be more staff, in particular night staff, because her biggest worry was the fear of Andrew wandering away from the house. This is one of the dangers associated with Alzheimer's, and of particular concern to Lambs with its location near a lake and major highway.

I made furniture plans and struggled to fit Andrew's Ethan Allen furniture and precious belongings into the floor plan of the smaller room in House Four. Before the move could be arranged, Andrew slumped over at work and became unresponsive. He was rushed to the emergency room at Condell Hospital where, after a battery of tests, the doctors concluded that the problem was caused by an exceptionally low heart rate (down to thirty). The cardiologist recommended a pacemaker. We spoke on the phone to several doctors and learned that it was not uncommon for someone with Down syndrome to have a pacemaker fitted and that they coped well with the device.

Andrew spent two weeks in the hospital. The surgery had to be delayed until his blood could recover from the Coumadin that he had been taking for a long time. His physical recovery was satisfactory, but he had a hard time dealing mentally with all the machines, tubes, monitors, and general strangeness. Pete and I both had bad colds, so we could not travel to visit him. I am sure the nurses and doctors were kind and caring, but we felt terrible thinking about him being in such a traumatic situation with no family to give him comfort. Visits from cousin Lolla and our close friends Nancy and Don provided some distraction for him.

The hospital social worker had expected to find a rehab facility in Libertyville where Andrew could regain his strength before returning to Lambs, but no one wanted to take a developmentally disabled patient with a psychiatric history and Alzheimer's. At one point the hospital had decided that he could return to Lambs. Everything was arranged. But the next day the decision was revoked when the doctor who attended Lambs on a regular basis reviewed Andrew's case and decided that Lambs did not have the staff to care for his needs. House One residents, who had been excited at the prospect of greeting their returning housemate, were so upset that they marched en masse to confront Dianne Yaconetti in her office and demand an explanation. At least they were prepared to take him whatever his condition, but they were only participants, not caretakers. Finally, Dr. Chicoine (director of the Down Syndrome Clinic), who was one of the attending physicians at Park Ridge Care Center (PRCC), persuaded the center to accept Andrew as a rehab patient. The care center was also a nursing home, and most of the patients were developmentally disabled.

We flew to Chicago a week after Andrew was moved to PRCC. We were shocked to see his feeble condition and soon realized that we needed to make the heart-wrenching decision that a nursing home now had to become his permanent home. It was especially difficult to realize that Andrew belonged with a group of disabled residents in various stages

Loving Andrew

of senility. He was very gaunt, stooped, and restless. He kept saying to us, "Let's go," meaning "Let's go home to Lambs." He made several attempts to leave the facility and on a couple of occasions made it out of the front door, setting off the alarm and surprising the nurses with how fast he could run. They were not amused when I told them that in 2005 Andrew had won a medal for a 220-yard race in Special Olympics.

During our visit, we met Dr. Chicoine and had an encouraging discussion with him about straightening out Andrew's medications, which the hospital had changed. They had taken him off Risperdal, the one antipsychotic medication that had kept his voices at bay, and added Keppra because they believed that a small cerebral bleed was putting Andrew at risk for seizures. Dr. Chicoine agreed to discontinue the Keppra, which can cause hallucinations and agitation, and to put Andrew back on Risperdal. This seemed to pay off: Andrew's agitation disappeared; he became less inclined to want to leave and began to adjust to his new surroundings.

An important key to Andrew's adjustment was Nadine, PRCC's social worker. Nadine was a pretty woman with large eyes and a mass of blonde, curly hair. She had a warm, outgoing personality and a certain pizzazz that must have helped her connect with her patients and get them involved in occupational therapies. With Andrew she was firm but loving in her efforts to keep him occupied and discourage his urge to run away. He fell in love with her and she with him. Nadine told us later that when Andrew came into her life, she was experiencing some personal challenges and her work had become quite burdensome. Gradually, she found herself captivated by Andrew's sweet personality, broad smile, and infectious laugh; he became her motivator, helping her get up in the morning and go to work.

Unfortunately, about six weeks after settling at PRCC, Andrew had a seizure. Dr. Chicoine started him on Depakote, but as happened several years ago, this made Andrew totally lifeless and lethargic, so the doctor prescribed Lamictal. We had continued our regular routine of phoning Andrew on Sunday morning. For a few weeks after he moved to PRCC, Andrew had a phone voice that was strong and cheerful. After he started the antiseizure medications, this disappeared, and he seemed unable to respond to our questions. He even stopped saying, "I love you too" when we ended the call by saying, "We love you."

During a visit at the end of April, we found that sometimes, unexpectedly, he would say four or five words in a row. They seemed to appear out of nowhere, and we would catch a fleeting glimpse of the old Andrew. Then, just as suddenly, they disappeared, and there was only silence. At other times he would say, "I have to tell you," and we waited, holding our breath for the great pronouncement, or even a word to give us a clue as to what might be coming. But there was nothing. It was like a child blowing soap bubbles through a ring; they formed and floated for a second, balancing on the air, and then flew away and dissolved, never to form again. At other moments, Andrew would smile or giggle with an infectious grin on his face, finding something intangible that was humorous. But most of the time he was in a fog, a lost soul living out his last years among a group of other helpless nursing home residents.

We wanted so much to give him a present for his birthday. Lisa had suggested a watch because his had disappeared in the confusion of the hospital stay and move to Park Ridge. After looking for something simple and inexpensive, we decided that such a gift would not work. The watch needed to be digital; it would need an elastic band for ease of putting on and off, but the metal pieces might irritate his skin; or he might take it off and forget where he put it. Finally, we concluded that time no longer had any meaning for him. The days passed with the routine of the nursing home care marking the hours.

Mealtimes were usually important and pleasurable. However, during one of her visits from Philadelphia, Lisa experienced a disgruntled Andrew. She had accompanied him into the dining room, so the staff had moved Andrew from his usual seat to another table where Lisa could sit with him. When Lisa tried to help him get into his place, he said angrily, "Don't push me." He fussed with his bib, groaned, and did not eat well, snatching utensils away from Lisa as she tried to help him. Lisa said she was sorry for upsetting him and finally just sat back and left him alone. He occasionally looked at her to make sure she was still there. One time when their eyes locked, he saw that she was sad and said tenderly with love in his eyes, "It's not you." It turned out that he was upset because being seated at a different table had interfered with his accustomed routine. Like many people with Alzheimer's, he was quite unable to put his dilemma into words.

On the last day of her weekend visit, Lisa, with limited time before she had to leave for the airport, had made no plans for an outing. For some reason, Andrew was agitated and grumpy and would not sit with her, even though the other residents made space for him. Lisa asked what was troubling him, but he did not or could not respond. Then when Lisa said she needed a coffee, he said, "OK, you can," and after a few minutes added, "Are you ready?" When Lisa said he could come with her in the car while she went for a coffee, he brightened up and walked to the car with a slight spring in his shuffling gait. He was happy to stay in the car while Lisa bought her coffee, and then he half dozed, checking now and then that he was with his sister, as she drove around the neighborhood. When they returned to PRCC, Lisa said, "Here we are," and Andrew replied, "Yes" with confidence and no regret. As they walked through the entry hall, Andrew grabbed the inner door and held it open for his sister. He smiled happily to see the staff waiting for him and giggled with pride when they exclaimed over his spontaneous chivalry. Lisa felt so pleased that the staff had caught a glimpse of the old Andrew, but at the same time she was immensely sad that most of what the nurses saw each day was the empty shell of her brother, formerly a high-functioning man with Down syndrome.

The Lambs staff and Andrew's housemates were devastated by his departure. After he was settled in the nursing home, Mike organized a pizza party as a birthday celebration. Eleven residents of House One and two staff members drove to Park Ridge, picked up Andrew, and took him to a pizza restaurant. They gave him a birthday card that they had made, and everyone had a great time. When the party was over, Andrew was quite amenable to going back to PRCC.

It was impossible to know what Andrew felt about his move to the nursing home and how much he missed Lambs. After taking him on an outing to Target, always one of his favorite excursions to buy soda pop and snacks, Lisa mentioned how nice it had been to see Mike, who had visited from Lambs the day before and taken Andrew for a haircut. Andrew said, "It's been a long time." Lisa asked if he was talking about being away from Lambs, and he said, "Yes, I think it's time I should go back." Lisa tried to comfort him by explaining that he had retired from his job at the Lambs Work Center and that his home was now PRCC. She knew he would miss his old friends, but he would soon make new friends in his new home. We, Andrew's family, probably found his departure from Lambs much more of an emotional drain than anything Andrew might have felt—one of the few benefits of Alzheimer's disease.

The pastor and congregation of St. Lawrence Episcopal Church, as well as Mrs. Lloyd, Andrew's faithful church friend and driver, were also sorry to see Andrew retire from his church duties and move to a nursing home. Many members of the congregation signed a poster-size card, which was placed on a bulletin board in his room. Pastor Patti Snickenberger wrote me a note saying, "He is a special and very precious person. I am so used to him at the altar, assisting as acolyte and being so proud of his ministry, and I will miss him terribly."

Andrew had now reached the lowest flight of the Down syndrome staircase, and we worried about his health and his state of mind. But we took comfort in knowing that in the later stages of their disease, most Alzheimer's patients lose all concept of time and place and live only in the past. In spite of his surroundings, which to us were depressing, Andrew seemed to be comfortable, content, and well cared for. He assured us, "I am happy."

Chapter 25:
Finale

On Monday, June 13, 2011, we received a call from the nursing home to say that Andrew had been taken to the emergency room (ER) at Lutheran General Hospital in Park Ridge with breathing and swallowing difficulties. This was followed by a call from Dr. Chicoine advising us to go immediately to Chicago, as Andrew's situation was ominous.

We alerted Lisa, and all three of us managed to get on flights the next day (Tuesday). Lisa arrived in the morning and Pete and I in the evening. By then it had been determined that Andrew had not suffered a stroke, seizure, or heart attack, but he definitely had pneumonia and pulmonary embolism. The doctors had started him on antibiotics and a blood thinner. Although he was on oxygen and looking very groggy, Andrew did recognize us. The next day he was moved out of the intensive care unit (ICU) to a large private room on the tenth floor of a new wing with clear views of the Chicago skyline. He was more alert, said hello, and occasionally managed a word or two. Lisa was especially moved when she sat by his bedside on her own and he looked into her eyes, touched her face, and said, "You are so lovely."

We had a long meeting with Dr. Chicoine to discuss all scenarios, including the chances for recovery, and at what stage we might consider a "do not resuscitate" order. The next few days were intense, marked primarily by Andrew's labored breathing, episodes of apnea, and swallowing difficulties, with frequent uncomfortable suctioning to remove mucus. The doctors inserted a filter into the inferior vena cava to prevent clots moving from his legs to his lungs, but because of more bleeding on the brain, the blood thinner had to be discontinued. Although Andrew was somewhat brighter on Thursday, he started having violent tremors that shook his whole body. At the same time he screwed up his eyes, putting his hands over them and on his head. It soon became clear that he was hallucinating and having severe withdrawal symptoms from being taken off his antipsychotic medications when he was admitted on Monday. It was a rough day. We held his hands and tried to comfort him as each spasm racked his body. We attempted to imagine what ghostly images he was seeing. At times he reached up with his hands as though he was trying to grasp some strange creature floating over him. All day he was unable to relax or sleep. Dr. Chicoine ordered him put back on the Risperdal, but it could only be given at bedtime with the tablet crushed up in applesauce. We waited impatiently for bedtime.

The next day (Friday) Andrew was calmer and the hallucinations seemed to have diminished, but at the same time he became disturbingly unresponsive. For a short time he was allowed some pureed food, and I fed him small spoonfuls of blended meats, vegetables, and even simulated bread along with a thick, milk-like drink. Unfortunately, this gradual progress did not last long. The speech therapist soon determined that his sluggishness inhibited him from being able to close off his windpipe when swallowing, and there was too much danger of him aspirating. More CT scans revealed bleeding between the folds of the brain and a white area in the front, probably indicative of dead cells.

When we said goodnight to him on Saturday evening, he seemed a little better, but I recall with great sadness how tightly he held my hand, as though he might not see us again. We all left Chicago on Sunday morning: Lisa to return to her home in Pennsylvania and Pete and I to fly the four hours to Los Angeles. This would give us one day to turn around, pack, and leave on our long-planned trip to Scotland to attend the sixtieth reunion of my matriculation year and the six-hundredth anniversary of the founding of St. Andrew's University. We agonized about continuing with our trip. I had asked Dr. Chicoine whether we should go or not and he said, "You have given fifty-two years to Andrew; it's all right to go."

Before boarding our Sunday flight to Los Angeles we learned that Andrew had had a bad night and needed an oxygen mask. We arrived home with heavy hearts. Late that evening, we had an urgent call from Lisa and from a hospital doctor to say they had to intubate Andrew because his blood oxygen level was dropping and he could not breathe. The situation was critical. The next morning we learned that Andrew had blood clots throughout his arms, and that his left lung was completely occluded. We discussed with Lisa what we should do, and together we agreed that the time had come to follow the guidance of Dr. Chicoine and the hospital doctors and take Andrew off the ventilator.

This is the most difficult decision for anyone to make — to cease medical intervention that postpones death. The doctors told us that even if he should recover from this episode, he would continue to be susceptible to pneumonia and other problems and would most likely be back in the ER in a short time. We realized that there was no quality of life left, and we recalled how much Andrew disliked machines and tubes, which he had struggled to remove during his hospital stay in January. Moreover, he would hate being dependent on a feeding tube or being restricted to a bed or wheelchair. Alarmed by the television reports of Terri Schiavo being maintained in a vegetative state, many Lambs Farm residents had signed living wills. Andrew had joined them in 2007 when he could understand, as much as he could understand anything, what it meant to be dependent on machines.

Lisa arranged to return to Chicago the next day (Monday), and we asked the hospital to keep Andrew on life support until she got there. I called Patti Snickenberger, the rector of St. Lawrence, and asked her to be present, along with our good friends, Don and Nancy, our cousin Lolla, and Andrew's favorite counselors at Lambs, Mike and Alan. Andrew's nurse took the group aside, explained the procedure, and stated firmly that she could not guarantee the outcome. She wanted to be sure that she should proceed with removal of all life support. Andrew would receive a dose of morphine to counteract any pain as the tube was removed, and his antibiotics and saline would be stopped. Everyone supported the family's decision that Andrew would not want to live in a severely compromised physical condition. They gathered around Andrew's bedside, with Patti leading the group in prayer. Stories, some humorous, of Andrew's stages in life were shared. To everyone's surprise, Andrew was able to breathe on his own after the tube was removed, and in spite of being groggy from the morphine, he acknowledged the group and managed one of his charming smiles. The nurses had been able to give him a deep suction when he was intubated, so his lungs were relatively clear. The group gradually trickled home, but the nurse made up a bed so Lisa could stay the night.

The next couple of days were confusing. Andrew was moved to general medicine, an older wing of the hospital where the nurses did not seem to know his history or that he was terminal. One nurse wanted to get him up and walking. Lisa was worried that he was starting to hallucinate again, but because of his swallowing difficulties, oral medication was not an option. Lisa asked that he be put on morphine or a tranquilizer to relieve any distress. On Tuesday night there was a terrible storm, with tornadoes threatened and warnings to stay away from the windows. Power went out, but the hospital generators took over. When Lisa finally left to go to the nearby hotel where we had all stayed the previous week, she saw the destruction wrought by the fierce winds. The hotel computers had been down, and Lisa had a long wait before she could check into a room, only to find no soap in the bathroom.

The next day (Wednesday) she returned to the hospital early to meet with Dr. Chicoine. She told him tearfully about the problems dealing with nurses and residents who did not know Andrew's history. Dr. Chicoine was very sympathetic and arranged for Andrew to be moved to the Rainbow Hospice nearby. It took another thirty-six hours for a bed to be available, but once he was moved and settled, Lisa felt greatly relieved.

The hospice was aesthetically pleasing, with fifteen large, private rooms arranged around a central lounge area for visitors. Each room was furnished with comfortable armchairs and a sofa upholstered in earth-toned, homey fabrics and occasional chairs that could be pulled up close to the bed. There was a minimum of hospital-type equipment, with no machines or beepers except for a small oxygen tank that emitted a kind of white noise. A pleasant perfume pervaded the room and the atmosphere exuded calmness. The nurses were gentle and attentive, turning Andrew every few hours, bathing him every night, and keeping him comfortable and free of pain. Most of the time Andrew seemed to be in a deep sleep and unaware of who was there, although he did protest gently when he was turned. Lisa stayed in Chicago until the weekend, when she finally had to go home to look after her own family.

Lolla visited soon after Lisa left and found Andrew strangely wakeful but not agitated. Although he had barely acknowledged Lisa's presence, he must have been aware of her continuing vigil and was possibly disturbed that she had left. Lolla sat by his bed, held his hand, and talked to him about their days as young children playing games together in Florida. She said, "He even smiled when I talked about dancing with him at my wedding. His eyes were open, and we had a lot of visual communication." When the nurse came to reposition Andrew, she sneezed, and Andrew said quite clearly, "Bless you." Lolla arranged for a volunteer music therapist to visit and sing to him, which the nurse said he enjoyed. During the next week, Lisa's husband Dean, who was on a business trip to Chicago, spent time sitting with Andrew, as did Nancy and Don, Nadine, Lolla, and the deacon from St. Lawrence.

Lisa had the brunt of Andrew's care, for which we are eternally grateful. She sat by his bedside, sang and prayed, and told him it was all right to leave this earth, that he would have a good time in heaven with his beloved Lael, his baby sister, Jean, his grandparents and uncles, and his dog, Pucci. Nevertheless, we spent anxious days in Scotland and London, phoning her every day to get an update. I kept my cell phone by my side day and night, expecting the call to say that Andrew had gone. But he held on for twelve days. We had a long talk with Lisa on Saturday, July 2. She had been home nearly a week and was trying to decide whether and when to go back to Chicago. Lolla visited Andrew in the afternoon and sensed a change. She sent a text to Lisa: "I know it's difficult to be away from Andrew. But I truly think he is traveling somewhere else now...You will be just as close to him through your thoughts and communications from home...Just set aside some time each evening to commune with him. He will feel your love. You don't need to be here for him to be aware of it. Be at peace."

Lisa told us, "Around 4:30 p.m. I woke up from a snooze by the pool and tried to do as Lolla had said. The sky was a beautiful shade of blue, with wispy white clouds. I imagined myself being with Andrew, praying for his comfort and hoping he was feeling our love and Christ's love, praying that he would leave these earthly bonds and go to heaven, where he'd be free of pain and suffering. Moments later my cell phone rang, and I knew it had to be Rainbow Hospice. Nurse Patti hesitated before telling me that Andrew had just passed. She had gone in to check on him and noticed his breathing was shallow and soft. She knew right away and just stayed with him instead of calling. She said it was very quick." Lisa called us at 10:00 p.m. London time. We all wept uncontrollably.

We returned to Pasadena on July 4 and pitched right into booking flights, hotels, and all that was needed for the funeral weekend. Before leaving on our trip, we had already discussed a date with St. Lawrence Church and with Lambs Farm. The funeral would be on Saturday, July 16, with a memorial service for the Lambs residents on Monday, July 18. Fortunately, we had followed Dianne Yaconetti's advice and put together a prepaid funeral plan in 2010 with a funeral home in Libertyville. All that was left were the details of the service, which I worked on with Patti.

Pete and I, Dean and Lisa, and John flew to Chicago on July 15 for a weekend of remembrance and celebration of Andrew's life. About fifty parishioners, including faithful Helen Lloyd, members of Lambs, Lisa's high school classmates, Dr. Chicoine, Nadine (the social worker at Park Ridge Care Center), and friends of the family attended the service of thanksgiving at St. Lawrence Church. The service, led by the Reverend Patricia (Patti) Snickenberger and the deacon, the Reverend MJ Lewis-Kirk, began with the acolytes, who had served with Andrew, proceeding up the aisle just as Andrew would have done, and taking their places behind the altar. MJ carried a brass urn containing Andrew's remains and placed it on a flower-encircled pedestal in front of the altar. She placed a white cloth with an embroidered cross over the urn and carefully wrapped Andrew's gold acolyte cincture around it.

The service consisted of hymns and psalms of praise, readings from the Scriptures, and tributes to Andrew. John recalled happy and humorous childhood incidents and his admiration for a brother who was always so friendly and socially bold and achieved so much more than was expected of him, reinforcing his parents' decision not to let him be whisked away at birth but be brought up as a fully involved family member:

We're not here today to say good-bye to Andrew. We're here to celebrate his life, his contributions, his accomplishments, the many people he touched, and to remember him always in our hearts, minds, and souls. He is now free from the challenges that the physical world dealt him and he is at peace. Godspeed, brother.

Lisa spoke of Andrew always feeling blessed in spite of the unfair burden of his challenges:

In Andrew's final days in the hospital, with communication minimized to single words, he did not use those few words he had to complain or lament. Instead he showed his love and devotion to those he knew with smiles and laughter. He was able to welcome friends with a hello and to deter nurses with a decided no when asked if he was in pain. He put four words together to tell me: "You are so lovely," and the last words he said to me were, "Thank you." As his sister, I take loving and appreciating Andrew for granted; it's a given. It is a blessing to see how many others loved him for all he offered in his simple and humble way.

We are so grateful to St. Lawrence Church for opening your hearts and minds to Andrew for all these years. You didn't just invite him to come and be a guest in the back of your church; you invited him to be an integral part of your community, representing the church by serving and leading. Andrew was thrilled to find Christ here at St. Lawrence and was honored to share his love and joy with such a gracious and generous congregation. Thank you for embracing him and making him a part of your family.

I read a poem called "High Flight" by John Gillespie Magee, Jr.:

Oh! I have slipped the surly bonds of Earth
And danced the skies on laughter-silvered wings;
Sunward I've climbed, and joined the tumbling mirth
Of sun-split clouds,—and done a hundred things
You have not dreamed of—wheeled and soared and swung
High in the sunlit silence. Hov'ring there,
I've chased the shouting wind along, and flung
My eager craft through footless halls of air...

Up, up the long, delirious, burning blue

I've topped the wind-swept heights with easy grace

Where never lark, or even eagle flew,

And, while with silent lifting mind I've trod

The high, untrespassed sanctity of space,

Put out my hand, and touched the face of God.

Patti completed the tributes with a stirring homily. She spoke of her visit to St. Lawrence just before she became rector four and a half years earlier. Sitting at the back of the church, she turned to watch the altar party enter and was profoundly moved by the sight of Andrew in his role as crucifer, leading the procession up the aisle with a smile on his face as broad as the sanctuary. As she came to know and love many things about him, she realized that "he had a rare gift, one most of us would envy. The gift was…absolute clarity about his vocation, first as a Christian and then as an acolyte, as one who serves God at the altar." Patti ended her homily with a reference to the appropriateness of the poem that I had read:

> It couldn't be more fitting, if you knew Andrew. Can't you just see him slipping the surly bonds of earth and dancing the skies on laughter-silvered wings? Or doing a hundred things that we've not dreamed of? I see him topping the wind-swept heights with easy grace, where never lark or even eagle flew. But the image most clear to me, the one I can envision with the most ease, the one that gives me hope, the one I hope comforts you in your grief, is one of Andrew putting out his hand and touching the face of God.
>
> And then—something else: God invites Andrew to the heavenly banquet, vests him in white, and wraps around him the cincture reserved for the lead acolyte in God's holy retinue.

Patti accompanied her words by holding up a red girdle for Andrew to wear in his new role in heaven.

The Lambs Memorial Service "Celebrating the Life of Andrew Wyllie"

on Monday afternoon was quite different but just as moving. After welcoming everyone, Dianne Yaconetti gave an overview of Andrew's life. She stressed how Lambs became an important component in his life, but Andrew was also important to Lambs Farm: "He represented the epitome of a Lambs Farm participant. He was everything that our co-founders fought to achieve." Dianne recalled with humor the determination of Andrew and two of his friends to stay together and have Mike Impastato as their house parent after the houses were renovated. The trio expressed their wishes not only in strongly written notes to the president but in follow-up phone calls, and finally, led by Andrew, the group stormed into her office. Dianne explained that it was now fitting that these best friends, along with Mike Impastato, were the principal players in the service.

Marc Natchman read a Psalm of David (Ps. 23:1–6), and Liz Alvary gave a carefully prepared tribute to Andrew saying, "He was the best friend I've known for many years...He was very caring and understanding." She recalled how Andrew helped her when they worked at Sunset Foods together, and how she lately would help him make his lunch or cut up his food. She mentioned his sense of fun and how much he enjoyed their outings to Wisconsin Dells. In his eulogy, Mike spoke of his fondness for Andrew and his long association with him. He said: "Andrew was a caring, helpful, and very special person. He was well liked by both the residents and the staff. He had a great sense of humor, was very intelligent, and was extremely determined to the point of being fearless. He simply loved life and everything about it." Mike told me later that he felt Andrew was watching over him to make sure he got through his speech with fortitude. Pete paid tribute to Lambs for providing Andrew with such a wonderful life. Before the final songs, the microphone was opened for anyone to speak about Andrew. About a dozen participants lined up and spoke of their friend and how much he will be missed. The speeches ranged from a couple of words to lengthy tributes. All were completely unrehearsed, spoken from the heart, and extremely touching.

Music included "Amazing Grace" sung with gusto accompanying Elvis Presley's version on a CD and "Let There Be Peace on Earth." In closing, "Peace in the Valley" was led by one of the participants looking highly professional as she held the microphone and walked up and down in front of the podium. Afterward everyone enjoyed juice and cookies and a chance to look at the display of photographs, Special Olympics uniforms, and the many medals that Andrew had won through the years.

— ★ —

Writing about Andrew's last weeks has been highly emotional but at the same time a cathartic exercise. I keep questioning our decision to continue with our trip to our homeland. It's easy to recite reasons or excuses. If Lisa had been unable to take our place and be with Andrew, we would certainly have cancelled. None of us expected him to survive for so long. He would have died before we left if the hospital personnel had not intubated him, but it would have been a painful end. Although the length of the dying process was stressful for his family and friends, for Andrew it was comfortable, peaceful, and dignified, especially once he was settled in the Rainbow Hospice. Lolla described it as "a peaceful way station— he never seemed agitated or distressed…the nurses were always gentle and sweet with him."

Pete and I found solace in returning to St. Andrews, the place where we had met and that had provided the source for Andrew's name. During the Sunday-morning chapel service, we both prayed for him. We found comfort connecting after many years with our university friends and close relatives. We spent an afternoon with my deceased brother's children in London and met a new generation of grandnephews and a grandniece, reminding us that life goes on. We returned jet-lagged and exhausted from the long journey but with a certain spiritual refreshment to get us through the final farewell.

Notes of their last days with Andrew by Lisa and Lolla helped immeasurably with the writing of this chapter. Lisa's diary concluded with the following:

> It was an honor and a gift to spend this precious time with Andrew. I wish I could have been with him when he died, but thankfully he had visits from Lolla, Nadine, Nancy and Don, and Dean, and that he was at Rainbow Hospice with such a caring and tender staff.… I've had some wonderful God moments during

my time with Andrew and since he passed. Each person can find meaning in events or not, but I find it brings comfort and a feeling of connectedness to listen to the sights, sounds, and messages in our experiences and environment. Yesterday I read Pastor Patti's beautiful homily about Andrew, based on Scripture and the poem that Mom read. She described Andrew soaring on the wings of an eagle, dancing on clouds, and touching the face of God. Out by the pool later that day, I was alone and second guessing all the decisions we'd made. What if we had just gotten Andrew's cocktail of medications right, so he could have been awake enough to function? He could have lived on since his body was so strong. What if, what if, what if. I cried and prayed for a sign to let me know we'd done the right thing. I looked up and there was an eagle soaring high in the clear blue sky, directly over me. There were no other birds around and no more eagles for the next three hours that I was out by the pool. I had to laugh the sign was so clear!

Lisa's diary referred to another special moment:

In church we are taught that God has a plan for our lives, He knows our birth and our death before we are even conceived. We are also taught that when we do what we are called to do, which in my case is ministering to others, people will see Christ's love shining through us. When Andrew touched my face and told me I was so lovely (which was a completely unique thing for him to do and say), he wasn't speaking to me. He was already seeing the plan laid out before him, and it was Christ's love he saw through my adoration and service to him. MJ put words to it by telling the congregation she had seen the face of Jesus in me when we talked. Andrew's gesture was such a gift to me on many levels. On the surface it was adorable and complimentary. But on the deeper level, I "saw" him reach out his hand and touch the face of God! His blue eyes were filled with love, adoration, and confidence, his speech was uninhibited and clear, there was no apparent handicap, and he was once again that lovely Andrew who shared his heart without reserve. A tiny glimpse of heaven, another gift to let us know he's all right.

We all take comfort in knowing that Andrew is finally free of his "troubles," as he called his mental demons, and is spared further ravages of

Alzheimer's disease. The bronze urn containing his ashes was placed in a vault in the Columbarium at St. Lawrence. A simple plaque on the outside wall of the sanctuary identifies its location. Andrew's role on this earth is finished. He is at peace and with God.

Epilogue

Andrew's story is finished, and the purpose of this epilogue is to review the main themes that are woven into the book. How did the experience of having a child with Down syndrome affect our family structure? With the advancements in prenatal testing techniques, is it necessary to bring a child with Down syndrome into the world? How did we succeed in helping Andrew master the skills of life and become a contributing member of society?

As we, Andrew's family, commiserated with each other over his steep decline and eventual death, we found consolation in looking back at his life and his many successes. It is in this context that I recalled a discussion I had in the mid-1990s with Lisa and John concerning their feelings about growing up with a brother with Down syndrome. Andrew contributed his own memories to some of the incidents. As in all family chatter, we slipped into calling Andrew "Andy."

The relationship of a Down syndrome person with siblings will vary from family to family. The majority of children with Down syndrome are born to older mothers, making them the youngest of several siblings, whose roles will automatically become caretaker or teacher. Andrew was our first child, making him big brother to his younger siblings.

Lisa, four years younger than Andrew, quickly established a motherly role and took on the position as protector and teacher before Andrew was old enough to understand what was happening. On the other hand, John, who was six years younger, was always the baby brother in Andrew's eyes.

I began our discussion by asking, "As small children, how did you feel about having a developmentally disabled brother?"

"I never really thought much about it because he was always there as part of our family," said Lisa. "We were always in the same neighborhood, but we went to a different school, so we didn't have to take care of him or protect him at school."

"What about when you were playing with other kids?"

"I think Lisa and I always had a strong feeling of protection, especially in our younger years," replied John. "For instance in the playgrounds, when kids couldn't understand what Andy said, we acted as his interpreters."

Lisa added, "It wasn't a big deal. We would repeat what he said, and then it was done with. Some of the older kids were very nice to him. Other times we would step in and be defensive when people would pick on him. I remember one instance when three black guys from his school were being mean to him in the alley. I had no fear and was ready to take on these big kids in order to protect Andy."

Andrew himself recalled an incident. "I was having fun on the swings. I tried to fit in with the other kids, but they weren't being nice to me, and Lisa came and stopped them."

"Was there a time when you hesitated to invite someone to the house because you would have to introduce your brother?"

Lisa replied, "There was certainly an initial feeling of anxiety, wondering how to get over the hump of saying, 'My brother is retarded' before they reached the house. I tried not to preempt their image of Andy by suggesting that he was different. I would introduce him just as I would introduce anybody else and hoped that they could handle it and weren't repulsed in any way."

Andrew had good memories of Lisa's friends, "They were always nice to me," he said. John remembers Lisa's friends being warm and motherly toward Andy. Four friends, who are still living in the Chicago area, came to Andrew's funeral.

I commented to Lisa, "I have the impression that you have carried on this practice of not telling people ahead of time about Andy."

"Unless he is there to be presented as a very normal, lovely person, then you don't want to tell your friends you have a Down's brother because it might give them images of something awful. It's like any prejudice," explained Lisa. "When someone with a big birthmark is described to you, you think how terrible; but when you know the person, you get beyond that birthmark, and you don't think about it anymore because you are focusing on the person's personality."

Lisa's attitude makes sense and has merit. She represents the modern generation who regard people with disabilities as equal human beings with a rightful place in society. Hopefully, this attitude has become more prevalent with the assimilation of special needs children into regular school classes. I, on the other hand, was anxious to forestall awkwardness by explaining Andrew's handicap before people met him. Perhaps this came as a result of our early years when we had to convince everyone that our baby, a "mongolian idiot," was not an oddity to be shut away in an institution.

Regarding our summer vacations in Florida between 1969 and 1973, I asked Lisa and John, "How did you and the cousins treat Andy?"

"Oh, he was just one of the group. Cousin Lolla really helped. She was the eldest and the leader of our gang," recounted John.

Andrew remembered Lolla with great fondness: "She helped me with my food. When I didn't want to eat something, she would say, 'Try it, you might like it.'"

John continued, "Lolla made sure everyone was involved. We spent so much time in the water and she taught us games like Red Light Green Light, Mother May I, and Marco Polo. Andy was just as much part of the activities, because he was a strong swimmer and could participate in the water games as an equal. When Lisa would go off and do something with Lolla, we guys were left on our own to play with crabs and turtles or water games with the canoe. We had such a good time, and I felt a lot of camaraderie with Andy."

I added, "That complete acceptance was so good for Andy. He really blossomed in Florida. What about summer camps? I know you were in your separate groups, but did it bother you to have a handicapped brother at the same camp?"

"It was more difficult than dealing with my own friends around school, where everybody knew and accepted Andy," said John. "At camp there were a lot of people who didn't try to understand someone who was different. Some people hesitated to involve him in the activities. For instance, in sporting events, like their annual Olympics, we let the counselors know that Andy could swim, run, or hit a ball."

I continued with my probing into the dynamics of those early years. John remembers the dichotomy of his relationship with Andy.

"Well, I was the younger child, but in many ways Andy was treated as the youngest. I attribute my overinflated sense of fairness to the interplay of this relationship. As a child I felt that a lot of times Andy would receive special treatment and I wouldn't. For instance, you were always trying to impress on us the importance of taking turns, whereas Andy would get away with exceptions. The excuse was that he didn't understand, but you'd always told us to just treat him normally. Perhaps Lisa and I tried to treat him too normally. We would expect more from him than he was capable of."

"That's probably true," I said. "Whereas Dad and I realized there were limitations. Maybe we should have worked harder at making him share. I think this changed when he moved to Lambs where everyone had to abide by the rules, as well as learning to share and be considerate of others. If Andy needed help with something, we tried to make it a family thing so we all worked at it. John, do you feel these efforts focused too much attention on him?"

"Andy would accept my help with hitting a baseball or with other sport things. I was capable of helping him with verbs or how to pronounce words, but he would refuse my assistance because I was his little brother. He would take help from Lisa with his homework, but never from me."

"I think more than John, I tried to be Andy's friend as well as his sister," said Lisa. "I would ask him about his day, his friends, and his relationships."

Lisa's natural instinct is to mother; John's is to teach. He has always enjoyed showing other people how to do things both as a teaching assistant in graduate school and in his present role in a business concern.

John continued, "Andy's life was dominated by television shows, and it was a constant battle with all of us. His room was right next to the TV room, so he often commandeered the set before we had a chance to turn it on. He watched all the soap operas and baseball games."

"Remember, he didn't have friends at school like you and Lisa did. Why do you think that was?" I asked.

"I don't really know. Many people at Kenwood High School knew him and would say hi to him," said John. "But if you asked him who they were, he didn't know."

Lisa remembers asking Andy, "Do you know why girls aren't interested in you?"

Andrew had answered, "Perhaps it's because they think I'm funny or different."

I suggested, "Maybe he didn't know how to go about developing a real friendship. Or maybe he didn't feel that other kids completely accepted him."

Andrew was aware of his handicap, but we never knew to what extent people's reactions bothered him. Many years later, he told us he disliked being called retarded.

John said, "Andy was never able to accept any guidance from me in terms of social behavior around women," referring to Andy's teenage years when he was developing sexually and became obsessed with hair.

"He was always writing notes to our female visitors asking them to come down to his room to have their hair done," recalled John. "I guess it was usually innocent, although I think he really wanted to kiss them. I was too shy to take such a bold approach, so I resented Andy being able to get away with it. When we had parties, I would turn to him as a brother and say, 'Let's behave ourselves and not make any passes.' But he would continue to write notes, and it embarrassed me."

Andrew commented on these memories, "John doesn't have to be embarrassed because that was my thing then. I didn't have a woman in my life in those days, not like I do now. Now I have been with Lael for sixteen years."

In defense of Andrew's behavior I said, "I think Andy's differences didn't matter so much when he was young because a small child can be forgiven for imperfect manners or behavior. But it was during his teenage

Loving Andrew

years that we all became more conscious of his actions in public. We wanted him to be socially acceptable and not stand out as different."

After Andrew left home, he started sporting different hairstyles, usually in the fashion of the day and over which we had no control. He had a variety of perms, sometimes short and neat, and at other times in the style of a big Afro.

I explained to Lisa and John, "Andrew was his own person. It was his life, and his head and his hair."

"I know you couldn't control him and he was going to do what he wanted. But John and I can complain about it," Lisa replied.

"I know—you grew up with a brother with straight hair."

And John added, "Who was named Andy. And then we had a brother called Andrew with curly hair."

I told John, "He had his hair straight for your wedding, and he did that especially for you."

John was surprised, "Oh, that was nice of him. Now we can look back on the photos and see Andy as we always knew him."

John continued reminiscing: "In his stubborn ways, he didn't really want to take advice from anybody. But Mum, you and Dad always seemed able to push a magic button and turn the advice around so that it was something he wanted to do, and I wished I could do the same." Although Andrew attained a high level of development, there was a limit to his understanding. We need to remember that pushing our special people to the edge of normalcy sometimes has repercussions. We encourage them to conquer difficulties, strive to do the same as others, and fit into a normal life. At the same time, we impose limitations.

Are we pushing too hard as we urge our children to reach for the stars yet impose limits on their achievements? To what extent should we change the rules or expect others to accommodate the handicapped so that they can fit within the guidelines created by society? Just as we all need to look for happiness and satisfaction within the boundaries of our personal spheres, we reminded Andrew that his goal was to do the best he could within the limitations of his abilities. Most of all we struggled to work within the limits of his reasoning powers. Normal children learn to reason or conceptualize in formal and abstract terms by the age of eleven, but a person with Down syndrome almost never reaches this level.

"Even as an adult, John, we still had to think how to persuade Andrew to do something that he'd decided he didn't want to do. We thought up reasons that would be acceptable in the context of his thinking."

John agreed with our successful methods: "You guys were always good at that. Andy might react stubbornly, but he was much more ready to accept what you would say. I was his little brother, and he felt he shouldn't have to listen to me. So it was this mix of big brother, little brother and the role flip-flops that bothered me most."

"But didn't this change in recent years?"

John agreed: "Yes, we became equal as brothers and uncles, and he regarded me as his pal. I even found a way of pressing that magic button. One time we were together, Andy wasn't taking instructions from you parents, but he was taking them from me."

"You asked him for help too, such as having him show you how to tie your tie."

John, who hardly ever wears a tie, said, "I could probably manage to tie it, but Andy could do it better because he practiced more."

"It's those kinds of things that made Andrew feel equal and accepted," I concluded.

"With today's prenatal testing techniques," Monica said, "it is no longer necessary for people to bear the burden of a child with Down syndrome."

Monica was one of Pete's scientific colleagues who knew us well while we were in Chicago. We were having lunch with her at a 2003 conference in Kyoto, Japan. She continued in what was more a statement than a question, "If you had had the advantage of such tests, surely you would have opted for an abortion?"

Although we were quite taken aback by Monica's forthright position, it is not untypical. During the span of our son's life, attitudes toward the mentally handicapped have changed dramatically as the torch of knowledge has illuminated the dark corners of a fascinating subject, and prenatal testing provides parental choice. According to a cover story in *USA*

Today (August 15, 1997), "Genetic testing is changing who gets born in America." As technology continues to improve, should women be pressured into testing? If the test indicates an abnormality, should they be encouraged to consider abortion? With more women pursuing demanding careers, childbearing may be delayed until the mid-thirties, increasing the potential for conceiving a baby with Down syndrome or another disability. However, most women, whatever their age, regard prenatal testing as an automatic part of pregnancy; the test is a means of reassurance or to prevent the birth of a severely malformed child.

As of this writing, a new test, the MaterniT21, can be given at ten weeks and is almost 100 percent accurate. By taking a sample of the mother's blood and counting fragments from the fetus's DNA, technicians are able to recognize a chromosome abnormality, including the telltale extra chromosome of Down syndrome. The test replaces the invasive and risky procedures of chorionic villus Sampling (CVS) or amniocentesis, although they can still be used for absolute certainty.

A couple having difficulty getting pregnant can choose to undergo in vitro fertilization (IVF). This procedure allows for embryo sorting or preimplantation genetic diagnosis (PGD). After the woman's eggs have been mixed with the husband's sperm, the embryos can be screened for a variety of abnormalities, enabling the parents to choose both perfection and sex before implantation.

The ongoing identification of disease-carrying genes, together with the technology to recognize fetal abnormalities early in pregnancy, is raising the specter of vitriolic debates about the ethical issues associated with abortion and the right to life. Few would challenge the position that parents should be given the opportunity to prevent the birth of a child with a fatal disease. However, as the technology to identify a defective fetus becomes simpler and more commonplace, society seems to be moving further down the slippery spiral of looking upon the birth of children with disabilities as an unnecessary burden.

Some couples who have weighed the pros and cons have valid reasons for feeling that they could not cope even with a mildly disabled child. Normal children challenge our parenting abilities, and a disabled child poses a far greater responsibility. However, there are couples that look on testing as an opportunity to prepare for a special child. Michael Bérubé wrote in his 1998 book, *Life as We Know It,* "There never has been a better time to be born with Down syndrome." With the surge of legislation during the last two decades, disabled people are becoming accepted into the mainstream of life. Fifty-two years ago we used our common sense to teach Andrew through stimulation and exercise; now parents have the benefit of early-intervention programs tailored to their child's special needs, followed by partial or full inclusion in regular classes during their school years.

These educational opportunities combined with improved medical care enable most people with Down syndrome to lead a useful and fulfilling life, with the majority being capable of working in a supportive employment setting. In spite of this upbeat picture, approximately 90 percent of parents who learn that their baby will be Down syndrome choose abortion, resulting in a significant drop in the Down syndrome population, which may in turn bring about a serious decline in support and services. Unfortunately none of the tests can foretell the severity of an abnormality, so children who might have led happy and productive lives are denied the chance to be born.

There is a fine line between the eugenics movement of the early 1900s, striving for perfection in the human race, and the pressure placed on parents in the twenty-first century to produce children free of abnormalities. Certainly it is the hope of all parents to have a normal, healthy baby, but are more women, preoccupied with careers and ambitious to win a place in the boardroom, looking only for trophy children? With increased costs of medical care and services, is society beginning to regard disabled children as luxuries? Are taxpayers resenting the cost of educating children with severe mental or physical handicaps who do not fit into a regular school program? Because medical technology is finding causes and developing cures, are we looking increasingly for perfection? As molecular biologists unravel the secrets of DNA, the soul-searching national debates about the prospects for and ethics of social engineering have ramifications at many different levels. We should remember that there is a fine line between testing for abnormalities and testing for behavioral patterns, intelligence, or sex. Perhaps we are forgetting that life is a game of chance, and we should not attempt to play God. No embryo selection or prenatal test, invasive or noninvasive, can guarantee a flawless product or rule out unexpected calamities.

Early diagnosis can tell a mother she is carrying a normal baby, but it is not able to predict premature deliveries and the complications that may result. Nor, as in our situation with a daughter who died of cancer at fourteen months, can testing foretell a serious illness or accident capable of killing a healthy child or leaving indelible scars. Children grow into promising teenagers or successful adults and then, without warning, fall victim to drugs, alcohol, mental disease, or other dire afflictions. However much we try to eliminate defects, we can never create a perfect world.

Many couples choose not to be tested. For most the gamble pays off and they are blessed with a normal, healthy child. For others the birth of a baby with Down syndrome or other abnormality brings shock, disappointment, and concern about the future. But with the help of extensive support services, most families, such as the Rodriguez and Yeager families, learn to cope and soon discover the compensating delights of their exceptional child.

Couples faced with the dilemma of prenatal evaluation should receive the best possible medical advice, including genetic and psychological counseling. But neither professionals nor the attitudes of society should take away an individual's reproductive freedom, including the right to abort or the right to produce a less-than-perfect baby. Ultimately, only the parents should make the final decision about whether the fetus should live or die. For those couples who feel unable to take on the responsibility of a defective child and who cannot deal with the trauma and guilt of abortion, there are parents waiting to adopt children with Down syndrome.

Awareness of the advances in medical technology led our friend Monica, during our luncheon conversation in Kyoto, to assume that if such sophisticated tests had existed in 1959, we would have chosen to abort a fetus with Down syndrome. Placing his coffee cup carefully in its saucer, Pete pondered his response. "That's a tough question. If we had been tested and given the prognosis of mongolism as it was described at the time Andrew was born, I might have voted for termination of the pregnancy. But having seen how different Andrew's life became from that early forecast, I know now that a termination vote was not justified. Would we have chosen a simpler life without the struggle of bringing up a mentally retarded child? Again I say no, because in spite of his present mental health problems, Andrew derived so much enjoyment out of the good years of his life and in return gave us so much pleasure and love. The compensations far outweighed the struggles."

"But if you had it to do over again, surely you would not still make the decision to bring him up as part of the family?" persisted Monica.

Pete was firm in his reply. "He was our child. We made him, he existed, and he was our responsibility to care for. We never wavered on that point."

"But what about your responsibility to each other, to the family unit? How could you do this to your other children? Surely they were affected by having a handicapped brother," insisted Monica.

"Of course they were affected," said Pete. "But there are many worse influences in life, like alcoholism, drug addiction, and divorce that affect a child's development. We believe that making Andrew part of the family, although stressful at times, was a positive influence. Lisa and John's participation provided them with a valuable experience and gave them a different outlook on life. I think this is evident from Lisa's choice of career and John's choice of a wife, who is a special education teacher."

Without a doubt, Lisa's and John's lives have been influenced and enriched from growing up with a developmentally disabled brother. Although John struggled with his role as the younger brother and felt frustrated that Andy wouldn't accept his help, he has developed into a sensitive, caring man with a special empathy for the disabled. "In many ways I was proud of having a brother with Down syndrome who grew up to be so capable and independent."

After graduating from the University of Chicago Laboratory School, John attended the University of California, San Diego, and majored in molecular biology. Following graduate studies at Utah State University, he joined a business communications company, where he now works as a programmer analyst. In 1994 he married Elaine Loken, who is a special education teacher in Logan, Utah. She has worked with severely disabled elementary children and is now a resource specialist who recently earned a teacher of the year award. John and Elaine have a son and a daughter.

In high school Lisa wrote an essay for her biology class entitled "Mongoloids Can Be Normal People Too." Among her sources, she listed, "Home experiences with my brother." Her conclusion stated, "People with Down syndrome should be brought up basically the same way as any other normal child. They just need a little more attention and emphasis on everything so that they can achieve the most normal position in society as possible and make a contribution to the community."

Lisa's early mothering and complete acceptance of her brother with Down syndrome led to a vocation working with special needs children. She attended Smith College in Massachusetts and graduated cum laude in special education in 1985. She is married to Dean Behm, and they have four children, three boys and a girl. When her older children went to college, Lisa began working as a special instructor for an early intervention program, providing the kind of support that was not available when Andrew was growing up.

In spite of the attitude of Monica and many others, our experience bringing up a child with Down syndrome was rewarding. We realize that we were lucky. Until his late thirties and the onset of his schizophrenia, Andrew was especially high functioning. But not all children with Down syndrome will reach Andrew's level of ability. Some may have serious medical complications or other disabilities. Whatever their potential, it seems that people with Down syndrome will be loving and happy individuals.

What gave us the strength to carry on and succeed? For Pete, it was the expectation that, as humans, we would learn how to cope with an aberration of nature; for me, it was the belief that God had a role for us to play; for both of us, it was our mutual love and friendship. We always met challenges as a team, and we shared the pain and sorrow. We respected each other's ideas and concerns; we discussed options and made decisions together. We were determined to overcome the hurdles and help our special child attain his potential.

Both of us had the advantage of secure childhoods encircled by caring families. Our upbringing and British schooling instilled into us a sense of moral obligation. We learned never to shirk our responsibilities. We were taught to work diligently and follow a project through to completion. My boarding school education and participation in team sports taught me to submerge my individualism and strive to do my best for the team, the school, and the greater good of others. My father's position as a caring and understanding surgeon, in particular his work making new limbs for crippled children, provided me with a strong role model. When I was a teenager, I remember him telling me that I had guts to keep tackling a challenge in the face of failure. I often think about how proud he would have been of our efforts in facilitating his grandson's success.

Certain experiences prepare us for the vicissitudes of life. Pete took off two years from university to join an expedition to Greenland. Learning to survive in the arctic wilderness with a sledge and team of husky dogs, and living through two winters of total darkness, minimized the impact of future challenges.

Our meeting at university was a blessed coincidence. I couldn't have found a better husband to father our children. Pete has a gentle and caring nature. He is dedicated to his work and highly successful in his profession, but he has never neglected his family to bury himself in the laboratory or to barhop with the boys. Family duties, from washing the dishes to entertaining the children, were always part of his routine, and he was never too macho to change a diaper or give a baby a bottle.

We accepted the challenge of Andrew's handicap and knew that we would spend many years helping him develop, but we never expected to have to cope with the loss of a baby to cancer. At the time, the suffering was overwhelming and we feared we could never be happy again, but our baby's tragic death helped us realize that Andrew was not such a burden. Remembering Andrew's zest for life after Jean's death, I think of the verse in Isaiah 11:

> The wolf also shall dwell with the lamb, and the leopard shall lie down with the kid; and the calf and the young lion and the fatling together; and a little child shall lead them.

Andrew took us by the hand, telling us that he had needs and a life to live. He was our little ray of sunshine that led us out of the darkness of the forest into the light of the open plain.

As our family grew, Andrew's presence strengthened our family togetherness and influenced our other children's approach to life and relationships. We were always open about his handicap, and we tried to enlist the help of Lisa and John in our struggles to teach him a new task. They learned to come to his aid when necessary, but they also demanded that he follow the same rules and perform the same chores.

Discussing his short story "Teach Us to Outgrow Our Madness" about his brain-damaged child, Japanese author Kenzaburo Oe says he developed the creed, "If we can live through our difficulties, we can find a new dimension in life." We feel that bringing up Andrew as an integral part of our family life has taught us a greater sense of humanity. Pete is a more human scientist in touch with the realities of life, and we are all more caring, considerate, and compassionate people.

Writing this book has helped me appreciate Andrew's role in our lives and the value of his own activities and happiness. As was clearly evident from the many tributes at his memorial services, Andrew touched the lives of many, helping them in his special way become better people. He also demonstrated that people with his disability can lead a relatively normal life until the effects of a cruel disease, such as Alzheimer's, forces them onto the lower steps of the Down syndrome staircase. Caring for him when he was a child taught me patience and understanding and an appreciation for simple things. I learned humility and a different outlook on the measure of success. It is not necessary to become a doctor, a lawyer, a professor, or a wealthy entrepreneur. Satisfaction and rewards can be found within the realm of each person's abilities. Whenever I think I am not doing well at something, I think of Andrew and his achievements, and a sense of peace permeates my soul.

Like the members of other groups that are out of the mainstream of life, Andrew showed that he could be an acceptable, contributing member of society. "I'm trying to be like a normal person and fit in because I got Down's." He knew that he had limitations: "Sometimes I talk too fast." But he was always proud of his achievements: "I can do things like hold a job as long as I can."

St. Augustine wrote, "Everywhere a greater joy is preceded by a greater suffering." We lived through our difficulties, built up a family who brought us many rewards, and helped Andrew be the best he could, being what he was with the gifts that he was given.

> God gave this child to you to guide,
> To love, to walk through life beside.
> A little child so full of charms,
> To fill a pair of loving arms.
> God picked you out because He knew
> How safe His child would be with you.
> —Anonymous

Appendix:
Discovering a Chromosome Abnormality

Much has been discovered about the cause and frequency of Down syndrome since Andrew was born in 1959, when my brother George wrote: "Mongolism, as you have probably already discovered, is associated with a chromosome abnormality recently discovered by British and French workers."

P. E. Polani, professor of pediatric research at Guy's Hospital, London, wrote in the *Journal of Physiotherapy* (1976) that mongolism (or Down syndrome) has probably always existed among humans. A report in the 1970s stated that Down syndrome had been found in apes and chimpanzees. A seventh-century Saxon skull with structures that could be mongoloid was discovered during excavations of a monastery in Nottinghamshire. Some sixteenth-century paintings show children with mongoloid facial features.

However, it was not until 1866 that the type of retardation, with its special characteristics, was clearly identified and separated from other types of abnormalities by Dr. John Langdon Haydon Down, medical superintendent of the Earlswood Asylum for Idiots in Surrey, England. Owing to the oriental appearance of his patients, Dr. Down used the terms *mongolism* and *mongolian idiot* in his description of the condition because he thought the group might be a throwback to a lesser species similar to Mongolian people, whom he regarded as primitive. Although the syndrome (the word means a collection of signs) became officially named after Dr. Down, the ethnically descriptive and derogatory names persisted for another hundred years and are still found in dictionaries today.

In the late 1800s, various references to and descriptions of the condition appeared in medical literature. Scientists observed that many patients with Down syndrome had congenital heart disease. Doctors began to look for the cause of the syndrome. In the 1930s, it was decided that something outside of the fetus might have affected its development and be related to the aging of the mother's womb. In some families, Down syndrome had occurred more than once, leading researchers to consider a genetic cause.

In 1932, P. J. Waardenburg, a Dutch ophthalmologist, suggested that Down syndrome might have a chromosomal cause. In 1952, Ursula Mittwoch of London studied the spermatogonial cells (primitive male germ cells) of a man with Down syndrome and found forty-eight (or twenty-four pairs) of chromosomes. At this time it was thought that normal people had forty-eight chromosomes, so it was concluded that the chromosome count of this Down syndrome subject was normal.

By 1956 the technology for culturing cells had been improved. The work of Swedish scientists Tjio and Levan, confirmed by researchers in England, showed that normal people had forty-six chromosomes. Four years later, an article from a British newspaper dated July 24, 1960, quoted Dr. D. H. H. Thomas, medical superintendent of Cell Barnes Hospital, as saying, "Dramatic and very important advances are taking place in one field [of mental deficiency] ... Mongolism is a condition associated with an abnormality of the chromosomes of the cell—the threads on which the genes are strung ...This discovery is barely twelve months old. In the normal human cell there are forty-six chromosomes. In the mongol there are forty-seven."

Dr. Thomas was referring to the 1959 work in Paris of Dr. Jérôme Lejeune and his colleagues, who discovered the chromosome irregularity of Down syndrome by grouping chromosomes of similar size and shape and arranging them in order from the longest to the shortest. This is called a karyotype. Lejeune observed that the count of forty-seven chromosomes was the result of the twenty-first chromosome occurring in triplicate instead of a pair. He called the anomaly trisomy 21 (*tri* for three and *soma* meaning "of the body").

However, it was not until 1970 that banding and staining techniques enabled scientists to identify accurately each chromosome or parts of chromosomes. Chromosomes carry the genes; each chromosome contains about five thousand genes. Recent discoveries have shown that only a small segment of the long arm of chromosome 21 is involved. Further identification of its genes should add to our understanding of Down syndrome. Genes are made up of DNA, the coded information or building blocks of life that determine a person's physical development and personality. It is the genes that decide our height, shape and sex, whether we have brown or blue eyes, light or dark hair.

The chromosomes of a person with Down syndrome are all present and normal. The problem is caused by an extra quantity of genetic material, which interferes with the development of the body and mind, causing the overall picture to be imperfect.

The new technology revealed three different types of Down syndrome: trisomy 21; translocation; and mosaicism. Before conception, a mistake can occur during the cellular process involving the sperm or egg. An individual receives half of his chromosomes from the father and half from the mother. In each sperm and egg (called the germ cells), there are only twenty-three chromosomes or half the number ordinarily found in other cells of the body. When the sperm and egg are united, the total chromosome count will be forty-six, but if either one of the germ cells has an extra chromosome, it will be passed on at conception.

Occasionally an error occurs after conception. Cells divide to make more cells. The chromosomes are duplicated and divide equally into the new cells. Sometimes the chromosomes get stuck together and divide unequally. This is called nondisjunction. One of the new cells gets an extra chromosome, and the other cell has one chromosome less; this cell will probably die. The cell with the extra chromosome can survive and go on multiplying, but now with an imbalance of chromosomes. If the extra chromosome is the twenty-first, the anomaly is called trisomy 21.

Down syndrome can also occur as a result of translocation. As the cells divide, one chromosome becomes attached or translocated to another chromosome, usually number 14, number 21, or number 22. This is not a separate or "free" chromosome; it is an extra piece on one of the chromosomes listed above. The total chromosome count is forty-six, but the extra attachment on one chromosome causes a problem. In about one-third of these cases the anomaly is inherited from a parent. The parent is normal but has only forty-five chromosomes because part of the twenty-first chromosome has become attached to another chromosome. All the necessary information is there but is laid out differently.

In about 2 to 5 percent of the Down syndrome embryos, some cells divide correctly and other cells incorrectly, resulting in a "mosaic" or mixture of normal and abnormal numbers of chromosomes. In mosaic children, the Down syndrome features and characteristics will probably be less pronounced and average intelligence may be higher.

The chances of giving birth to a baby with Down syndrome vary with the age of the mother, but parents who already have a child with trisomy or mosaic 21 have a 1 percent chance of having a similar baby, because the mechanism that brought about the first error could occur again, although researchers do not know the cause. About one-third of transloca-tion trisomy 21 cases are inherited because the mother or the father is a carrier. The chances of having another baby with Down syndrome are one in five if the mother is the carrier, and one in twenty to fifty if the father is the carrier.

The National Down Syndrome Congress stated: "The incidence of Down syndrome in the United States is approximately one in every 800 to 1,000 live births." Although the genetic condition is the most common chromosomal disorder, nondisjunction in the cell division causes about 80 percent of fetuses to be miscarried during the first trimester of pregnancy.

Since the 1930s it was thought that the mother's age influenced the chances of having a baby with Down syndrome. In fact both parents' cells are more likely to divide unequally as they age. It is now considered that in 5 percent of cases, the error can be attributed to the men's sperm cells. The likelihood of the problem occurring in the egg will always be higher because of the large number of sperm involved in fertilization and the fact that men's sperm is being constantly renewed. In contrast, all of a woman's eggs are present at birth. Between puberty and menopause, some will ripen each month and be discarded or fertilized. So the older a woman becomes, the older the eggs are, and the mechanism of cell division is more likely to become faulty. It is like a favorite car: the longer you drive it, the more parts will rust or deteriorate.

In his 1996 book *Understanding Down Syndrome*, Dr. Cliff Cunningham explains that in women under thirty the risk of having a Down syndrome baby is about 1 in 1,500; the risk rises gradually until the woman is thirty-five, after which it doubles approximately every two and half years. Between thirty-five and forty the incidence is 1 in 280 to 290; in the forty to forty-five age group, it is 1 in 35 to 50; over forty-five years, it is between one in 20 to 65.

Selected Bibliography

Books on Down Syndrome and Special Needs

Batschaw, Mark L., MD. *Your Child Has a Disability: A Complete Sourcebook of Daily and Medical Care.* Boston: Little Brown & Co., 1991.

Beck, Martha. *Expecting Adam.* New York: Times Books, 1999.

Bérubé, Michael. *Life As We Know It: A Father, a Family, and an Exceptional Child.* New York: Pantheon Books, 1996.

Chicoine, Brian, MD, and Dennis McGuire, PhD. *The Guide to Good Health for Teens & Adults with Down Syndrome.* Bethesda, MD: Woodbine House, 2010.

Cunningham, Cliff. *Understanding Down Syndrome: An Introduction for Parents.* Cambridge, MA: Brookline Books, 1996 (first American edition).

Kogan, Rick, and Mark Joseph. *Lambs Farm: Where People Grow.* Chicago: Lambs Farm, 2011.

McGuire, Dennis, PhD, and Brian Chicoine, MD. *Mental Wellness in Adults with Down Syndrome: A Guide to Emotional and Behavioral Strengths and Challenges.* Bethesda, MD: Woodbine House, 2006.

N[ewitt], I[sabel]. *For the Parents of a Mongol Child.* Clent, Worcestershire, England: Sunfield Children's Homes, 1946.

Oe, Kenzaburo. *Teach Us to Outgrow Our Madness.* Translated by John Nathan. New York: Grove Press, 1977.

Pueschel, Siegfied M., MD, PhD, MPH. *A Parent's Guide to Down Syndrome: Toward a Brighter Future.* Baltimore, MD: Paul H. Brookes Publishing Co., 1990.

Rapp, Rayna. *Testing Women, Testing the Fetus: The Social Impact of Amniocentesis in America*. New York: Routledge, 2000.

Ross, Bette M. *Our Special Child: A Parent's Guide to Helping Children with Special Needs Reach Their Potential*. Nashville, TN: Thomas Nelson Publishers, 1993.

Sandel, Michael J. *The Case against Perfection: Ethics in the Age of Genetic Engineering*. Cambridge, MA: Harvard University Press, Belknap Press, 2009.

Shorter, Edward. *The Kennedy Family and the History of Mental Retardation*. Philadelphia, PA: Temple University Press, 2000.

Unsworth, Tim. *The Lambs of Libertyville: A Working Community of Retarded Adults*. Chicago: Contemporary Books, 1990.

Books on Mental Health

Jamison, Kay Redfield. *An Unquiet Mind: A Memoir of Moods and Madness*. New York: Alfred A. Knopf, 1995.

Nasar, Sylvia. *A Beautiful Mind: A Biography of John Forbes Nash, Jr., Winner of the Nobel Prize in Economics, 1994*. New York: Touchstone, 1998.

Saks, Elyn R. *The Center Cannot Hold: My Journey through Madness*. New York: Hyperion Books, 2007.

Author Biography

Romy Wyllie has had her own interior design business for thirty-five years. She is the author of two books on architecture: *Caltech's Architectural Heritage: From Spanish Tile to Modern Stone* (Balcony Press, 2000), and *Bertram Goodhue: His Life and Residential Architecture* (W. W. Norton, 2007). Wyllie is an Honorary Alumna of Caltech, where she leads a volunteer architectural tour service. She lives in Pasadena, California, with her husband, Peter.

16824902R00163

Made in the USA
Charleston, SC
12 January 2013